Katherine Murray
Author of 40+ computer books

Microsoft

P9-CAL-117

Faster Smarter

Microsoft®

Office XP

Take charge of your Microsoft Office programs—
faster, smarter, *better*!

PUBLISHED BY
Microsoft Press
A Division of Microsoft Corporation
One Microsoft Way
Redmond, Washington 98052-6399

Library of Congress Cataloging-in-Publication Data
Murray, Katherine, 1961-
    Faster Smarter Microsoft Office XP / Katherine Murray.
        p. cm.
    Includes index.
    ISBN 0-7356-1862-3
    1. Microsoft Office. 2. Business--Computer programs. I. Title.

   HF5548.4.M525 M873   2002
   005.369--dc21   2002029535

Printed and bound in the United States of America.

1 2 3 4 5 6 7 8 9   QWE   8 7 6 5 4 3

Distributed in Canada by H.B. Fenn and Company Ltd.

A CIP catalogue record for this book is available from the British Library.

Microsoft Press books are available through booksellers and distributors worldwide. For further information about international editions, contact your local Microsoft Corporation office or contact Microsoft Press International directly at fax (425) 936-7329. Visit our Web site at www.microsoft.com/mspress. Send comments to *mspinput@microsoft.com*.

Acquisitions Editor: Alex Blanton
Project Editor: Kristen Weatherby
Series Editor: Kristen Weatherby

Body Part No. X08-95130

Table of Contents

Part I: Microsoft Office XP Basics

This section of the book gets you started quickly by learning about the features all the Microsoft Office XP applications have in common. You'll find out how to start and exit programs, get Help, work with files, print documents, and more.

Part II: Word Power, Made Simple

Unleash the power of Microsoft Word by learning how to create, edit, and format your documents. In addition to everyday tasks, you'll master special tasks such as working with sections, graphics, and more.

Part III: Excel the Easy Way

This next part of the book appeals to your left-brained, analytical side as you work with numbers in Microsoft Excel. From starting a simple spreadsheet to working with functions to formatting columns and rows, adding headings, and setting print ranges, this part gives you everything you need to know to feel comfortable in the numbers game.

Part IV: Simply PowerPoint

Want to jazz up those Word bullet lists and Excel charts? Microsoft PowerPoint gives you the chance to create professional presentations and wow your audience with the data you've prepared. In this part, you'll learn how to create a quality presentation, arrange slides, add transitions, time the slide show, and produce the show for an audience.

Part V: Organize with Microsoft Outlook

Everyone needs a little help getting organized. This part shows you how to use Microsoft Outlook as your start and end point for organizing e-mail, appointments, to-do tasks, journal entries, and more.

Part VI: Managing Data with Microsoft Access

Microsoft Access isn't the intimidating, high-end database new users often think it is—it's actually a pretty friendly, powerful program that walks you through the process of creating tables for storing data and creating reports, queries, and much more. This part of the book shows you how to do the basics in Access so you have what you need to explore further on your own.

Part VII: Fast Web Pages with Microsoft FrontPage

Web pages are everywhere in Office XP; you can create Web pages from Word, from Excel, and from PowerPoint. But when you want a real Web page—a complete site with multiple pages, numerous links, and slick text, graphics, and rollover effects—Microsoft FrontPage is your program. This part of the book shows you how to create a simple or sophisticated Web page quickly.

To my boys, Christopher and Cameron.
Thanks for a fun summer.
Love, Mom

Acknowledgments

Kristen (project editor extraordinaire) would tell me not to say this, but I will anyway: This was a dream project. After writing literally dozens of technical books, I've learned that you've got to roll with the punches on these things. Sometimes you have a team that never quite clicks; other times you are blessed to work with a group of people you'd like to keep working with forever. This was one of those projects. I enjoy writing for Microsoft Press because it's truly a collaborative effort—a team of professionals who treat each other with respect and truly care about giving you the best book possible. As we come to the end of this project, my special thank-yous go something like this:

First and foremost, to Kristen Weatherby, who is a smart, straight-shooting, fun, dog-loving publishing professional. Her guidance and suggestions are always right-on and she delivers even the bad news (we're *still* over on page count?!) in a way that inspires me to think of solutions. I'm looking forward to working with you again, Kristen. :)

Thanks also to Alex Blanton, my acquisition editor at Microsoft Press, for thinking of me for this project and being wonderful (with an eye on deadlines, of course) all along the way. Again, a smart fellow who knows publishing and has a keen sense of how this can all fit together in the larger scheme of things.

More thanks to the folks at nSight, Inc., who did a fine, even-handed edit and kept working with that terrific design (and my chatty text) until everything fit in the pages you see before you. (And believe me, that was no small job.)

Thanks also to the tech editor, Eric Faulkner, who netted out the small bugs I accidentally left floating in some of my procedures and who were a great help in letting me know where things could be clarified and improved.

As always, thanks to Claudette Moore, my agent and friend at Moore Literary Agency, for providing just the right mix of support, encouragement, and push. She knows me well. :)

Introduction

Welcome to *Faster Smarter Microsoft Office XP,* a book that puts you in the driver's seat of Microsoft Office XP, the multidimensional productivity suite from Microsoft. The various applications in Office XP enable you to do just about anything you need to do with your computer—at work, at home, or at school.

Sending e-mail? Try Microsoft Outlook. Creating a report for a major presentation? Create the report document in Microsoft Word and put the key points on attention-getting slides in Microsoft PowerPoint. Tracking sales projections for your national accounts? Microsoft Excel has the power you need to analyze, report, and chart your financial data. Knock out a professional-level Web site with Microsoft FrontPage in a single afternoon. And for doing close-to-miraculous things with your data—organizing, managing, sorting, organizing, filtering, reporting, and more—you can put Microsoft Access on the job.

In Office XP, you've got all the software power you need to get where you want to go. Now you simply need the map to show you the quickest, smartest route (and of course, you don't want to miss the great sights along the way). *Faster Smarter Microsoft Office XP* is designed to help you tap the most important features in each of the primary applications so that you can get productive quickly—and we'll touch on some of the add-in programs as well. Because Office XP has a lot of ground to cover, you'll find that we move through the different applications at a pretty quick pace, touching on all the basics so you know how to do the most important things first.

Not only will you find the tasks you're likely to use most often in each of the different programs, but you'll also discover tips and workarounds that help you accomplish things faster and with a minimum of effort (that's where the *smarter* comes in). And because Office XP is a suite of complementary applications that share some common features and procedures, you'll find that what you learn in one application easily transfers to another. That means a shorter learning curve for you, which translates to better productivity sooner.

Ready to get started? There's no time to lose! By this afternoon, you could be working faster and smarter with Office XP.

Versions of Office XP

You may be wondering whether you've got the right book for the version of Office XP you are using. Let's answer that right now: Yes, you do—no matter which version you've got. Chances are that you are using (or thinking about purchasing) one of the following versions of Office XP:

- Microsoft Office XP Professional, which includes the primary core programs (Word, Excel, Outlook, PowerPoint, and Access)

- Microsoft Office XP Standard, which includes Word, Excel, Outlook, and PowerPoint and also is available in a special discounted version for teachers and students

- Microsoft Office XP Developer, which includes all the programs in the Professional version plus FrontPage, SharePoint Team Services, and Developer tools

You might also have one of two versions of Office XP that are preinstalled on new computers. Office XP for Small Business includes Word, Excel, Outlook, and Microsoft Publisher, and Office XP Professional with Publisher includes all the programs in the Small Business version plus PowerPoint and Access.

In this book, you'll find everything you need to know to get up to speed with the core applications, which are the central focus of each of the three Office XP packages—and discover quickly how to do what you most want to do with these powerful programs. Whether you want to create a simple document, print a lengthy analysis of your cost-to-sales ratio, or whip up a Web page in 30 minutes or less, you'll be able to find what you need—and hopefully have some fun—following along in this book.

This Book Could Be for You

Chances are that you've had some experience with computers but you just haven't had the time or inclination to look too closely at Office XP. Perhaps your office just licensed the program for the first time. Or maybe you decided after a number of years in your own small business that it was time to upgrade to a program that can truly do it all.

Whatever your reason for learning Office XP now, welcome! You will find that *Faster Smarter Microsoft Office XP* has something for you if you are:

- Comfortable with computers but new to Office XP

- Skilled in one program (perhaps word processing with Word or creating spreadsheets with Excel) but unfamiliar with the rest of the applications

- Interested in learning how the various Office XP applications can be used together to make you more productive at work

- Wanting to learn skills that complement those you already have

- Working in a corporate environment in which you are responsible for producing professional-looking reports, spreadsheets, and presentations

■   In a work situation where you need to master a specific task in Word, Excel, PowerPoint, Access, Outlook, or FrontPage quickly (although being familiar with the others would be helpful, too)

■   Needing to get up-to-speed with the latest versions of the Office programs so that your small business can collaborate with client companies

Whether you use Office XP in your business, at home, or at school (or all three), you'll find that the suite has everything you need for working with words, numbers, multimedia, Web pages, and e-mail. In short, Office XP offers all the work tools you could need—and in *Faster Smarter Microsoft Office XP,* we've attempted to give you a great road map for discovering and using the tools that will help you get where you want to be in the fastest way.

What's in This Book?

Because there's so much information between the covers of this book, we thought it would be helpful to organize the sections by application. In other words, each major part of the book focuses on one of the primary applications you'll be working with. Specifically, here's the breakdown:

Part I, "Learning the Basics of Microsoft Office XP," introduces you to the suite and shows you how to start and exit the various programs, use the Shortcut Bar, perform tasks that are common to all applications, run multiple programs, switch among open programs, and get help when you need it.

Part II, "Word Power, Made Simple," shines a spotlight on Word 2002, the word processing component of Office XP. In this part of the book, you learn all the document basics you'll ever need—starting a new document, working with templates, entering and importing text, editing and formatting text, creating lists and tables, and more. You'll also learn to do some high-end tasks with Word, including creating special layouts, working with sections, inserting graphics, creating links, adding bookmarks, generating a table of contents, and inserting codes, and creating an index.

Part III, "Excel the Easy Way," takes a focused approach to building a basic spreadsheet and shows you how to enter and format data, organize rows and columns, create data ranges, and work with functions. Once you create the basic spreadsheet, you learn to improve its accuracy by editing your information and boost its visual appeal by changing the format, adding borders and shading, choosing a different font, style, and size. When the spreadsheet looks the way you want it to, you learn how to select areas of the sheet for printing. Last but not least, in this part you learn to plot and chart spreadsheet data using any one of the collection of chart styles—pie, bar, line, area, and more—offered in Excel 2002.

Part IV, "Simply Powerpoint," gets you right into the fun world of presentations by showing you how simple it can be to put your thoughts in slide form.

In this part of the book, you learn to create a simple presentation by using the professional designs built into the program. You then add your own text and graphics, set the order and timing of slides, and choose eye-catching transitions that will keep your audience interested. Finally, you learn to add multimedia effects to your presentations—sound, video, and more—and find out how to turn a presentation into a Web page and how to broadcast your presentation live, online, to an invited audience. Fun stuff!

Part V, "Organize with Microsoft Outlook," illustrates how much easier life is with a personal information manager such as Outlook working for you. In this part of the book, we begin by using Outlook to handle online communications—creating, sending, receiving, and filtering e-mail. But the capabilities of Outlook go far beyond simple messaging; you can use the Calendar, Journal, Address Book, Notes, and Task features in Outlook to further organize your time, thoughts, contacts, and to-do lists. Your only excuse for being disorganized after reading this section of the book is that you haven't found time to import the data you need to organize.

Part VI, "Managing Data with Microsoft Access," focuses on the difference that smart data management makes, giving you the power to know what's going on in your business by seeing for yourself how data hangs together, who's buying what, and how you can best anticipate and respond to trends that affect your business and your life. This part walks you through the process of creating a database, working with data tables, creating data-entry forms, sorting information, working with queries, and then preparing and printing reports.

Part VII, "Fast Web Pages with Microsoft FrontPage," gives you the straight story on creating Web pages you'll be proud of. The part starts with a basic discussion of creating a simple site and moves to ideas about finding graphics, working with color, creating and managing links, adding tables and frames, creating rollovers, and viewing the source code for the page. You'll also learn to publish your pages and troubleshoot errors when they occur.

Finally, the book winds down with two appendixes. Appendix A provides a blow-by-blow description of the installation and upgrade process of Office XP. (You'll also learn how to uninstall and reinstall features here.) Appendix B lists the Office XP shortcut keys in one handy reference.

Tips, Notes, and Other Special Elements

To make your trip through the book as easy and informative as possible, we've provided special elements to draw your attention to information that can save you a few steps, clarify terms or concepts, or provide additional information that can help you learn more about the topic at hand. You'll find the following elements in each of the chapters in the book:

- **Tips**   offer quick techniques, workarounds, or suggestions that can help you perform tasks faster.
- **Notes**   provide additional information related to the task at hand. A note might provide background on a feature, an idea about ways a certain task might be used or a Web site you can visit for more information.
- **See Alsos**   list a reference to another section in the book that provides complementary techniques.
- **Cautions**   help you avoid trouble by pointing out what could go wrong (or introducing ways you can prevent problems) in a given procedure.
- **Lingo tips**   define concepts and technical terms referred to in the text.
- **Try This! elements**   provide real examples of how you can use the different features of Office XP. You'll find some interesting stories and suggestions here.
- **Key Points**   help you review what you've learned by listing the important concepts introduced in each chapter.

In addition to these special elements, you'll find throughout the book a fast-but-friendly tour of all the major features in the primary applications. You'll also find a healthy mix of explanation and how-tos—the numbered lists indicate a process you can follow to learn a particular task. In addition, you'll find that screen shots (pictures of my computer screen as I write) help illustrate where we are in a process, and tables help you see at a glance information that can be compared and contrasted.

So now that you know the lay of the land, let's check out the system requirements you need so we can get down to work.

What You Need

For Office XP to run optimally on your system, Microsoft recommends that you have the following hardware and software capabilities:

- Pentium 133 or Pentium III computer
- At least 128 megabytes (MB) of random access memory (RAM)
- Microsoft Windows XP Professional (Office XP also runs on Windows 98, Windows Millennium Edition, Windows NT, Windows 2000 Professional, and Windows XP Home Edition)
- 210 MB hard disk space for Office XP Standard (245 MB for Office XP Professional)
- CD-ROM drive

- SuperVGA monitor (or better) with 800-by-600-pixel resolution and 256 colors
- Mouse or other pointing device (trackball, touchpad, and so on)

In addition to these system basics, you might need other devices, depending on what you want to do with Office XP. Check out this list and see whether there's anything you're missing:

- A Windows-compatible printer
- A scanner or digital camera for importing graphics
- Microphone for speech recognition
- Graphics tablet for handwriting recognition and drawing input
- Extra RAM for media-intensive operations
- 14,400-baud modem (or faster)
- Internet connection with an Internet service provider

Note   If you have questions about system requirements or want to double-check and make sure that your computer makes the grade, check out the Office XP system requirements online at *http://www.microsoft.com/office/evaluation/systreqs.asp.*

Now, if you're ready to get started, let's kick into high gear and move on to Chapter 1, "Getting to Know Microsoft Office XP."

Support

Every effort has been made to ensure the accuracy of this book. Microsoft Press provides corrections for books at the following address:

http://mspress.microsoft.com/support/

If you have comments, questions, or ideas regarding this book, please send them to Microsoft Press via e-mail to the following address:

mspinput@microsoft.com

or via postal mail to:

Microsoft Press
Attn: Faster Smarter Series Editor
One Microsoft Way
Redmond, WA 98052-6399

You can also contact the author directly at kmurray@iquest.net or her BlogOfficeXP Web site, *http://www.revisionsplus.com/blogofficexp.html,* with any comments or suggestions. Please note that product support is not offered through the above addresses.

Part I

Microsoft Office XP Basics

Ready to get started using Microsoft Office XP? If so, you're in the right place. This first part of the book helps you get comfortable with all the basics of Office XP. Chapter 1, "Getting to Know Microsoft Office XP," starts right off with a discussion of the ways in which you launch the individual programs. We then talk about what you can do with the programs in Office XP and encourage you to think about the things you'd most like to try. Finally, the chapter gives a tour of the Office XP toolbar and the new features that Office XP offers.

In Chapter 2, "Working with Programs," you begin to explore one of the great benefits of Office XP: the ease with which you can work with several different programs at once, sharing data and features. This chapter teaches the nitty-gritty of multiple window management—how to display multiple open windows, switch among them, and close them when you're through. Also in this chapter, you learn how to perform some of the tasks that the applications have in common—tasks such as opening, saving, printing, and closing files.

By the time you reach Chapter 3, "Finding Help at Every Turn," you'll want to explore a little more on your own. In this chapter, you learn about the various ways you can find help in Office XP. Whether you prefer asking a quick question in the Ask A Question field, using conventional context-sensitive help, relying on one of the animated assistants, or going online to get in-depth help from the Microsoft Knowledge Base, this chapter gives you so many help choices that you'll be certain that you never work alone in Office XP.

Chapter 1

Getting to Know Microsoft Office XP

If you're like many of us, you may have thought about Microsoft Office for a long time before you decided to try it. If you're the owner of a small business, Office is a pretty expensive program—how can you be sure it's worth the cost? If you're an employee in a business that has recently switched to Office from another application suite, you may be wondering with some trepidation how much you have to learn and how steep the learning curve will be.

This first chapter of the book answers those questions. By the time we're finished here, you will know more than one way to launch an Office XP application and you'll have a broad-based understanding of what makes Office XP unique and the kinds of wonderful things you'll be able to do with it.

Note First things first. If installing the program is up to you and you haven't done it yet, take a moment now and, using Appendix A as your guide, install Office XP. If you are using Office XP on a network and you are not the network administrator, talk to the powers that be so you can get the program installed and begin using it as soon as possible.

What's Included with Office XP?

Office has been around in one form or another for more than a decade, and Office XP is the latest and greatest release in a long line of successful programs.

Office XP is actually a *suite* of applications, meaning that it is a collection of complementary programs that work together to help you accomplish what you need to do. These are the core programs that make up the Standard version of Office XP:

■   Microsoft Word 2002, a word-processing program you will use to write letters, create reports, publish newsletters, and more.

■   Microsoft Excel 2002, a spreadsheet program capable of simple-to-complex financial operations, sorting and analyzing data, and charting and reporting.

■   Microsoft PowerPoint 2002, a presentation graphics program you'll use to create slide shows for presentations, kiosk displays, and even broadcasting on the Web.

■   Microsoft Outlook 2002, an information and communication manager you'll use to send and receive e-mail, organize your calendar, and keep track of notes, tasks, and your personal and business contacts.

In addition to the core programs, the following applications are included with Office XP Professional:

■   Microsoft Access 2002, a relational data management program that enables you to organize, track, sort, filter, and report on your data.

■   Microsoft FrontPage 2002, a professional-level Web page creation program that gives you everything you need for generating multifaceted Web sites.

And, if you *really* get into Office XP and find you want to develop your own tools and applications, you can upgrade to Office XP Developer, which includes all the programs available in Professional, plus the SharePoint Team Services and Developer tools.

Note   Other versions of Office XP may have different configurations of programs. For example, Microsoft Publisher is included in some Office XP versions that are installed on new computers, and Microsoft FrontPage is not available with all versions of Office XP Professional but has been offered as a special add-in with some promotional packages.

What Can You Do with Office XP?

By now you're probably getting a pretty good idea of the various capabilities wrapped up in this one software suite you're preparing to use. Whether you want to work with words, numbers, images, Web content, or data, there's a program in Office XP that was created just to do what you want to do. No matter what kind of result you need to produce—a report, a Web page, a spreadsheet, a database, a presentation, or an e-mail campaign—Office XP has the tool to help you produce it.

Here are just a few of the ways in which you might use Office XP:

- You can create the company newsletter in Word, turn it into Web content using FrontPage, and send out an e-mail version using Outlook.

- You can store the inventory records for your small bookstore in an Access database; track sales and accounts receivable and payable in Excel; and do a mass mailing to your entire customer base using the mail-merge feature of Word.

- You can create a professional-level corporate Web site using FrontPage, compose the annual report in Word, and import charts you created in Excel to portray the company's happy financial picture.

- You can use Outlook to help you organize your calendar, schedule meetings with your staff, track employee information, assign tasks (for yourself and others), add notes to reviewed documents, and manage your ever-growing contact list.

Tip The best use of Office XP is, of course, whatever you plan to do with it. How will the Office XP applications help you in your day-to-day work? Thinking through the tasks you do either manually or with another program and asking yourself now how you would like to improve or streamline those tasks can help you get the most out of Office as we go along.

One of the biggest benefits of using Office XP as a suite of applications is the easy way in which you can use the programs together. The individual programs are so seamlessly integrated that you can move data from Word to Excel to PowerPoint to Access without a second thought. You can edit a table in Word and have its information—which originally came from Excel—updated automatically. You can create a Web page in FrontPage, then make some changes in Word, and then move back to FrontPage again, all simply and easily—and with no glitches or format conversions to worry you.

And not only will your facts and figures transfer smoothly from one application to another, but your understanding of the different features the programs share is also transferrable knowledge. From the basic look and feel of the screen to using the Help system to saving, printing, renaming, and deleting files, the similarity between the applications will lessen your learning curve and give you a leg up each time you use a new program.

Starting Office XP

Once Office XP is installed on your computer, you can choose any number of ways to open an application and get busy. This section shows you how to start Office XP and open an application or two.

You can begin working with Office XP applications in different ways (as shown in Figure 1-1):

- By opening a new or existing Office document.

- By choosing the program directly from the All Programs option in the Start menu.

- By displaying the Office XP Toolbar and clicking the program icon you want to use.

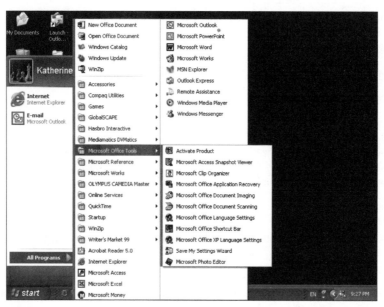

Figure 1-1   You can launch an Office XP application three different ways. Take your pick.

Opening a New Office Document

To open a new Office XP document, perform the following steps:

1   Click Start on the *taskbar* and then click All Programs.

2   In the displayed program list, click New Office Document.

3   In the New Office Document dialog box (shown in Figure 1-2), click the application you want to open, and then click OK. The application starts and a blank document opens on your screen, ready for your use.

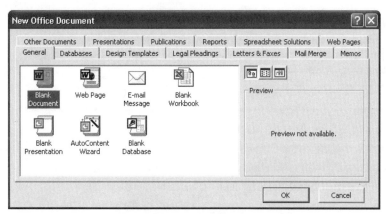

Figure 1-2   Start a new Office XP document by clicking the program icon and then clicking OK.

Lingo   The *taskbar* refers to the Windows taskbar, the horizontal bar across the bottom of your desktop. The taskbar displays the Start button on the left, tabs for any open applications in the center area, and the system icons on the far right.

Other Possibilities in the New Office Document Dialog Box   The New

Office Document dialog box includes a huge range of tabs behind the General one, which is selected by default. What's in those tabs and do you need to worry about them?

Each of the 13 tabs in the New Office Document dialog box gives you ready-made templates you can use as a starting point for your documents. Whether you are working on a legal brief, a database for tracking inventory, the company balance sheet, a new Web page, or a presentation for your next sales conference, the Office templates help you work smarter by doing all the startup work for you. You can begin with a designed, formatted file that is simply ready to accept your data.

When you begin working through the examples in the part of the book focused on individual applications, you may want to come back to the New Office Document dialog box and select a template to try. Familiarizing yourself with the available files now can be a real time-saver when you're faced with creating those files yourself for the first time.

Launching Programs from the Start Menu

Starting one of the applications—Word, Excel, Outlook, PowerPoint, Access, or FrontPage—from the Start menu is about as simple as it gets. Just follow these steps:

1   Click Start on the taskbar.

2   Click All Programs. In the displayed list, click the name of the application you want to launch (for example, Microsoft PowerPoint). The program opens and displays a new, blank document in the work area of the window.

Tip   Because Windows XP has "smart" menus that customize themselves to show choices you've recently made, the next time you open the Start menu you may see the Office application you just opened available in the top portion of the Start menu. To start that application, simply click it.

And Don't Forget Windows Explorer   There's yet another way to launch an Office XP program we haven't mentioned. When you are working with Windows Explorer, the file management utility that is part of Windows XP (and other versions of Windows as well), you can launch one of the Office XP applications by double-clicking the file's icon. Each file in the Windows Explorer window has a different-but-similar icon to show that the file is part of the Office XP suite. Here's the way the different icons appear:

Microsoft Word

Microsoft Excel

Microsoft PowerPoint

Microsoft Outlook

Microsoft Access

Microsoft FrontPage

     After you double-click the icon, the file you selected opens in its own application window on the desktop.

Using the Office Shortcut Bar

Now that you know the menu sequences, you may opt instead to start an application from the Office Shortcut Bar. You'll like working with the bar if you frequently start and work with different programs. For example, suppose that you're putting together a report in Word. You are writing about the sales results of a recent competition in the Eastern division. What were those totals again? You start Excel to look at the sales figures. Then you remember that you really liked what the director of sales suggested as the slogan for the sales campaign—it's right on the tip of your tongue, but you can't quite remember it. Better look it up in the presentation she created. You start PowerPoint.

If you are working with the Office Shortcut Bar, you can start these programs quickly, with a single click of the mouse. Then it's simply a matter of navigating to the files you need.

Follow these steps to put the Office Shortcut Bar into action:

1   Click Start on the taskbar.

2   Point to Microsoft Office Tools. From the submenu, click Microsoft Office Shortcut Bar. After a moment, the bar appears along the right edge of your screen (as shown in Figure 1-3).

Figure 1-3   The Office Shortcut Bar puts all the installed Office XP programs at the tip of your mouse.

Tip   Depending on how you've set up your version of Office XP and how you elected to install the different components, you may get a message the first time you use the Office Shortcut Bar, asking whether you'd like Windows to display the Shortcut Bar as soon as Windows launches. If you want to do this (this is a time-saver if you think you'll use the bar often), click Yes; otherwise, click No. If you're irritated that Windows would even *ask* you such a thing, click the check box to the left of Please Do Not Ask Me This Question Again.

To launch an application from the Office Shortcut Bar, simply click the application icon you want. The new document then opens in the work area, leaving space for the Shortcut Bar to remain visible to the right of the document window. This enables you to open another application easily by clicking the icon you want. Table 1-1 gives you a quick look at the tools on the Shortcut Bar.

See Also   *Six of the tools on the Office Shortcut Bar launch utilities that are part of Outlook. For more about working with Outlook features, see Part V, "E-Mail and Organize with Microsoft Outlook."*

Table 1-1   Shortcut Bar Tools

Icon	Name	Description
	New Office Document	Displays the New Office Document dialog box
	Open Office Document	Displays the Open Office Document dialog box so that you can choose an existing file
	New Message	Launches Outlook and opens a new message window
	New Appointment	Launches the Outlook Calendar and opens a new appointment window
	New Task	Starts Outlook and displays the Task window
	New Contact	Starts Outlook and opens the New Contact dialog box so that you can add a new contact
	New Journal Entry	Opens an Outlook Journal Entry window so that you can log a new entry
	New Note	Displays an Outlook Notepad so that you can type notes as needed
	Microsoft Word	Starts Word
	Microsoft Excel	Starts Excel
	Microsoft PowerPoint	Starts PowerPoint
	Microsoft Outlook	Starts Outlook
	Microsoft Access	Starts Access

Tip   If you decide that displaying the Shortcut Bar wasn't such a great idea and you want to hide it, right-click on the folder icon at the top of the bar. A pop-up menu appears. Click Hide Toolbar. The bar will remain hidden until you select it again in the Microsoft Office Tools submenu of the All Programs list.

Exiting Programs

Now that you've got all these programs open on the Windows desktop, how do you get rid of some of them? When you're finished working with a program, you can close it in one of two ways:

- You can click the Close box in the upper-right corner of the application window.

- You can open the File menu for the application window and choose Exit.

If you have entered information or modified the file, the program will ask you whether you want to save the file. If you do, enter a file name (or, if you are working with an existing file, leave the file name as it appears) and click Save.

New Features of Office XP

One of the primary goals in Office XP was to make daily tasks easier to perform—and easier means fewer menu selections and fewer mouse clicks. One way Office XP has streamlined everyday tasks is with the introduction of the *task pane* (shown in Figure 1-4), a panel that appears along the right side of the work area when you do common things such as start a new file, apply styles, add clip art, or search for information.

Figure 1-4 The task pane brings common operations to you, enabling you to continue working in your document without interruption.

Now you can compose as easily as you speak and write with voice and handwriting recognition. You can teach Office XP applications to recognize your handwriting and respond to your voice commands. You also can dictate documents after training the applications to understand your pronunciation patterns.

Another addition in Office XP—which goes along with making tasks easier and helping your data go farther—is the introduction of smart tags. *Smart tags* are context-sensitive tags that present you with options based on what you are trying to do. For example, suppose that you are typing a date in a letter about an upcoming meeting. Word will recognize the date and display a smart tag indicator (a dotted purple underline). When you position the mouse pointer on the indicator, the Smart Tag Action button appears. Click it to see your choices. Because Word recognizes the information you typed as a date, your smart tag options include Schedule A Meeting and Show My Calendar. You can move right to Outlook, set up the meeting, and enter it in your calendar right now, while you're thinking about it.

Similar context menus appear when you are correcting and copying information as well. The AutoCorrect Options button appears when you have entered data that Office thinks might need correcting, and the Paste Options button provides you with choices for the way in which you want to paste the text into your document, spreadsheet, presentation, or e-mail message (as shown in Figure 1-5).

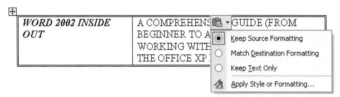

Figure 1-5   Context-sensitive features, like the Paste Options button shown here, enable you to choose options for the data you're working with while you're working with it.

Here are some additional features that improve your daily work with Office XP applications:

- Help is easier to find because of the new Ask A Question box in the upper-right corner of the application windows.

- A newly revised Clip Organizer enables you to search for, organize, and add clip art using the new task pane.

- Built-in diagramming enables you to illustrate your ideas more easily, building conceptual diagrams to show processes and relationships.

- The capability of adding digital signatures to Word, Excel, and Power-Point files helps you ensure that the files are accessed and modified only by authorized people.

- Now you can easily save Office XP documents in a form ready for the Web, whether you are creating Excel spreadsheets, Word documents, or PowerPoint presentations.

■   A new Document Recovery task pane appears whenever you have a system failure, preserving your files in their last state and giving you the option of saving them so you don't lose your most recent work.

As you can see, there's a lot to explore in Office XP. Throughout this book, you'll work with the best Office has to offer—in easy-to-follow, fast-paced chunks. We start the next chapter with the bare beginnings: working with multiple applications in Office XP and performing some of those common operations that make up the ABCs of file handling, such as opening, saving, printing, renaming, and deleting files.

Key Points

■   Office XP is available in three versions—Standard, Professional, and Developer.

■   The Office XP suite includes a complement of programs that include Word, Excel, Outlook, and PowerPoint as core applications. Other applications in some versions of Office XP include Access, FrontPage, and Publisher.

■   You can start Office XP many different ways: by choosing New Office Document in the All Programs list, by selecting the application you want to launch (also in the All Programs list), or by using the tools on the Office XP Shortcut bar.

■   You exit a program by clicking its Close box in the upper-right corner or by choosing Exit from the File menu.

■   Office XP applications share many features and the similar interface makes it easy for you to learn them.

■   The easy exchange of data from program to program adds to the power and flexibility of Office XP.

Chapter 2

Working with Programs

Now that you know how to start the various Microsoft Office XP programs, you're ready to learn how to juggle the different applications you can have open in Office XP at one time. The tasks we cover in this chapter aren't difficult, but they are necessary. You'll learn that the trick is to become coordinated, as you do when learning to drive a stick shift, so that you'll have the program you want open on the screen when you want it. Once you've mastered these procedural basics, you'll be ready to move on to the more exciting tasks ahead.

One of the great advantages of working with the Office XP suite of programs is that many of the basic tasks you perform—opening and saving files, printing documents and reports, and using the Clipboard—are the same from program to program. That means you can learn a task once and use it many times (there's that "working smarter" theme again).

Using Multiple Applications

Even if you think you purchased Office XP to work primarily with one program (to write articles with Microsoft Word, for example, or to create spreadsheets with Microsoft Excel), as you discover the many things you can do—easily and quickly—with all the Office applications, you'll want to try all the core programs. The way in which you can move data from one program to another is almost effortless; and sharing that data can save you hours you might otherwise spend retyping, re-entering, or reconfiguring data you already have.

You may wonder when you'd need or want to have more than one program open at a time. Here are a few scenarios:

- Someone sends you the latest sales figures and they are saved in a Word table. No problem—you can simply copy and paste them into your Excel spreadsheet and do the necessary calculations.

- You write the company newsletter in Word and want to send it out company-wide. You can send the file as an e-mail message in Outlook and then import it into FrontPage to add to your company's Web site.

- There's a policy change in your company's Human Resources hand-book and you need to send the information to all HR personnel in your six offices worldwide. You write the change in a Word document, use your Access database to find the names and addresses of the HR per-sonnel, and then mail merge and print the information from Word. And if you want to send out e-mail messages about the upcoming change in the handbook, you can use Outlook to do that.

- You're applying for a small business loan and you want your application to look as professional as possible. Both your income-and-loss statement and balance sheet are already saved in an Excel spreadsheet; you have created charts that show your lenders at a glance that your business is a good investment. You create the final application in Word, inserting the Excel spreadsheet and chart at the appropriate places.

Tip   Of course, you might switch between programs for much less noble reasons than these. Sometimes when I'm feeling lazy and I need to add a column of numbers in a Word document that I'm working on, I simply drag and drop the numbers into an Excel spreadsheet, enter a function, and have Excel do the math. It saves me from having to open the Windows Calculator and clicking all the individual digits. (When you're trying to save work for yourself, every little bit helps.)

In Chapter 1 you learned to open Office XP applications. If you plan to follow along with the examples in this chapter, open two or three applications. For my pur-poses here, I'll work with Word, Excel, and Microsoft PowerPoint. But you can choose the applications you'd most like to explore instead.

Working with the Taskbar

If you've worked with any of the last several incarnations of the Windows oper-ating systems, you are familiar with the taskbar. It's that strip along the bottom of your screen that houses the Start button on the far left and a set of icons on the far right. In the middle is a blank area that fills with application names as you open them. Figure 2-1 shows how the taskbar appears when you have a Word file and an Excel file open.

Quick Launch bar

Start menu   Program area   Icon area

Figure 2-1   The Windows taskbar is where the action begins in Office XP.

There are four important areas on the taskbar—three of which you're likely to use regularly:

■   The Start menu is the beginning point for many of the applications, utilities, and documents you work with in Windows.

■   The Quick Launch bar lets you open programs quickly.

■   The Program area shows the programs you have open.

■   The notification area displays the icons for utilities and system controls on your computer. You won't use this area often, but you can refer to it to see which system utilities are running on your system.

Tip   The Quick Launch bar shows Microsoft Internet Explorer and Microsoft Outlook Express as the default icons, but you can add your favorite Office XP applications to the Quick Launch bar so that you can open them with a single click of the mouse (without the Office Shortcut Bar taking up space on your screen). To add an application to the Quick Launch bar, simply drag the program icon from your desktop to the Quick Launch bar. The program icon will stay on the desktop, but a smaller version will appear in the Quick Launch bar.

If you don't have a program icon on the desktop, you can drag the icon from the All Programs menu. Click Start, point to All Programs, and then drag the program icon from the menu to the Quick Launch bar. The next time you want to start the program, just click it on the taskbar. Simple, isn't it?

To switch from one open program to another, simply click the program name on the taskbar. Windows brings the program you selected to the forefront so that you can work in that application window. Figure 2-2 shows the desktop when Word is the selected application. Notice that the Word button is darker when Word is selected.

Tip   One of the great conveniences of the taskbar—besides the fact that you can switch among programs easily—is that you can temporarily "put away" programs you're not using to give yourself more room for on-screen work. When you want to reduce a program to a button on the taskbar, click the Minimize button in the window controls in the upper-right corner of the program window. The program window shrinks to a button, clearing the way for other programs. When you want to redisplay the program window, click its button and you're back in business.

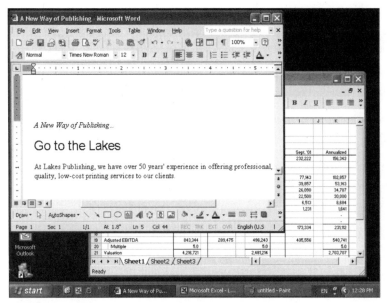

Figure 2-2 When you click the taskbar button for the application you want to use, Windows brings it to the forefront.

Making the Taskbar Go Away Yes, the taskbar can be helpful, but as you get more comfortable working with Office XP applications, you'll also notice that it takes up room on the screen. You can set the taskbar so it disappears when you don't need it and reappears when you do. To make the change, position the pointer on the taskbar and right-click. Choose Properties from the menu that appears. In the taskbar And Start Menu Properties dialog box, make sure the taskbar tab is selected and then click Auto-Hide The taskbar to instruct Windows to hide the taskbar when you're not using it. Click Apply, and then click OK.

The next time you move the mouse pointer off the taskbar, the taskbar disappears. When you want to use the taskbar again, simply point to the area of the screen where the taskbar *would* be if it weren't hidden. The bar reappears, ready for use.

Switching Among Applications

In addition to the point-and-click method of using the taskbar, there are four other ways you can move from program to program. Three of the methods involve the use of shortcut keys, and the third is a window procedure (which we'll cover in the next section).

- Pressing and releasing Alt+Tab takes you back to the previous application window you were using. For example, if you are working in a Word document and switch to Excel, pressing Alt+Tab takes you back to Word; then pressing Alt+Tab a second time takes you back to Excel. If you have more than two programs running, you can use the Alt and Tab keys to move among them by holding down the Alt key and then pressing Tab. This action displays a pop-up window that displays the icons for your current open applications. To choose the application you want, continue to press and release Tab (while still holding down the Alt key) until the program icon you want is highlighted (a description of the item appears along the bottom of the pop-up window). When the program icon you want is highlighted, release both keys and that program window is displayed.

- Pressing Alt+Esc cycles through all the applications you have open. This means that if you have Word, Excel, PowerPoint, and Outlook all open in your current work session, Windows will display each window in turn as you press Alt+Esc.

- Just a few years ago, Ctrl+Alt+Del used to be the dreaded "reboot" key combination that dumped all your open files and restarted your computer. Now, however, Ctrl+Alt+Del brings up the Windows Task Manager, which lets you check the status of your programs (such as when you have a program that seems to be locking up) and enables you to switch to a different program if you'd rather not use one of the other methods. Figure 2-3 shows the Windows Task Manager. To change to a different open application, select the file in the Task list and click Switch To.

Figure 2-3   You can use the Windows Task Manager when you want to check the status of your programs or switch to a different one.

Arranging Application Windows

What happens when you have several programs running at once and you need to see more than one of them on the screen at once? You might be comparing the sales figures in that Word table with the ones you created in your Excel report to determine which ones are correct. To be certain, you need to see those sets of figures side by side. To do that, you need to resize and rearrange the application windows.

When you first start an application, it opens full-screen, taking up the entire desktop area. This gives you the maximum amount of space on-screen so that you can work on the file you need to create. When you want to work with multiple applications, however, you need to be able to shrink the application's window size to make room for other windows. Then you rearrange the windows to display what you want to see. Here are the steps to do this:

1   Click the Restore Down button in the upper-right corner of the application window (it's the middle one of the three window control buttons). The window is reduced in size.

> **Note**   How much smaller the window gets depends on whether you've already reduced the size of the window. If you were previously working in the window at a smaller size, clicking Restore Down returns the window to that size.

2   Position the mouse pointer at one corner of the reduced window and drag inward toward the center of the window. The window grows smaller as you drag.

3   Release the mouse button when the window is the size you want.

4   Rearrange the program windows the way you want them by using the techniques described in Table 2-1. Figure 2-4 shows the desktop with Word, Excel, and PowerPoint files all neatly arranged.

> **Note**   After you've worked with an application and closed it once, the program remembers the window size you used before. The next time you start the program, Office will open the application to the window size previously used. You can then resize it however you like.

Table 2-1   Window Arranging Techniques

If You Want To...	Do This
Make a window shorter or longer	Drag the top or bottom of the window in or out
Make a window narrower or wider	Drag either side of the window in or out
Resize the entire window	Drag a window corner
Move a window	Drag the title bar of the window
Reduce a window to the taskbar	Click the Minimize button in the window controls
Close a window	Click the Close box in the window controls

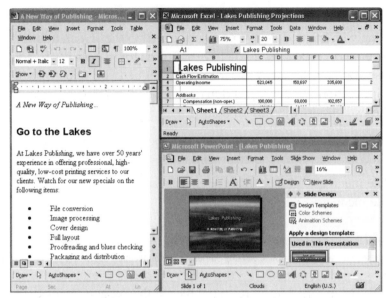

Figure 2-4   You can resize multiple windows so that you can see the necessary data for the work you're doing.

Tip   When you want to work in an application and give it the full desktop screen, click the Maximize button to enlarge the window. The other application windows are still open but they are hidden by the full-size window. To get back to those applications, use the taskbar or one of the shortcut key combinations.

Try This!   Windows also gives you a quick way to arrange two or more applications on your desktop: by tiling multiple windows. Begin by opening at least two programs, and then follow these steps:

1   Click the taskbar button of the first program you want to work with.

2   Press and hold the Ctrl key while clicking additional taskbar buttons (you can use this technique for as many windows as you like). This selects the windows you want to arrange.

3   While still holding down the Ctrl key, right-click one of the taskbar buttons you selected in step 2. A context-sensitive menu appears.

4   Choose Cascade, Tile Horzontally, or Tile Vertically to choose the type of arrangement you want. Cascade overlaps the windows so that each of the title bars are showing; Tile Horizontally places the windows one on top of another; and Tile Vertically positions the windows side-by-side.

Exiting Programs

Of course, working with many different programs open on the screen at one time can be cumbersome, especially if you have to search for the taskbar button you need because you have so many programs open. When you find yourself stumbling over application windows you don't really need, it's time to close a few. Here are the two easiest ways to do that:

- Click the Close box in the upper-right corner of the program window. This is marked as a red X so you can't miss it.

- Open the File menu and choose Exit (or alternatively, press Alt+F to open the File menu and X to exit).

Note   The small X to the right of the Ask A Question box in the application window (just beneath the Close box) closes the file in which you're working but leaves the application open.

If you have made any modifications to the files in the program windows since the last time you saved the files, the Office application will display a warning message, asking whether you'd like to save the changes you made to the file. If you want to save your work, click Yes (and read on to the "Saving Files" section). If you want to let your changes go, click No or Cancel. The application discards your changes and closes the program window.

Now that you know the basic procedures for working with applications once you get into them, you're ready for some of the common tasks that all Office XP applications share. These operations include opening files, working with the Clipboard, saving files, and printing files.

Opening Files

You've already seen that when you start a program in Office XP, a new document opens on the screen. But not every file you work with will be a new file. When you want to work with an existing file, you have the option of opening the document as an Office document, or opening it within the specific application you'll be using. This section gives you the how-tos for each of those situations.

Opening Files the Office Way

If you want to start right up with the Office document you plan to use, choose the Open Office Document option in the All Programs menu (or in the Office Shortcut Bar). This action brings up the Open Office Document dialog box, which shows all the different application files in the current folder, each with an icon showing which application it belongs to (as shown in Figure 2-5).

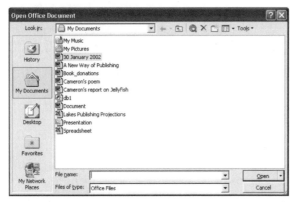

Figure 2-5   The Open Office Document dialog box lists all the Office files in the current folder and shows their program icons.

To open the file you want, navigate to the folder you want by clicking the Look In down-arrow and choosing the folder you want from the list. Then select the file you want to open in the files list and click Open. The file appears in a program window on your screen.

Tip   The Open button has a small submenu that offers you the option of opening a copy of a file (which enables you to keep the original safe). Additionally, if you select a Web page file in the list, the Open button includes an option that allows you to open the file in a browser window. To display the Open submenu, click the small arrow to the right of the button name.

Opening Files Within Applications

But suppose that you're working in Word and you want to look up the report you submitted last week—which you also created in Word. When you're using an application (any Office XP application), you can open a file in any of three ways:

- Open the File menu and choose Open
- Press Ctrl+O
- Click the Open tool on the toolbar

Note   You'll learn more about the different tools in the chapters on each of the individual programs. For now, just know that most common tools—New, Open, Save, and Print—are available on the toolbar of every Office XP application.

Any of these methods brings up the Open dialog box, which looks almost identical to the Open Office Document dialog box. To open the file you want, navigate to the right folder, select the file from the list, and click Open. The document opens in the application window.

I want to call your attention to one aspect of the application's Open dialog box: You have other choices available in the Open submenu. When you open a document in Word, for example, and click the small arrow to the right of the Open button, you see the submenu shown here:

In addition to the regular Open command, you can use the Open As Copy command, which creates and opens a copy of the document, and the Open As Read-Only command, which opens the document in the application window but won't allow you to revise it. This is a good option for those times when you want to review something without inadvertently modifying it. Also, Open And Repair lets you open a file that may have been damaged due to a badly timed crash or lockup. (The new Document Recovery feature in Windows XP helps you recover quickly from those times when your computer crashes, but the Open And Repair option is a nice safeguard to have.)

Working with Stackable Documents   Something really neat that's a new feature of Windows XP is the ability to "stack" documents on the taskbar. Now when you have several files open in Word, for example, you can see each of the file names in a pop-up list that appears when you click the Word button on the taskbar, as shown here:

To choose the one you want, simply click its button.

You can rearrange, tile, or cascade the documents in individual windows by right-clicking the Word taskbar button and choosing the look you want. You can also close all the documents at once by right-clicking and choosing Close Group.

Using the Clipboard

The Office Clipboard is one of the tools Office XP uses to help you move data, pictures, paragraphs, charts, and more from one document to another. The Clipboard functions like a 3-D clipboard—you take a document out of a file and put it on the Clipboard until you need it. When you're working with the file you want to add it to, you take it off the Clipboard and slip it in the file.

Microsoft Windows XP—and now Office XP—improved the way the Clipboard operates, enabling you to save as many as 24 different items from any and all applications. You also can display the Clipboard in the task pane along the right side of the program window so that you can easily see what you want to paste into the current file.

How do you put something on the Clipboard? Simple. Whenever you use either the Copy or Cut command in an application, the item you cut or copied is placed on the Clipboard. For our purposes here, we'll use Copy. Start by selecting the item—text, image, or data—that you want to copy. Then you can choose your favorite of three methods:

- Open the Edit menu and choose Copy

- Press Ctrl+C

- Click the Copy tool on the toolbar

Each of these actions places the selected item on the as-yet unseen Office Clipboard. When you're ready to see what you've put there, you can open the Edit menu and choose Office Clipboard, or click the down-arrow in the upper-right corner of the task pane and select Clipboard from the submenu. The Clipboard opens in the task pane area of your window (as shown in Figure 2-6).

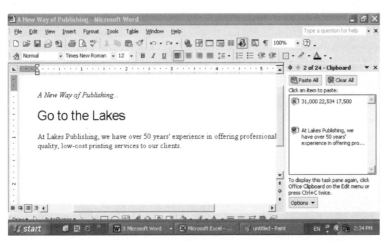

Figure 2-6 The Clipboard opens in the task pane and displays as many as 24 items you've copied from all applications.

Here are a few things worth knowing about the Clipboard display:

- Program icons appear to the left of the Clipboard items, showing you the application in which they were created.

■ A small Clipboard icon appears on the taskbar to let you know items are currently stored on the Clipboard, and a small pop-up message tells you how many items are on the Clipboard each time you add a new one.

■ You can elect to paste all the items on the Clipboard at once by clicking Paste All, or you can select the item you want to add to the current document and choose Edit, Paste; press Ctrl+V; or click the Paste tool.

■ You can customize the way the Clipboard works on your system by clicking Options and choosing the settings you want.

When you're ready to erase the contents of the Clipboard (which is a good idea to do regularly because storing large items—especially graphics—on the Clipboard eats up disk space), click Clear All. Office XP clears the Clipboard and you can start again.

Saving Files

When you've created a file worth saving, you can save the file using one of—you guessed it—three methods. (Starting to see a pattern here? The procedures are similar enough that what you learn in one task instantly transfers to the next.) The methods are as follows:

■ Open the File menu and choose Save

■ Press Ctrl+S

■ Click the Save tool on the toolbar

Each of these actions brings up the Save As dialog box (shown in Figure 2-7). The Save As dialog box resembles the Open dialog box.

Figure 2-7   When you want to save a new word document for the first time, use the Save As dialog box.

Here are the steps for saving your file:

1 Click the Save In down-arrow to display the folders list. Navigate to the folder in which you want to store the file.

2   Enter a name for the file in the File Name box.

3   Click the Save As Type down-arrow and choose the format in which you want to save the file. If you are saving the file in the same format used to create it, you don't need to do anything here. But if you're saving the file to be used with a different program, or with an earlier version of a program (such as Word 6.0/95), choosing the Save As Type setting is important.

4   Click Save to save the file. The file is stored in the folder you selected under the file name you entered.

Saving Office Documents as Web Pages Everything's going to the Web these days. And you don't have to be handy with Hypertext Markup Language (HTML) or FrontPage in order to publish your Office documents online. In fact, you can save your Office documents as Web pages just by using the Save As command in the File menu. Here's the process:

1   Prepare your document as usual in Word, Excel, or PowerPoint.

2   From the File menu, choose Save As.

3   In the Save As dialog box, choose Web Page in the Save As Type box.

4   If you want to change the title for the page (the name displayed in the window's title bar), click Change Title, enter the name, and then click OK.

5   Enter the name for the file in the File name box and then click Save.

The program creates an HTML file along with the necessary folders and you can then post the document to the Web using your File Transfer Protocol (FTP) or favorite upload utility. (If you are working on a network and are unsure how to upload documents to a Web server, check with your system administrator for more information.)

Printing Files

Ready for another set of three? Oops—not everything is as predictable as it seems—there are actually *four* ways you can print from within an Office XP application:

■   Open the File menu and choose Print.

■   Press Ctrl+P.

■   Click the Print tool on the toolbar. Be forewarned, though—this action sends the document directly to the default printer without stopping to show you the Print dialog box, so the document will print according to your default options.

■   Open the File menu and choose Print Preview. The document is displayed in a preview window on your screen so you can see how it will appear in print. If everything looks good, click the Print tool on the Preview toolbar to complete the print operation.

When the Print dialog box (shown in Figure 2-8) appears, you can choose which printer you want to use and what portions of the file you want to print (all applications enable you to print the entire file or a selected portion of the file). You can specify the number of copies you want and determine the order in which they are printed. When you've set all the print options the way you want them, click OK. The file is sent to your printer and you should have a nice, clean printout in a matter of seconds.

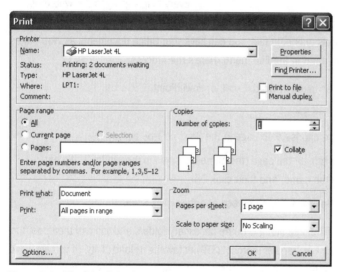

Figure 2-8   The Print dialog box lets you choose your printer, decide how much you want to print, and in what order.

Note   Although the basic printing process works the same in all Office XP applications, each program has its unique print features. For more about printing in each of the Office XP progams, see the program-specific chapters later in this book.

Now you've been through all the basic tasks you need to know to really start moving with Office XP. This chapter showed you how to work with multiple applications—switching among them, arranging and resizing windows, using the Clipboard to share data, and shutting them down. We finished the chapter with a discussion of the basic procedures that are common to all applications. What else is there to do before we dive into the individual application chapters? Only one thing—you still need to know what to do when it's time to yell "Help!" Luckily, that's the subject of the next chapter.

Key Points

■ Having different Office XP applications running at once gives you an easy way to share data among programs.

■ Use the taskbar to switch among open applications and also to start progams and get system information.

■ The shortcut keys Alt+Tab and Alt+Esc, as well as the Task Manager, give you alternate ways of switching among progams.

■ Resize and rearrange program windows when you need to see more than one application on the screen.

■ You minimize, resize, restore, maximize, and close windows using the window controls in the upper-right corner of the program window.

■ The procedures for opening, saving, and printing files are similar in all Office XP applications. You can begin the procedures by opening the File menu and selecting the command you want, by using a shortcut key, or by selecting the appropriate tool on the toolbar.

■ The Office Clipboard saves as many as 24 items from all applications. You can view the contents of the Clipboard in the task pane.

Chapter 3

Finding Help at Every Turn

Everybody needs a little help now and then. Maybe you've forgotten how to insert index entries in Microsoft Word. Or maybe you can't remember the function for figuring percentages in Microsoft Excel. Or maybe you're about to use Microsoft Access for the first time and you have your queries and criteria mixed up. Whatever the reason, having a resource right there to help you figure things out is a real saving grace. And Microsoft Office XP has it in spades.

Help in Many Colors

The Help system in Office XP was designed specifically to meet the needs of very different kinds of users needing very different kinds of help. Some users want to be walked through a process, getting guidance each step of the way. Other users want to see a quick write-up and then—Aha!—the lightbulb goes on. Still other users just need a little reminder now and then, telling them the name of this tool, the function of that button, and so on. Table 3-1 lists the different ways you can get help in Office XP and gives you a brief description of each method.

Whether you like to have a help companion at your side, want to do the research and then tackle the task, or just want a little nudge when you need it, you'll find that at least one method of getting help in Office fits the way you work. This chapter introduces you to these various help channels so you'll know how to find it when you need it.

Table 3-1   Ways to Get Help in Office XP

Help Method	Shortcut Key	Description
Application help	F1	Displays the Help system related to the particular program you are using
Office Assistant	None	An animated companion that leads you through common tasks and anticipates your help needs
What's This?	Shift+F1	A help feature that displays descriptive tags providing the name and function of items on the screen
Detect And Repair	None	Scans Office files to locate and fix any errors

Using Ask A Question

Wouldn't it be nice to be able to ask a simple question and get a simple answer—*fast*? That's the idea behind the Ask A Question box, located in the upper-right corner of each application window. Wondering how to create a border around cells in an Excel spreadsheet? Type **border cells** and press Enter, and the list displayed in Figure 3-1 appears.

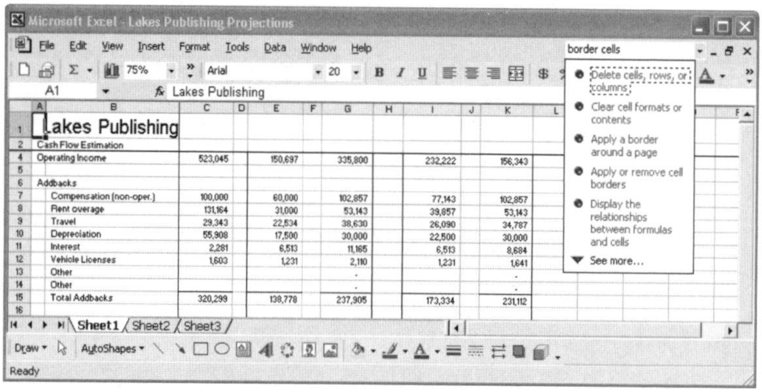

Figure 3-1   The Ask A Question box enables you to get quick help while you work.

If you see a Help topic that seems close to what you need, click it. The Help window opens in the task pane area, giving you more information and the steps you need for that particular operation. If you don't see a suggestion that fits what you're looking for, you can click See More at the bottom of the help list to view additional topics. If you review the entire list of help items and you *still* don't see the Help topic you need, you can click None Of The Above, and then search for more information on the Web.

Tip   Sometimes it can be difficult to find the specific help you need if the words you are using are too general. Try narrowing your terms to identify the specific issue as concisely as possible; for example, *format header, number images, export workbook,* and so on.

Working with the Office Assistant

When you fired up Office XP for the first time, it's likely that you were met by the antics of the Office Assistant, an animated guide eager to lead you through common procedures in the application program you started. The default assistant is Clippit, the paperclip. His blinking eyeballs and crooked smile (*is* that a smile?) are endearing, and his help is practical and direct.

When the Office Assistant is displayed on the screen, you begin the process of asking him a question by clicking his image. A pop-up box appears, asking what you would like to do. You can simply type your question (as shown in Figure 3-2) and click Search.

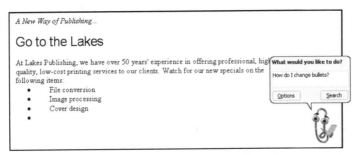

Figure 3-2 You can ask the Assistant a question specific to the program you are using.

Training Your Assistant Are you wondering what's behind the Options button in the Assistant pop-up box? You can customize things the Assistant does for and with you, and also tailor the kinds of tips the Assistant offers. To display your choices, click the Assistant to display the pop-up box and click Options. The Office Assistant dialog box appears.

In the top half of the Options tab, you can control when and where the Assistant appears. You can also disable the Make Sounds option if the little sound effects get under your skin. In the bottom half of the Options tab, you make choices about the kinds of tips that are displayed. You can add to the tips already selected or reset the tips to their default settings by clicking Reset My Tips.

When you're finished changing the Office Assistant settings, click OK to return to your work.

Changing Assistants

Although Clippit is pretty easy to get along with, you might want to try one of the other Assistants, which come in a variety of characters. To change the Assistant, click the Assistant to display the pop-up box (or if the Assistant is not displayed on the screen, choose Show The Office Assistant from the Help menu). Click Options and select the Gallery tab (as shown in Figure 3-3).

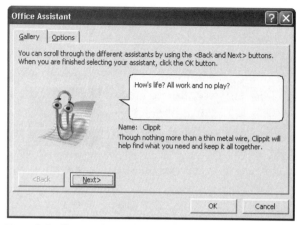

Figure 3-3   You can change the Office Assistant to find a personality best suited to your own.

You can view each Assistant by clicking Next to page through the selections. When you find the one you want, click OK. Your new Assistant joins you in the work area of your document window.

Note   Depending on the way you installed some of the features in your version of Office XP, not all your Assistants may be available right off the bat. If you select an Assistant that isn't installed, your current Assistant will let you know and ask whether you'd like to install the new Assistant now. Click Yes to continue or No to cancel. If you click Yes, the Windows Installer will add the new Assistant. You may be prompted to insert your Office XP CD if it is not already in the CD-ROM drive.

Hiding the Assistant

It's not unusual for users to enjoy the companionship of the Assistant for the first few weeks as they learn a new program, but once they move beyond the just-figuring-it-out stage, they are ready to go it alone. When you get to this point and you want to put the Office Assistant away, you can do it two ways:

■   Right-click the Office Assistant and choose Hide from the pop-up menu.

■   Choose Hide The Office Assistant from the Help menu.

Turning Off the Assistant

But be forewarned—hiding an Assistant is not the same as disabling the Office Assistant feature. The next time you press F1, your companion reappears. And, depending on how many options you've selected, the Assistant may also appear when you are working with wizards in Office applications and when the program wants to alert you to something you need to know.

If you want to do away with the Office Assistant completely so that it's not appearing uninvited and unannounced, right-click the Office Assistant and click the Options button. On the Options tab of the Office Assistant dialog box, clear the Use The Office Assistant check box; then click OK. That puts away the Assistant once and for all—or at least until the next time you choose Show The Office Assistant from the Help menu.

Tip   If you decide you want to try again with yet a *different* Assistant, you can check out the Microsoft Office Download Center (*http://office.microsoft.com/Downloads/default.aspx*) to see whether there are any additional Office Assistants available.

Using the Help System

Although the Office Assistant and the Ask A Question box are two ways to get quick help that you can apply as you work, sometimes you need an answer that is more detailed. If you're trying to learn how to add footers to your slides in Microsoft PowerPoint, for example, a simple question might not do the trick. You'll want to use the Office XP Help system to find a description of the whole procedure to guide you. You can open the Help system by doing either of the following:

- Press F1.
- Choose Microsoft PowerPoint Help from the Help menu.

Note   When the Office Assistant is enabled (which is the setting by default), pressing F1 brings up the character with the pop-up question, "What would you like to do?" When you have turned off the Office Assistant (see the section entitled "Turning Off the Assistant" for the steps on how to do this), pressing F1 brings up the Office XP Help system.

Figure 3-4 shows the Help panel that appears the first time you access the Help system in PowerPoint. This panel gives you everything you need to know about Help—telling you about the new features in Office XP, the Office Web site, the ways in which you can get help. In addition, the Help introductory window offers you a few suggestions for topics you might want help with (none of those applies to adding footers, however, so we need to keep looking) and links to sites you can visit for more information.

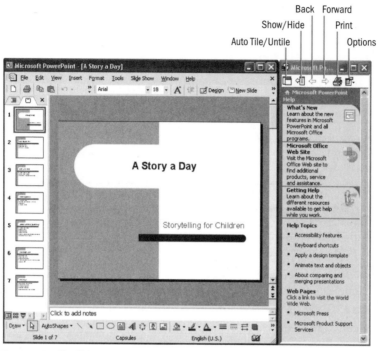

Figure 3-4   The Help panel offers you a wide range of choices, including Help topics and Web pages.

At the top of the Help panel is a set of tools. Table 3-3 describes each of these tools and tells you when you'll use each one.

Table 3-2   Microsoft Office Help Tools

Name	Description
Auto Tile	Resizes the application window so it can be visible beside the help panel
Show	Opens the Help panel to a double-width which displays the Contents, Answer Wizard, and Index tabs
Back	Enables you to return to the Help page you previously viewed
Forward	Enables you to move forward to the next page in a sequence you've already visited
Print	Prints the current Help topic
Options	Displays many of the tools in command form (you can choose Print, Back, or Forward from this menu, for example); also enables you to set Internet options and refresh the display

The following sections take you through each of the different ways you'll use the Help system to find the information you seek.

Expanding the Help Panel

The first step in chasing down your answers involves displaying the Help tools. They are neatly tucked away in the tab section hidden in the left side of the Help window. To display those options, you first need to expand the window by clicking the Show tool. This opens the Help window to show a series of topics and subtopics in a vertical list on the left side of the Help panel.

Once you expand the Help panel, you see three Help tools you can use to find what you're looking for. The Contents tab displays a list of topics and sub-topics you can click for more information. The Answer Wizard enables you to ask a question and find an answer. The Index lets you search for the help you need by entering specific keywords. The first time you open the Help panel, the Answer Wizard is the default; from then on, the default is whatever you were working with the last time the panel was displayed.

Arranging On-Screen Windows

If you intend to continue working while you have the Help panel open, you'll need to use Auto Tile to arrange your windows on the screen. Simply click Auto Tile and the Help panel (with or without the left panel displayed) and the application window will be positioned side-by-side on the screen.

Tip   You can resize the different columns in the Help panel to give the Contents tab more room if you like. Simply position the pointer over the vertical dividing line in the center of the panel. When the pointer changes to a double-headed arrow, drag the center line to the left, redistributing the size of the Help panel columns.

Reviewing Help Contents

When you want to get step-by-step instructions for a particular procedure (such as adding footers to your PowerPoint presentation), the Contents tab is a good place to start. Here's the path that gets you to the Adding Headers And Footers topic:

1   Click the + to the left of Creating Presentations. A list of subtopics appears.

2   Click the + to the left of Formatting Slides And Presentations. Additional subtopics appear in a list below this selection.

3   Aha! Click the + beside Adding Headers And Footers, and additional subtopics appear.

4   Click the Add Headers And Footers subtopic and the help information is displayed in the left panel of the Help window. To choose the procedure you want, click the Add Headers And Footers To Slides link and the steps appear in the Help window (as shown in Figure 3-5).

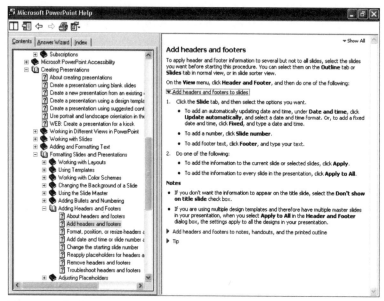

Figure 3-5   Getting to a procedure may require clicking through several levels of topics, but it's worth it.

Tip   Don't forget that you can expand the Help window to full-screen size if you want to read through a help section without having to scroll the panel. To display the panel so that it fills your screen, click the Maximize button in the window controls in the upper right of the Help panel. When you're ready to return the Help panel to its normal size, click Restore Down.

Using the Answer Wizard

The Answer Wizard isn't much different from the "What do you want to do?" help the Office Assistant offers, except that it's offered in the Help window instead of floating over your application. You type the question you want answered and click Search; the Help system then displays a list of topics that are likely to give you the information you want (as shown in Figure 3-6). You simply click the topic you want to view and the text appears in the left Help panel.

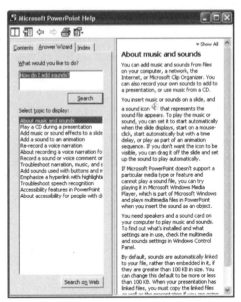

Figure 3-6   The Answer Wizard answers your question by displaying Help topics.

Tip   Just in case the Answer Wizard doesn't have the answer to everything, you can take comfort in the fact that you can click Search On Web to find online information related to your search question. You know the saying: Where there's a Web, there's a way.

Searching the Index

The Index is helpful when you want to search for help by entering a specific word or phrase. The Index is the third tab in the Help window. To use the Index, click the Index tab and then follow these steps:

1   Type the word(s) you want to search for, or scroll through the keyword list and click the word or symbol you want to use.

2   Click the Search button.

3   Choose the topic in the list you want to view. The help information appears in the right panel (as shown in Figure 3-7).

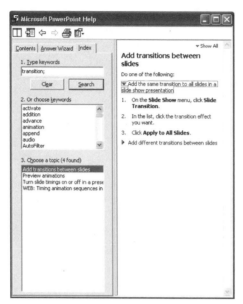

Figure 3-7   Index allows you to search for help by entering keywords.

Try This!   You can print a Help topic at any time you're using the Help system by clicking the Print tool on the Help toolbar. Here are the steps:

1   Using the Help feature of your choice, navigate to the topic you want to print.

2   Make sure your printer is online and ready.

3   Click the Print tool. Office displays the Print dialog box so that you can choose your printer, specify the number of copies you want, and click Print. That's all there is to it—and now you have a page to refer to as you work on the procedure for which you needed help.

Using What's This? for As-You-Work Help

Suppose you're working in Access for the first time in months. The last time you did anything in Access you were just playing around, trying to get comfortable with the program. But now your boss has asked you to create a New Customer log and you need to use Access for a real-world application. But you sit at your desk, looking at the application window, wondering what in the world all these tools on the toolbar do.

When you position the mouse over the tools that are puzzling you, the names of the tools appear. The mystery tools are Analyze and Relationships. But seeing the tool names doesn't tell you what they *do*. That's where the What's This? help comes in handy.

To use What's This?, open the Help menu in the program you are using and choose What's This? The pointer changes to an arrow with a question mark. Direct the What's This? pointer to the item you want to know about and click the mouse button. A pop-up message box appears, giving you a full explanation of the item you've selected. For example, when you click the What's This? pointer on the Analyze tool on the Access toolbar, the message box shown in Figure 3-8 appears.

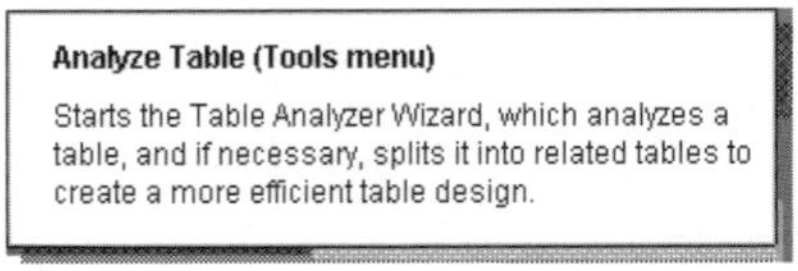

Analyze Table (Tools menu)

Starts the Table Analyzer Wizard, which analyzes a table, and if necessary, splits it into related tables to create a more efficient table design.

Figure 3-8   What's This? helps you learn more about features and tools available on-screen.

Tip   What's This? also provides more than basic descriptive info. In some circumstances—such as when you're working on a document in Word—What's This? also displays in the Reveal Formatting task pane formatting information about the item you're pointing to. This can be helpful when you're wondering whether the headings in your document have been formatted identically. You can select What's This? and point to each heading in turn to display and compare their formatting settings. You can also use the Compare To Another Selection option in the Reveal Formatting task pane to check and compare formats. For more about working with formatting in Word, see Chapter 6, "Formatting in Microsoft Word."

Finding Help Online

One of the major improvements Office XP includes over its ancestors is the seamless way that Web access is built into the program. You may find yourself moving online and offline all day as you work with your Office applications, and this is true when you're working with the Help system as well. You have a number of different ways to find help online while you're working with Office Help:

■   You can open the Help menu and choose Office On The Web. This selection takes you to the Microsoft Office Assistance Center (as shown in Figure 3-9).

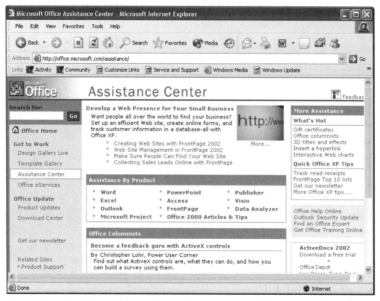

Figure 3-9   The Office Assistance Center offers product-specific support and lots of tips and ideas.

■   When you are working with the Answer Wizard, you can click Search On The Web to find out more about the topic that interests you.

■   When you see a Help topic beginning with the word Web: shown in the topic list of any of the Help features (Contents, Answer Wizard, or Index), click it to move online to an article related to your search topic.

Even if you find yourself rarely needing to use Help in Office XP, it's a good idea to check out the Web offerings every so often using Office On The Web. The Assistance Center page gives you answers, tips, offers, and more. And the information is continually updated, so visit regularly to avoid missing something that might help you work faster and smarter.

Detecting and Repairing Problems

Sometimes your version of Office may just start acting squirrelly. Not long ago, after months and months of use, I found that I could not quit Outlook without an error occurring. Each time I tried to close the program, a dialog box would appear, telling me that the program was not responding and asking me whether I wanted to send an error report. What happened? Most likely, a file that Outlook regularly uses to quit the program was damaged in some way. The solution? Detect And Repair.

The Detect And Repair option is available in the Help menus of all the Office XP programs. In each case, you begin the process by opening the Help menu and selecting the command. The Detect And Repair dialog box then appears (as shown in Figure 3-10), giving you two basic choices:

- You can have Office restore your shortcuts while doing the repairs (this returns the original shortcuts to your Windows desktop).

- You can have the utility discard any changes you've made to the program and return the program to its default settings.

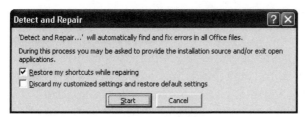

Figure 3-10 Detect And Repair can be your answer when an Office program is behaving strangely.

Click Start. The first thing Detect And Repair will ask you to do is quit all open Office programs. A list appears in the Close Office Programs dialog box; quit the programs and return to the dialog box, and then click Retry. The Microsoft Office Profile Wizard scans your hard disk, restores any damaged files, and displays a message saying everything's fine. Click OK to close the message box and return to your cleaner, healthier program.

You Know You Need Detect And Repair When... Refer to the following list to determine when you need to use the Detect And Repair tool:

- Your program keeps locking up at a certain point in a familiar process.

- The program seems to take an inordinately long time to do a routine task (such as opening or saving a file).

- The screen update in an application is very slow—for example, a dialog box "blocks out" part of the application window which is not immediately refreshed.

- The program is acting inconsistently; for example, Word might begin substituting odd styles for styles you *know* you've created correctly; information might appear in the wrong formats or disappear altogether (don't panic—most likely the data isn't really *gone*; the screen just hasn't updated its display).

Getting Product Updates

Programs are never really done—they are continually morphing into sets of more fully integrated features, stronger security measures, and so on. Office XP has periodic program updates that streamline processes and fix problems. You can make sure your copy of Office XP is as up-to-date as possible by following these steps:

1   Establish a connection to the Internet.

2   Get to the Office XP Web site by choosing Office On The Web from the Help menu or by pointing your browser to *http://office.microsoft.com /ProductUpdates/default.aspx*.

On the Product Updates page (shown in Figure 3-11), you can click the Go button to enable the Web site to check your computer to ensure you have the most current program files. If the utility finds that you do not have the most current version of a file, a page appears, displaying the additional updates that you can review. Select the ones you want and download them on the spot.

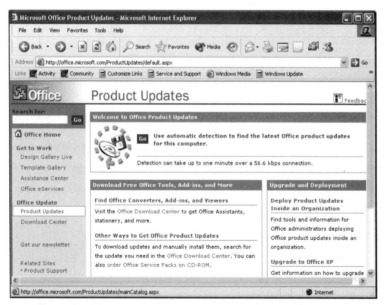

Figure 3-11   The Office XP Product Updates Web page will evaluate your system to see whether you need any new update files.

When you are asked whether you want to open the download file or save it to your hard disk, choose Save The File. Then, after the file is downloaded, use Windows Explorer or the Run command in the Start menu to start the new update. Onscreen prompts will lead you through the process for installing the file. Figure 3-12 shows an example of a setup utility launched automatically when I used the Run command to select an Office update file.

Figure 3-12 The update files include their own setup/install utility, so all you need to do is open them to start the process.

Because Microsoft digitally signs all its updates—thus verifying that the files come directly from Microsoft and are safe for your system—you can simply click Open and install the update while connected to the site, if you want to forgo saving the file to your hard disk. Generally, however, you should save files to your hard disk before installation so that you can protect your system against viruses.

Click Next to continue through the process and the update will automatically install. When the installation is finished, a message appears telling you so, and you can click OK to close the utility and continue on with your program, with the new features intact.

Key Points

- Office XP includes several different kinds of help to give you the answers you need the way you want them.

- The Ask A Question box gives you quick, topic-centered help related to the program you are using.

- The Office Assistant is an animated on-screen character that answers questions and walks you through common tasks.

■ The Help system is a comprehensive support system that offers three tools—Contents, Answer Wizard, and Index—that allow you to locate the information you seek.

■ What's This? is a quick-point method of defining important program elements and settings.

■ Use the Office On The Web option on the Help menu to go online to the Office Assistance Center and to get the latest program updates for Office XP.

Part II

Word Power, Made Simple

Now that you understand the basic workings of Microsoft Office XP and can navigate your way through the Help system, let's explore Microsoft Word, one of the best known programs in Office XP. In Chapter 4, "Creating and Saving a Document," you'll learn all the basics for getting your thoughts onto the electronic page. Chapter 5, "Using Microsoft Word's Editing Tools," assumes that you've entered text in the document and you're ready to start editing with the many tools at Word's disposal. Chapter 6, "Formatting in Microsoft Word," introduces you to the fun, easy-to-use formatting features of Word. By the time you get to Chapter 7, "Special Features (and Challenges!) in Microsoft Word," you'll be ready to tackle the specialized features you may not need in your everyday documents, such as sections, headers and footers, graphics and diagrams, hyperlinks, tables of contents, indexes, and macros.

Chapter 4

Creating a Simple Document

Whether you're just dying to start that Great American Novel or you've got a simple press release to produce, Microsoft Word has the power, the tools, and the know-how to help you get off to a good start. In this chapter, you'll become familiar with Word features, tools, and views, and you'll create a document (both from scratch and by using a template). You'll also find out how to enter text in different ways, giving you the flexibility you need to use Word in the way that works best for you.

What Can You Do with Microsoft Word?

Perhaps an easier question to answer would be, "What *can't* you do with Microsoft Word?" If your project has anything to do with words—typing them, arranging them, enhancing them, or checking them—Word can take care of it. Here are just a few of the tasks you can accomplish with Word:

- Compose the monthly sales letter to your field reps.

- Pull together a team to collaboratively produce your company's annual report.

- Create the weekly lesson plan for your classroom.

- Write, edit, and publish an entire book.

- Create a grocery list (no kidding).

- Compile your research on the behavior of army ants.

- Design Web pages and post them on the Internet.

- Publish a multicolumn newsletter.

- Create, print, and send a mass e-mail campaign.

Individuals use Word for projects at work, school, and home. Companies use Word as their word processor of choice. Word is used on stand-alone and networked systems alike; it's a standard format for files sent hither and yon all over the Internet, worldwide. If you want to use a simple-but-powerful word-processing program that is compatible with the majority of programs on the globe, you're in the right place.

A Walk Around the Word Window

The Word window has lots of open area, giving you plenty of room to think about the text you are composing. Your tools are positioned within easy reach along three sides of the work area. Take a look at Figure 4-1 to see the important elements in the Word window.

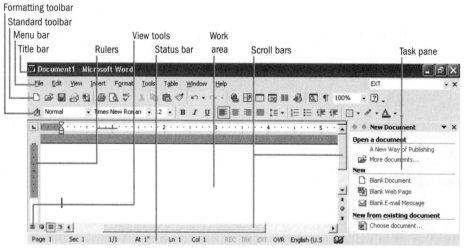

Figure 4-1   The Word window positions all the tools you need nearby so you can access them easily as you work.

These are the items you'll work with regularly in Word:

- **Title bar.** The title bar always lists the name of the document you are working on. If you have just started a document and have not yet named it, *Document1* shows as the default title.

■ **Work area.**   This is the open area of the screen in which you type your text, insert graphics, and so on.

■ **Rulers.**   The work area is bordered on the top and left by two rulers; you will set tabs, work with margins, and align text elements using the rulers.

■ **Scroll bars.**   Two scroll bars—horizontal and vertical—line the bottom and right sides of the work area. You'll use the scroll bars to move to areas of the document outside the current display.

■ **Menu bar.**   The Word menus contain commands related to a different aspect of creating a document.

■ **Standard toolbar.**   These tools enable you to work with files; cut, copy, and paste content; undo and redo your actions; and add special elements such as tables and spreadsheet sections.

■ **Formatting toolbar.**   You'll use these tools to change the look, style, size, and alignment of the text you enter.

■ **Task pane.**   The task pane anticipates the next operation you might want to perform and displays choices accordingly.

■ **Status bar.**   The status bar gives you information about the current file—the number of pages, the current cursor position, and whether Insert or Overtype mode is turned on (more about that in the section entitled "Entering Text," later in this chapter). Additionally, if you are using the spelling checker or printing the document, small icons appear in the right side of the status bar to show that those operations are in progress.

■ **View tools.**   Along the left side of the horizontal scroll bar, you see four tools that enable you to display your Word document in four ways.

The following sections go into a bit more detail about the items in the Word window you're likely to use most often.

Tip   Although the task pane appears when you first start Word and begin a document, you can put it away to give yourself more room to work on-screen. To close the task pane, click the Close box in the upper right corner of the pane.

Checking Out the Word Menus

Word includes nine menus, each of which contains commands related to a specific task you'll be accomplishing in Word. You open menus either by clicking the menu name or by pressing and holding the Alt key while pressing the underlined letter in the menu name (for example, Alt+F opens the File menu). Table 4-1 gives you a quick rundown of the types of commands you'll find in Word menus.

Table 4-1   Word Menu Commands

Menu	Shortcut Key	Description
File	Alt+F	Contains commands for anything related to working with Word documents—such as opening, saving, printing, importing, setting up, and previewing documents.
Edit	Alt+E	Includes everything you need for selecting, finding, cutting, copying, pasting, and clearing text. In addition, you can undo and redo recent operations.
View	Alt+V	Lets you choose the different ways in which you view your Word documents; also controls other items that are displayed on the screen (toolbars, the document map, headers and footers, and the task pane).
Insert	Alt+I	Enables you to insert just about anything you can imagine into your Word document. Want to add a page break? The date and time? A photo? A hyperlink? This menu contains those commands and many others.
Format	Alt+O	Controls the way your document looks—from text to background to graphics to frames. You can change the style, size, color, and alignment of text; create numbered and bulleted lists; change spacing; choose themes; and much more.
Tools	Alt+T	Gives you access to all the add-ins you can use to improve and extend the capabilities of your document. You can run the spelling and grammar checker, count words, track changes, set up speech recognition, add templates, do a mail merge, work collaboratively, and create macros.
Table	Alt+A	Lets you create, modify, format, sort, and customize tables in your Word document.
Window	Alt+W	Enables you to arrange or split open windows or select a different open document that is displayed in the menu list.
Help	Alt+H	Displays the Help menu options you can choose to find out more about your current task.

Try This!   Word uses smart technology to customize the menus according to the way you work. (So do all the other Office programs, for that matter.) This means that you are shown only the commands you are likely to want, which keeps the menu clear and the operation simple. When you click the menu name, the full menu does not open right away; instead, you see only the primary commands and any commands you have selected recently. An extend button (a double down arrow) appears at the bottom of the menu; if you don't see the command you want, click the button (or simply wait a second or two with the menu open and it will extend to full-size on its own). Give it a try by performing the following steps:

1   Click the Edit menu. The partial menu appears, with the extend button at the bottom.

2   Click the extend button (or just keep the menu open for a few seconds). The menu opens to its full length, displaying all available commands in their proper order.

3   Click outside the menu to close it.

Understanding Toolbars

When you first start Word, only the Standard and Formatting toolbars are displayed on the screen. Those are the ones we'll cover here because they are the ones you'll use most often.

The Standard toolbar gives you common tools for working with files; copying, cutting, and pasting; and adding tables, graphics, and more. Each tool has a corresponding command in one of the Word menus, as shown below:

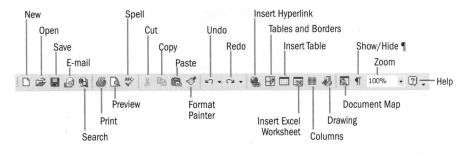

Tip A quick way to find out which tool is which is to use the ScreenTips built into each Office program. Simply position the pointer over the tool you're wondering about and wait a second. A tag appears telling you the name of the tool. You can add to the ScreenTips so that they also tell you what shortcut key to use for that task (for example, you can press Ctrl+C instead of clicking the Copy tool on the Standard toolbar). To add the shortcut keys to your ScreenTips, open the Tools menu, choose Customize, and, on the Options tab, select the Show Shortcut Keys In ScreenTips option; and then click Close.

The Formatting toolbar, shown below, contains the selections you need to enhance the appearance of your text. You can choose the font, size, and style; change the alignment and spacing of text; create numbered and bulleted lists; add borders and shades; and highlight and change the color of your text.

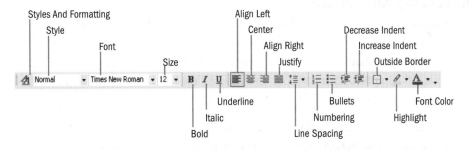

Tip Don't like the way the toolbars are arranged? You can move them around on-screen any place you like. The toolbars are *dockable*, which means that you can remove them from their current place beneath the menu bar and put them someplace else. To do this, click the small column of horizontal lines at the left end of the toolbar and drag toward the center of the work area to release it; then place the toolbar wherever you want. You might want to put the toolbar along the right edge or just leave it, palette-style, in your document window. You can resize the toolbar by dragging an end of the toolbar toward its center.

You will notice that, as you begin to try different features of Word, other toolbars will appear. When you insert a picture file, for example, the Picture toolbar appears. When you decide to track changes in a document, the Reviewing toolbar appears. To get the full effect of all the toolbars Word offers you, open the View menu and click Toolbars. You'll see the massive list shown in Figure 4-2. To display one of the toolbars, simply click the one you want to use.

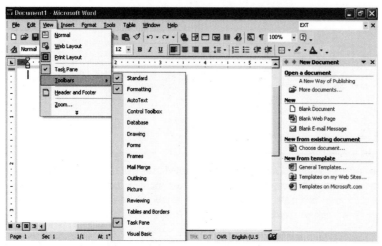

Figure 4-2   Word displays these toolbars by default but you can select others any time you choose.

When you're ready to hide the toolbar again, right-click the toolbar and choose its name from the list to deselect it. This puts the toolbar away until you want to use it again.

Introducing Word Views

Word gives you a number of different ways to look at the same document. You'll discover that some views enable you to focus only on text; others let you see how the layout is shaping up (both for print and for the Web); and still others let you check the organization of your document. You can choose the different views in two ways:

■   By clicking the view tool you want in the lower left corner of the Word work area (use ScreenTips to help you identify the one you want)

■   By opening the View menu and choosing your view from the displayed options

The following list explains what you can expect from each of the views in Word:

■   Normal view is the view you work with when you are entering text and creating your document. This view does not show special formats or column layouts if you've applied them, but it allows you to enter text quickly now and fuss with formats later.

- Web Layout view shows the way the page will look after it's saved as a Web document. Any formats and images you've placed will appear here, but as you can see, the margins of the page are different (as they will be on the Web).

- Print Layout view is the view selected by default when you begin using Word. In this view you can see all formatting changes you make, as well as any added graphics, lines, and so on. You also get a realistic idea of how the page will look when printed.

- Outline view shows how the document looks when it's arranged according to heading levels. Working in Outline view is great when you are creating a long document that you (and perhaps your team) are building from an outline.

Other Looks for Other Tasks   The four views described in this section—Normal, Web Layout, Print Layout, and Outline—are the primary ones available to you as you create your documents, but you have other options as well. While you're exploring the features of Word, be sure to check out these alternate looks:

Print Preview mode enables you to see the document as it would be printed. You can zoom to different page sizes and display more than one page on the screen if you like. Try Print Preview by choosing the command in the File menu or by clicking the Preview button on the Standard toolbar.

The *Document Map* divides your Word window into two panels. On the left you'll see all the headings in your document; and on the right you'll see the regular document, displayed in the view you were using. The Document Map feature is great for checking the headings you've used and for jumping to other sections in a long document. You can move directly to another section simply by clicking the heading in the panel on the left. To turn on the Document Map feature, open the View menu and choose Document Map or click the Document Map tool on the Standard toolbar.

The *Show/Hide Paragraph Marks* tool on the Standard toolbar displays your document in the selected view but adds paragraph and tab characters wherever you have pressed Enter or Tab in your document. This can be helpful if you are looking for an errant tab code that's knocking a list out of alignment, but otherwise it can make you cross-eyed. Leave this feature off until you need it.

The *Zoom* control on the Standard toolbar allows you to enlarge or shrink the display until the page is a size you're comfortable working with. Yes, it's true—you can put away those bifocals and work with your text zoomed to 150 percent if you choose! (Of course, that means you'll have to scroll the page back and forth to read your entire document, which can be a pain.)

Full Screen view is what Word enthusiasts who can't stand to have the screen cluttered with toolbars prefer. When you choose Full Screen view (by opening the View menu and choosing Full Screen), Word removes *all* the menus and toolbars and displays a Close Full Screen button floating over the work area. When you're ready to return to the menu/toolbar system, click the button and you're back.

Starting a New Document

When you start Word by clicking Microsoft Word on the Office Shortcut Bar or clicking Start, pointing to All Programs, and then clicking Microsoft Word, a new document opens automatically on your screen. On the right, the task pane offers you a number of choices for starting a new document.

Tip   If for some reason you *don't* see the task pane along the right side of your Word window, you can display it by choosing Task Pane from the View menu.

The task pane offers you three ways to create a new document:

- In the New area, you can choose whether to open a blank document, Web page, or e-mail message.

- In the New from Existing Document area, you can tell Word to open a new document based on one you've created (this is great for those times when you need to create a new brochure that has the same look and feel as the last brochure but with new content).

- In the New From Template area, you can choose a ready-made template available within Word or you can go to your favorite Web sites (or perhaps the great and mighty *www.microsoft.com*) to find templates that fit your project.

Note   In Chapter 2, you learned to start Office by choosing New Office Document from the All Programs menu. Although I give you the steps for starting a new document within the program here, remember that you can also begin a new document—whether it is a Microsoft Word document, a Microsoft Excel spreadsheet, a Microsoft PowerPoint presentation, or a Microsoft Access database—by making your choice in the New Office Document dialog box.

Choosing a Blank Document

When you first start Word, all you've *got* is a blank document, so that's simple enough. But when you are working on an existing document and want to start a new one, you can start the process by displaying the task pane in three ways:

- Open the File menu and choose New.
- Press the shortcut key Ctrl+N.
- Click the New tool on the Standard toolbar.

When the task pane appears, click Blank Document. A new, pristine electronic page appears, ready for your next project.

Another One of Those, Please   If you really like what you created in one document, you can create another one just like it by using the New From Existing Document command in the New Document task pane. When you click Choose Document, the New From Existing Document dialog box appears. Navigate to the folder containing the file you want to use, select it, and click Create New. Word then displays what appears to be the document you selected in the new document window. Notice, however, that the title bar says Document2, indicating that the file has not been named and saved. You can now modify the copy of the file to your heart's content and then name and save it when you're through. The original file remains intact.

Working with a Template

Word includes a huge selection of *templates* that can help you shortcut the process of creating a new document. In fact, you can use a template for everything from memos to Web pages to full-blown reports. Why start from scratch when you can just work with something already created by professionals? You save some keystrokes and get a professional design in the bargain. To use a template, follow these steps:

1   Click General Templates in the task pane.

2   In the Templates dialog box, click the tab containing the type of document you want to create. (As Figure 4-3 shows, you have quite a variety to choose from!)

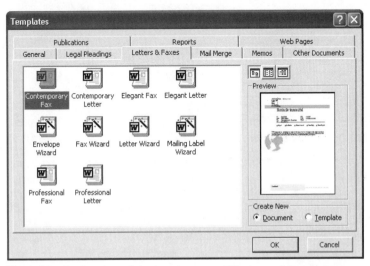

Figure 4-3   The Templates dialog box shows you all the types of documents you can create.

3   Select the template you want to use. The Preview window displays the template file you've chosen so that you can decide whether it's the one you want. If it's not, click a different one and check it out in the Preview window.

4   When you find the template you want to use, make sure the Document radio button is selected (this creates a new document, not a new template file), and click OK.

Once the document is open on your screen, you can simply click in the places it says [*Click here and type*] to add your own information. Figure 4-4 shows a fax coversheet template in use. The first item, in the To: line, has already been entered. The Fax: line is now selected. Continue making your changes (you can also change the format, colors, background and more—whatever you choose); when you're finished, press Ctrl+S to display the Save As dialog box so that you can name and save the file.

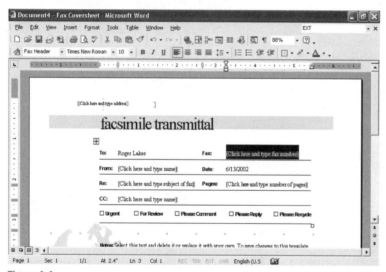

Figure 4-4   Using a template gives you a fast, easy way to start a professional-looking document.

Lingo   Are you wondering what a *template* is? A template is a ready-made file included with Word (and also Excel and PowerPoint) that enables you to build your document on what's already there. Templates include placeholder text that you replace with our own, and the formatting—such as headings, lists, body style, and so on—is already done, saving you time and trouble. You can use the templates built into Word or get more on the Web by clicking the options in the task pane.

Entering Text

How many ways can you type a memo? The answer used to be, "One keystroke at a time." Today, however, Word has expanded our data-entry horizons by offering additional ways of getting text into our documents. You can enter text in a Word document in the following ways:

- You can use the good, old-fashioned hunt-and-peck typing method.

- You can allow the AutoText feature in Word to help you speed text entry by anticipating what you're going to say and entering it for you.

- You can use the dictation feature in Word to *speak* text into the program.

- You can use your drawing tablet to *write* text (this is good primarily for adding your signature to documents or jotting a short note on a report).

- You can import text you've created in other programs.

Which method do you want to try first? The following sections walk you through several examples of the different text-entry methods. Have fun!

Caution   Be forewarned: Speech dictation and recognition is new with this version of Word, and although it's a great feature (and fun, too), you'll have to spend quite a bit of time "training" Word to recognize your speech patterns before it actually saves you time. The program needs to learn how you say things before it can enter your words and phrases accurately.

Typing Text

When you open that blank document (or template, for that matter), the cursor is blinking expectantly on your screen. When you type, the characters appear at the cursor position. Nothing mysterious about that. Type a sample paragraph now (here's one to use in case you can't think of one):

Mrs. Smith, the typing teacher, had never seen a new student type so fast or so well. Her eyes gleamed in admiration.

Notice that the sentence wrapped to the next line automatically. That's a feature called *word wrap*, and it's something Word takes care of automatically. You can continue entering text to get the feel of the keys, if you like, or simply press Enter to complete the paragraph and move the cursor to the next line.

One important consideration when you're typing text in your document is whether you're working in Insert or Overtype mode. Insert mode *inserts* characters at the cursor position, pushing existing characters to the right. Overtype mode *types over* existing characters and can sometimes create a mess in your document if you're not paying attention. By default, your document is in Insert mode (which means characters won't be replaced). You can toggle Overtype mode on and off by

pressing the Insert key on your keyboard. When Overtype mode is on, the symbol
OVR appears in the status bar along the bottom of the screen.

Using AutoText

The AutoText feature in Word is great for helping you streamline the typing of
often-used words and phrases. The feature comes with a whole slew of choices
already included—from headers and footers to mailing instructions to saluations
and signature lines. You can add the text by using the dialog-box method or by
displaying an AutoText toolbar in your work area (this is the best choice if you
plan to use AutoText for a number of entries). Here's how to do it:

1   Open the Tools menu and choose AutoCorrect.

2   Choose the AutoText tab in the AutoCorrect dialog box. Choose the
       AutoText entry you want to add by selecting it from the list, as shown
       in Figure 4-5.

Figure 4-5   Use the AutoText tab of the AutoCorrect dialog box to enter common phrases you'd
rather not type or those you tend to misspell.

3   Click Insert. The word or phrase is added at the cursor position in the
       document and the dialog box closes.

If you plan to use AutoText regularly, display the AutoText tab and choose
Show Toolbar. The AutoText entries are displayed on a short toolbar positioned
just above the work area. You can choose the text you want to insert by clicking
the All Entries button, selecting the category you want, and clicking your selection, as shown in Figure 4-6.

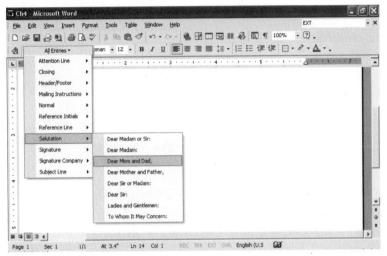

Figure 4-6   My folks aren't crazy about typed letters (too impersonal), so I probably won't really send this.

Your Own Custom AutoText   You can also use AutoText to customize your own ho-hum phrases. Suppose, for example, that the title of your official report is *A 12-Month Study of the Behavior of Army Ants* and you've been asked by your boss to refer to it by name every time you cite it in your summary report. How often will you have to type it? Dozens of times. Luckily, you can use AutoText to insert it for you at the click of your mouse. To do this, display the AutoText tab (if you're using the AutoText toolbar, you can simply click the AutoText tool to display it), type your phrase in the Enter AutoText Entries Here line, click Add, and then click OK. Now, when you want to insert the phrase, click the All Entries button on the AutoText toolbar, choose the Normal category (where customized entries are stored), and click the entry. Word inserts it at the cursor position.

Speaking Text

The speech recognition and dictation features in Word are exciting and fun. As I mentioned earlier, however, they require a lot of up-front preparation and training (for your computer, not for you). For Word to understand what you're trying to say and record it accurately, you need to teach it how to recognize your speech patterns and the fluctuations and intonations of your voice.

Tip   Before you work with speech in Word, you must have set up the feature in Microsoft Windows XP. To do this, click Speech Tools on the right side of the Language Bar, and then choose Options. This displays the Speech Properties dialog box, where you can create a training profile, test and adjust your microphone, and modify speech settings.

To start using the speech feature, follow these steps:

1 Position your cursor at the point in the document where you want to add the dictated text.

2 Open the Tools menu and choose Speech. The Windows XP Language Bar appears across your document.

3 Make sure your microphone is turned on and positioned properly.

4 Speak clearly and slowly into the microphone. The text appears on the screen.

Figure 4-7 shows you what appears on my screen in a quick trial session. I didn't say anything at all about baseball (or *The Simpsons*, for that matter), so I don't know what Word was thinking here. One thing is obvious—I need to spend more time training!

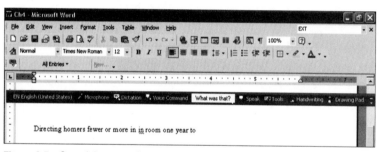

Figure 4-7   Speech is a great feature with tremendous potential—so long as you're willing to invest the preparation time. In the beginning, Word will be bound to make some errors, as you can see here.

We focused on dictation here, but Word will also respond to your voice commands: "Open File" opens the File menu. To activate voice commands, click Voice Command on the Language Bar, and then speak clearly into the microphone.

Caution   Depending on the power of your microphone, Word might pick up any little sound and interpret it as either a command or a word to be entered. While I was working on this section, for example, the telephone rang and I answered it. Somehow during that brief exchange, Word got the idea I was commanding it to print the document, so it opened the Print dialog box and tried sending the file to the printer. The moral: Turn the microphone off when you don't mean to speak into it.

Writing Text

Another fun feature in the Word toolkit is handwriting recognition. Now, this may not be practical for you for any long passages of text unless you have a graphics tablet (and pretty good handwriting, to boot).

To get the process started, click Handwriting on the Language Bar and choose Writing Pad from the menu that appears. The Writing Pad appears on the screen and you can write the text you want Word to insert. Word recognizes what you write and adds the typed characters on the screen, as shown in Figure 4-8.

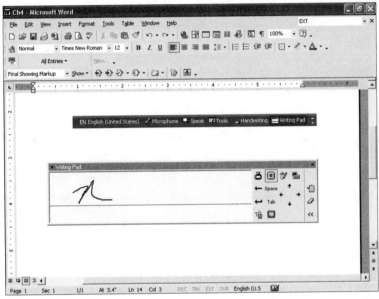

Figure 4-8 You can use handwriting recognition to jot notes into your document.

Tip You'll have a good time experimenting with the different handwriting features—and you can draw on the screen, too. The whole process will be much easier if you use something other than a touchpad as a pointing device (which is what I do when I want to add my signature to documents or draw highlighting marks on documents). A graphics tablet, a stylus, or even a mouse would be a much friendlier drawing instrument than a touchpad.

One more thing—how do you get rid of that infernal Language Bar when it seems to want to stay smack dab in the middle of your Word document? Click the small minimize button on the upper right corner of the bar. You'll see a Language Bar message box, telling you that the bar will be minimized and displayed as an icon beside the clock in the taskbar. Click OK and the Language Bar disappears.

Note Don't forget to save the file once you've finished it. Remember how? Press Ctrl+S to display the Save As dialog box, navigate to the folder in which you want to save the file, enter a file name, and click Save.

As this chapter has shown, the basic tasks for creating your first document are simple—you just open a new document and enter text. But the range of choices for the *kind* of document you create and the *way* in which you enter text require some exploration. By now you should have enough of a foundation to really begin cranking out those words in Word.

Key Points

- You can create all kinds of documents—from short and sweet to long and complicated—in Microsoft Word.

- The Word window is arranged to give you maximum work space and yet position all tools within easy reach of the mouse.

- Word includes nine menus that contain all the commands you need for different document tasks.

- You can choose most common commands by using the menus, tool-bars, or shortcut keys.

- Word offers four views that enable you to see your document in different perspectives: Normal, Web Page Layout, Print Layout, and Outline views.

- You can start a new document by choosing the command you want in the task pane.

- Use one of the many templates in Word to start right off with a document that has been designed and formatted in advance.

- You can enter text a number of different ways in Word: by typing, using AutoText, speaking into a microphone, or writing on the Word Writing Pad or a graphics tablet.

Chapter 5

Using Microsoft Word's Editing Tools

So now that you know how to create documents easily in Microsoft Word, you've probably been up half the night typing, right? Most likely, you've got a report full of typos and an oddly organized cover letter you need to fix before you hand them to the boss at the meeting tomorrow afternoon. Luckily, this next chapter is all about the best features for cleanup detail in Word: the editing toolset.

What Kind of Editing Can You Do with Word?

Because there are different kinds of errors in a document, Word gives you the following ways to correct those errors:

- **Line-by-line corrections.** Your common typo is the kind of correction for which you must position the mouse pointer where the error occurs, erase the errant character, and type the correct one. Other line-by-line corrections are simple text editing, deleting and adding words, and revising phrases. This kind of correction always involves positioning the cursor and then deleting text, retyping text, or both.

■ **Block corrections.**   When you need to move a paragraph, change the location of a heading, or change the order of sections in your document, you will select the text you need to work with, which highlights it as a block. Word has a number of shortcut keys and tools that make working with blocks of text easier.

■ **Automatic corrections.**   Word builds in a number of corrections that take place without your doing anything at all. AutoCorrect is a feature that corrects common errors as you type. The Spelling And Grammar checker scans through your document and evaluates the words you've used and the way you've used them.

■ **Collaborative editing.**   Word also makes it easy for a number of people to leave their mark on a team document. Using the Track Changes feature, one person can write the document, another can edit, a third can review it, and all three people can see the comments and changes that others have made. In addition, the Online Collaboration feature enables those people to meet online and have a discussion about the document in progress.

AutoCorrecting Your Document

The first kind of editing you may notice with Word is the kind that happens right before you eyes as you type. The AutoCorrect feature in Word is your silent helper, fixing such things as month names you forgot to capitalize or repeated letters in a common word.

Try it now. Follow these steps to see AutoCorrect in action:

1   Start Word and begin a new document, if necessary.

2   Type **I was plannning on january 1**. (Be sure to enter three *N*s in *planning* and leave *january* lowercase.)

As you type, Word corrects the errors automatically. Pretty neat, eh? Let's take a look at the AutoCorrect feature and find out how you can add your own entries to help catch your most common editing faux pas.

Changing AutoCorrect Options

As you might expect, AutoCorrect has its own dialog box. (In fact, you worked in the AutoText tab of the AutoCorrect dialog box in the last chapter, if you're reading this book sequentially.) You can display the AutoCorrect dialog box in one of two ways:

■   Choose AutoCorrect from the Tools menu.

■   Right-click a red-underlined word in your document (Word is telling you there's something wrong). When the pop-up menu appears, click Auto-Correct and then choose AutoCorrect Options, as shown in Figure 5-1.

Figure 5-1   Click a red-underlined word or phrase in your document to display the pop-up context menu.

Lingo   A *context menu* is a pop-up menu that displays options that relate to the task you are trying to perform. Right-clicking always makes the context menu appear.

Tip   If you don't see a wavy red line, chances are that someone has changed a setting in your spelling options. To find out, choose Options from the Tools menu and click the Spelling And Grammar tab. If the Hide Spelling Errors In This Document check box shows a check mark, click it to clear the mark, and then click OK. Now any spelling errors should appear with those funky wavy lines.

The AutoCorrect dialog box lists the various changes Word automatically makes for you (as shown in Figure 5-2). Many of the options have to do with capitalization, but in the Replace and With boxes, you have the opportunity to enter words, symbols, or phrases you want Word to catch for you. This is great for those times when you just *know* you are going to spell your new supervisor's name wrong or when you have a long product name you'd rather abbreviate as you type, knowing that Word will fill in all the missing characters using AutoCorrect.

To enter your own AutoCorrect entries, click in the Replace box and type the word or phrase you want Word to find. For example, if your company name is Consolidated Financial Publishing Group, Ltd., you could enter CFPG in the Replace box and the full name of the company in the With box. Then click Add and AutoCorrect adds the entry to the list. Now the next time you type **CFPG** in your document, AutoCorrect will substitute the full name of the company for the characters you entered, saving you time and keystrokes.

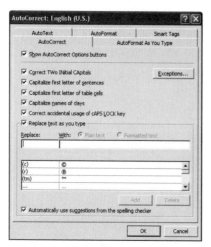

Figure 5-2   AutoCorrect checks for a number of errors automatically, but you can always add your own.

Turning AutoCorrect Off

AutoCorrect is a nice feature, but you may find that some of the "help" you receive isn't exactly what you'd hoped for. In some documents you may want to type (c) and have it stay (c) instead of automatically substituting the copyright symbol, ©, which is one of the changes AutoCorrect makes by default. When you want to turn AutoCorrect off, you do so by following these steps:

1   Display the AutoCorrect dialog box by choosing AutoCorrect Options from the Tools menu.

2   Clear all the check boxes in the AutoCorrect tab and then click OK.

For the best results, you may want to simply clear the check boxes of those items that interfere with the tasks you are trying to perform. For example, if you are writing a review of a new band called *tuesday* (which is meant to appear in all lowercase letters), you could simply clear the Capitalize Names Of Days check box and leave the others selected.

Tip   If AutoCorrect makes a change you don't like, you can use the Undo function (either by choosing Undo from the Edit menu or by hitting Ctrl+Z) to remove that change while still leaving AutoCorrect fully functioning. AutoCorrect learns from your correction and it won't make the correction again in that document.

Starting Simple: Correcting Typos

As you edit your documents, you will likely use different editing techniques for different things. Some words you'll let Word correct for you; others you'll retype.

Or perhaps you'll select the word and delete it by pressing Delete. This section shows you how to complete simple editing tasks.

Common Editing and Navigation Keys

Simple line-by-line editing really involves two steps: Detecting the error in the document and correcting it. This means you'll use a combination of navigation keys and editing keys to make the changes you need to make. Table 5-1 lists the keys you'll use to get around within the document, and Table 5-2 highlights the most common editing keys.

Table 5-1   Keys for Moving Around Within the Document

Pressing This Key	Performs This Action
PageUp	Scrolls the document up one screen
PageDown	Scrolls the document down one screen
Home	Moves the cursor quickly to the left end of a line of text
Ctrl+Home	Moves the cursor to the beginning of the document
End	Moves the cursor quickly to the end of the current line
Ctrl+End	Moves the cursor to the end of the document
Right arrow	Moves the cursor to the right one character or space
Ctrl+Right arrow	Moves the cursor to the right one word at a time
Left arrow	Moves the cursor to the left one character or space
Ctrl+Left arrow	Moves the cursor to the left one word at a time
Up arrow	Moves the cursor one line up
Down arrow	Moves the cursor one line down
F5	Displays the Find And Replace dialog box with the Go To tab selected so that you can enter the number of the page you want to go to

Table 5-2   Keys for Simple Line Editing

Pressing This Key	Performs This Action
Backspace	Erases the character to the left of the cursor
Enter	Completes a paragraph and moves the cursor to the next line in the document
Delete	Deletes the character immediately to the right of the cursor
Insert	Toggles the typing mode from Insert to Overtype mode

Browsing by Object   Word gives you yet another way to move through your document: the Browse Object feature. This feature enables you to browse through the document by a specific type of object. For example, suppose that you have been working on a document with two other team members and you want to review the document and see what others have said about it. You can choose Browse By Comment to move from comment to comment and read the comments your teammates have inserted.

When you click Select Browse Object (the circle in the lower portion of the vertical scroll bar), a palette of objects appears as follows. You can then click the object you want to use:

{a}	Field
	Endnote
	Footnote
	Comment
	Section
	Page
	Edits
	Heading
	Graphic
	Table

In addition, the Browse Object palette enables you to click GoTo to display the Go To dialog box and Find to display the Search dialog box. Once you've selected your object of choice, move forward or backward in the document by clicking Previous or Next.

A Little Editing Practice

Now that you know which tools to use, let's try a little editing. Open a document you want to play around with. I went back to the text I started earlier in the chapter and added the following:

I really hadn't thought about asking whether the moovers would be available for the holiday, but I guess I'd better find out. Let's sit on our plans to move the office until early next week so that I have a chance to find out for sure.

Two things need to be changed in this paragraph. First, the typing error *moovers* should be *movers*, and second, exchange the casual word *sit* for the more businesslike word *wait*. To make the correction, you simply click to position the cursor and use the Backspace or Delete key to delete the unwanted characters; then, retype the corrected word.

See? When I say *simple*, I mean simple. It really doesn't have to be any harder than that. In the next section, you learn to do a different kind of editing that requires you to select blocks of text.

Working with Paragraphs

The last section focused on making changes when you're working with individual lines, words, and characters. Another type of editing involves marking a section of text as a block and moving it, reformatting it, deleting it, or copying and pasting it.

Lingo   A *block* of text is any text (including a character, a word, a line, a paragraph, a section, or an entire document) that you highlight.

Selecting Text

You can select the text you want to work with in several ways. Depending on the size of the text selection, you may be able to use one or all of the following methods:

- To select a single word, double-click it.
- To select a sentence, press Ctrl and click.
- To select a paragraph, position the mouse pointer in the margin to the left of the paragraph and double- or triple-click the paragraph.
- To select a phrase, click at the beginning of the text you want to select; then drag the mouse to the end of the selection and release the mouse button.
- To select all text from the cursor position to the beginning of the document, press Ctrl+Shift+Home.
- To select all text from the cursor position to the end of the document, press Ctrl+Shift+End.
- To select the entire document, press Ctrl+A or choose Select All from the Edit menu.
- If you have added graphics, a table, or a chart to your document, you can select those items by simply clicking them.

Once you select the text you want to work with, you need to specify what you want to do with it. Some of the more common block edits involve copying, pasting, moving, or deleting text. The next sections show you how to do those basic tasks.

> **Tip**   In Word 2002, you can now select multiple blocks of text in different parts of the document (called *noncontiguous* blocks because they are not located together in the document). You might do this, for example, when you want to change the format of several headings in your document. You could select the first heading normally (triple-click the text to select it); then press and hold Ctrl. Scroll to the next heading and triple-click it; this text is selected too. Finally, still holding Ctrl, scroll to the additional headings and select them. Once the text blocks are selected, you can make whatever changes you were going to make and the edits are applied to all the selected blocks.

Copying and Pasting Paragraphs

Copying and pasting are two common tasks that use the Office Clipboard. Copying, of course, makes a copy of the text you select and places the copy on the Clipboard. Paste, on the other hand, takes a copy of the item on the Clipboard and inserts it in your document wherever the cursor is positioned. After you select the text you want to work with, you can copy and paste using three methods:

- Choose Copy (or Paste) from the Edit menu
- Click the Copy or Paste tool on the Standard toolbar
- Press Ctrl+C (for Copy) or Ctrl+V (for Paste)

The only trick to pasting is to make sure that you have positioned the cursor at the point you want the copied text to be placed before you choose the Paste command. Otherwise, the added text will be inserted at the current cursor position. (If you accidentally paste text in the wrong place, simply press Ctrl+Z to undo the change.)

> **Tip**   Remember that you can also display and work with the contents of the Office Clipboard by choosing Office Clipboard from the Edit menu.

Understanding Paste Special   Word also enables you to do a special kind of paste with some items you'll paste from the Office Clipboard. Choose the Paste Special command from the Edit menu when you are adding information such as text, graphics, a chart, or an HTML document and you want to preserve the format of file from which you originally copied the data. In the Paste Special dialog box, you can choose whether you want to embed the file or create a link that allows users to move to the application that created it.

Deleting Paragraphs

After all the trouble it takes to write and edit a good paragraph, you may be dismayed to find out how easy it is to get rid of it. Simply select the paragraph (triple-clicking the paragraph is the easiest way) and press Delete. If you prefer, you can press Ctrl+X, which "cuts" the text to the Clipboard, just in case you change your mind and want to use it somewhere else.

Using Undo and Redo

Especially when you are rushing to complete the editing of a project, the Undo feature in Word can be a real life-saver. Undo offers you the choice of undoing (no big surprise there) your most recent editing operations. You can undo your most recent action in any of three ways:

- Click Undo on the Standard toolbar.

- Choose Undo from the Edit menu.

- Press Ctrl+Z.

Word wipes away the change as if it were never made. If you decide that you liked the change after all and want to add it back again, you can *redo* the change using any of these methods:

- Click Redo on the Standard toolbar.

- Choose Repeat from the Edit menu.

- Press Ctrl+Y.

Both Undo and Redo offer a drop-down list that enables you to choose the point to which you want to return (as shown in Figure 5-3). Click the down arrow to the right of the Undo or Redo button and the drop-down list appears. Choose the edit to which you want to return, but remember—everything you've done since that point will be undone (or redone).

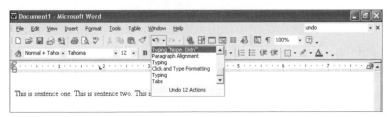

Figure 5-3   Undo and Redo let you go back (or forward) in time to change the changes you've already made.

Using Find and Replace

The Find and Replace features are tools that you can't do without. They enable you to search for a particular word, phrase, or format and replace it with something else. For example, suppose that your company's new product was referred to as RatPackX during its development stage. Now that the product is getting close to its release date, the official name, Mouse Manager, needs to be printed on all product specification sheets and documentation. It's your job to make the change. This is an ideal candidate for find-and-replace. Here's what you do:

1 Open the document you want to edit.

2 Press either Ctrl+F or Ctrl+H to display the Find And Replace dialog box. (You can also open the Edit menu and choose Replace if you prefer.) Figure 5-4 shows the Find And Replace dialog box.

Figure 5-4   The Find And Replace dialog box enables you to make changes quickly throughout your document.

3 In the Find What box in the Find And Replace dialog box, type the word or phrase you're looking for.

4 In the Replace With box, type the word or phrase you want to replace it with.

5 Click Replace All to replace all instances of the original word or phrase with the new entry.

If you want to check each occurrence before you replace it, you can click Find in the Find And Replace dialog box to locate the next item so you can read its context before you change it; then click Replace to change the found item.

Just Find, Please

You won't always want to replace a word or phrase you find with something else. Sometimes you just want to find specific text. Perhaps you want to read what you wrote about Mouse Manager so that you can be consistent with the Web content you're writing. Or maybe you are returning to a document you started last week and want to find your initials, which you used as a bookmark for the place you stopped last time.

To use Find by itself, press Ctrl+F. (You also can display the Find dialog box by opening the Edit menu and choosing Find or by clicking Find in the Select Browse Objects palette.) You will see that Find is just another tab in the Find

And Replace dialog box. The options are similar, with one exception: The Highlight All Items Found In option enables you to highlight all found words or phrases at once. You can then change the format or make a different editing change (click the Replace tab if you want to replace the highlighted words with something else).

Special Find and Replace Considerations When you click More in the Find And Replace dialog box, a number of additional options appear that help you get more specific about the text you're searching for. Here's a quick rundown:

- **Match Case.** Looks for words and phrases that are capitalized exactly the way you entered them.

- **Find Whole Words Only.** Locates only those words that stand alone, not the ones that include the entered phrase as a part of the word. If you were going through the document to replace the word *if* with *whether*, for example (an old editing pet peeve), selecting this option makes sure that only the word *if* is highlighted—not *life*, or *miffed* or *cliff*.

- **Use Wildcards.** Enables you to enter a partial phrase and wildcard characters to narrow your search.

- **Sounds Like (English).** Locates words that sound the same but are spelled differently (there and their, scene and seen, and so on).

- **Find All Word Forms (English).** Lets you find words that have the basic root in common. The word *light*, for example, would find *highlight*, *stoplight*, and *lightly*.

- **Format.** Allows you to search for text formatted a certain way, perhaps in a font, size, or style you want to edit.

- **Special.** Enables you to find special characters such as line spaces, em dashes, ellipses, or blank spaces.

Checking Your Spelling and Grammar

Even if you were the champion in your fifth-grade spelling bee, chances are that, sooner or later, you're going to spell a word incorrectly. Word has a tool that can help you postpone that fateful day. The Spelling And Grammar Checker is a simple but robust utility that runs mostly behind the scenes as you work in Word. Along the way, if you type a spelling that Word doesn't recognize, it will alert you that the word looks strange by underlining it with a wavy red line (grammar errors get a green line). You can see what Word's trying to tell you by right-clicking the word. A pop-up menu of spelling alternatives appears, and you can choose one of the words displayed if you find that it offers the correct spelling.

But that's just for individual, correct-as-you-go kinds of errors. What about those times you want a reputable editor to look over your shoulder and make sure your spelling and usage are correct? When you want to run the spelling checker on the entire document, follow these steps:

1 Press Ctrl+Home to move the cursor to the beginning of the document. (The Spelling Checker will begin checking at the cursor position.)

2 Choose Spelling And Grammar from the Tools menu (or press F7). The Spelling And Grammar Checker appears, as shown in Figure 5-5.

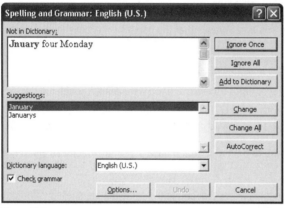

Figure 5-5   Spelling and grammar all at once! Let's see my fifth-grade teacher grade papers this fast!

3 The first thing Word considers odd is found in your document and the Spelling And Grammar dialog box appears. In the Not In Dictionary window in the top of the dialog box, you see what's stumping Word. In the Suggestions box in the bottom of the dialog box, you see what Word holds out as possible alternatives.

4 To select one of these suggestions, click it and choose Change. If you want to make this change for all occurrences in the document, click Change All. If you want to add the edit to your AutoCorrect list, click AutoCorrect.

5 If you don't need to change the phrase or word, you can click Ignore Once to skip this occurrence of this word. If you want to skip every occurrence of the word in the document, click Ignore All. If you want to add the word to the dictionary so that Word won't keep catching it in the Spelling And Grammar Checker, click Add To Dictionary.

Word will continue checking the document. When Word has finished, you'll receive the message: *The spelling and grammar check is complete.* Click OK to return to your document.

Spelling and Grammar Options We've only skimmed the surface of what the Spelling And Grammar Checker has to offer. You can set up the checker to do a number of other things by selecting the options you want in the Spelling And Grammar tab of the Options dialog box. (When you are working in the Spelling And Grammar dialog box, you can also display this dialog box by clicking Options.)

- Add your own custom dictionary by clicking Custom Dictionaries, selecting Add, and choosing the dictionary file from the displayed list.

- Check the Show Readability Statistics box to display a report of your document that gives you data such as word count, sentence length, and readability level.

- Click the Settings button in the Grammar area to customize the types of grammar issues that are found by the checker.

- In the Writing Style box, choose Grammar And Style to add a style checker that catches clichés and jargon, passive voice, sentence fragments, split infinitives, and more.

- Turn off the grammar checker so that it does not run at the same time the spelling checker runs by clearing the Check Grammar With Spelling check box.

Tracking Changes

When you are working with a team to prepare a document, it's imperative that you be able to see what each of the team members has contributed and know what you want to keep and what you want to discard. You can turn on tracking in your document three ways:

- Choose Track Changes from the Tools menu,

- Press Ctrl+Shift+E,

- Double-click the TRK symbol on the status bar to select it.

Tracking is now on, and any changes you make in the document will appear in red and underlined (although if you like, you can you change these default settings to display changes in a different color and style, as described in the section entitled "Setting Tracking Options," later in this chapter). A bar along the left side of the document also points out places in the document that have been edited. Figure 5-6 shows an item that has been added to a list after Tracking has been turned on.

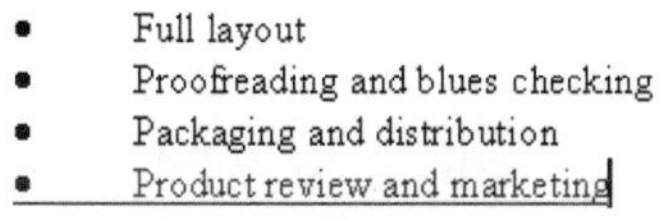

- Full layout
- Proofreading and blues checking
- Packaging and distribution
- Product review and marketing

Figure 5-6   Tracking enables you to see what has been done to a document during the editing process.

Using the Reviewing Toolbar

When you turn on Tracking, the Reviewing toolbar appears by default. You use the Reviewing toolbar for both tracking comments and adding, reviewing, and resolving comments. Figure 5-7 gives you a look at the Reviewing toolbar, and Table 5-3 tells you a little about each of the tools.

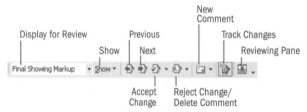

Figure 5-7   You use the Reviewing toolbar to control the way the document looks, show comments, track changes, and accept or reject changes.

Table 5-3   **Using Reviewing Tools**

Tool	Description
Display For Review	Click the down arrow to choose the version of the document you want to see: Original, Original Showing Markup, Final, or Final Showing Markup.
Show	Click the down arrow to choose what you want to display in the document (Comments, Insertions and Deletions, Formatting, Reviewers, and Reviewing Pane).
Previous	Jumps to the previous change.
Next	Jumps to the next change.
Accept Change	Adds the selected change to the document.
Reject Change/Delete Comment	Discards the current change and returns the document to its original state at that point. If a comment is selected, this tool removes the comment.
New Comment	In Normal view, displays the Reviewing Pane; in Web Layout and Print Layout views, displays a comment balloon. Either way, simply type in the comment you want to add.
Track Changes	Toggles tracking on and off.
Reviewing Pane	Displays the Reviewing Pane along the bottom of the document so that you can scroll through the changes and comments added to the document.

Setting Tracking Options

Especially if you are working with several people on a project, it is helpful for each to choose a color or style for his or her changes. That way the person compiling the final document can easily see which changes were made by which team member. You can set these colors and more options in the Track Changes dialog box (shown in Figure 5-8), which you display by clicking the Show down arrow on the Reviewing toolbar and choosing Options.

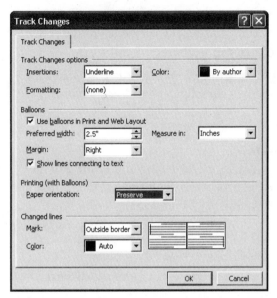

Figure 5-8   You can change the color and style of your changes, as well as the way in which changes appear, in the Track Changes dialog box.

These are the tracking options you can change:

■ You can change the way your inserted text is displayed by clicking the Insertions down-arrow and choosing a different style. Underline is the default, but you can choose Color only, Bold, Italic, or Double underline as well.

■ Choose a different color for your changes by clicking the Color down-arrow and making your choice.

■ If you want to change the indicator used to show formatting changes, click the Formatting down-arrow and choose the style you want.

> **Tip**   You may prefer to leave Formatting set to None because tracked changes can easily pile up if you have several people making changes on a document—and adding formatting changes can magnify the swirl of color in the document in progress. Formatting changes are typically secondary to added or deleted text, so you might want to leave this option disabled so that you can focus on the content.

■ You can do away with the balloons used to display tracked changes in Print and Web Layout views by clearing the Use Balloons check box. (In addition, you can change the balloon width and placement using the options in this section.)

■   You can set up the way you want documents to print with tracked
    changes by selecting Auto, Preserve (the default, which keeps the doc-
    ument's current setting), and Force Landscape.

■   You can alter the bar indicator along the left edge of the page that
    shows changes have been made by changing the location and color of
    the bar.

Accepting or Rejecting Changes

When you have received a document and are reviewing and evaluating the
changes and additions, you need to be able to accept or reject the changes and
suggestions everybody made. Two buttons on the Reviewing toolbar make that
a simple matter: Accept Changes and Reject Changes. The process goes like this:

1   Click Next to move to the next change in the document.

2   Review the change and decide whether you want to keep or discard it.

3   Click Accept Change to keep the change or Reject Change to discard it.

4   Click Next to move to the next change.

Note   Instead of working through the changes one by one, you may prefer to accept or reject all
the changes in the document at once. To choose those options, click the down arrow to the right
of either the Accept Changes or Reject Changes tool. Then choose Accept All Changes In Document or Reject All Changes In Document to complete the task.

Adding Comments

As part of the review process, team members may be more interested in adding
their suggestions than in making actual changes. Comments are perfect for that.
When you position the pointer over each comment, a pop-up box displays the
reviewer's name and the date and time the comment was added. Comments
appear in balloons on the right of the document in Print and Web Layout views,
as you see in Figure 5-9. (In Normal view, you must have the Reviewing Pane
open to view the comments.)

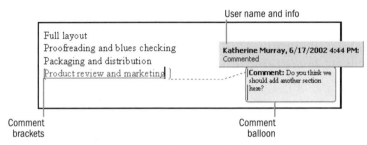

Figure 5-9   Comments are visible in balloons in Print and Web Layout views.

Resolving Comments

You can move from comment to comment in a document by simply scrolling through and reading the balloons, by clicking Next on the Reviewing toolbar, or by clicking Browse By Comment using the Browse Object feature.

After you review a comment, you can discard it by right-clicking the comment and choosing Delete Comment from the displayed menu. If you want to delete all comments at once, click the down arrow to the right of the Reject Change/Delete Comment tool on the Reviewing toolbar and click Delete All Comments In Document from the menu that appears. All comments are removed and your document is ready for a final review.

Displaying and Hiding the Reviewing Pane

The Reviewing Pane is a scrollable area of the document window that you can open to display the comments and changes in your document. This is a log of all of the changes and comments that appear in balloons in Print and Web Layout views. To display the Reviewing Pane, click the Reviewing Pane tool on the Reviewing toolbar. To hide the pane, click the button a second time.

I find that Reviewing Pane more difficult to work with than the text balloons on the document, but that's just me. If you find it easier to scroll through a list of changes (you can also use Next and Previous to move from item to item in the Reviewing Pane), you may prefer this view. If you want to work solely in the Reviewing Pane, you can do away with the text balloons (and thus reclaim more open document space) by clicking the Show down arrow, choosing Options, and clearing the Use Balloons In Web And Print Layout check box.

This chapter has covered a lot of ground. From simple line-by-line text corrections and larger block-style editing to the automated spelling and grammar checker and features for group editing, we've discussed a wide range of tools that will help you prepare your document for final production. The next chapter takes you into the world of formatting by helping you consider the look and feel you want your documents to convey.

Key Points

- AutoCorrect does on-the-spot corrections as you type. You can customize this feature to fit your own style and typing foibles.

- You use a combination of navigation keys and simple editing keys to perform simple line corrections.

- When you copy, move, cut, paste, delete, and format text, you first mark it as a block.

- The Find And Replace feature enables you to search for specific words or phrases in your document and replace the found items with other text.

- The Spelling And Grammar Checker is a full-featured utility that checks not only spelling and simple grammar but style and usage as well.

- You can use Word in a workgroup to develop a document and track changes so that you can see what each team member has added.

- Comments allow you to insert notes and suggestions in a collaborative document.

Chapter 6

Formatting in Microsoft Word

You can write the best prose in the world, but if it appears cramped and crowded and readers have to work to decipher it, chances are that it won't be read. This chapter shows you how to use the formatting features of Microsoft Word to make your document look like something that people will want to read. As you'll see, Word includes some automatic features (such as AutoFormat and themes) that can make formatting less of a chore; Word also gives you a wide range of options so that you can tailor your documents to look just the way you want them to look. We've got lots of ground to cover in this chapter, so let's get started.

Knowing When to Use What How important is formatting for those e-mail messages you send to your friends, the simple weekly update you send to your sales managers, or the syllabus you pass out to your fourth-period class? You'll have to make the call on that. But if you want a simple, quick format with a professional look, try creating your document based on Word's ready-to-use templates. You'll find templates for memos, fax cover sheets, reports, Web pages, and more. To see what templates are available in Word, choose New from the File menu, and then click General Templates and choose the document style you want to see. Remember, too, that you can make your own templates from favorite documents you create.

Letting AutoFormat Do the Work

AutoFormat is a great feature that sometimes gets a bad rap. AutoFormat can help you by automatically adding bullets to your lists as you type, changing heading styles, numbering steps, changing quotes and dashes, and more. But because AutoFormat is occasionally over-eager, changing what you'd rather not have changed, some people prefer to turn off the feature completely and format things by hand. I think the best way to handle AutoFormat is to teach it to do what you want it to do. You do this by setting the AutoFormat options to your preferences.

AutoFormat is turned on by default when you begin working with Word. To display the AutoFormat dialog box (shown in Figure 6-1), choose AutoFormat from the Format menu.

Figure 6-1   You can have Word do a quick AutoFormat based on the document style you select.

The two primary choices in the AutoFormat dialog box allow you to determine how you want the formatting to be done. If you want Word to go through the whole document and make any changes that are needed, leave AutoFormat Now selected. If you want Word to alert you about each formatting change before it is made and give you the option of accepting or rejecting the change, click AutoFormat And Review Each Change. When you click OK, AutoFormatting begins.

Note   Word gives you the option of applying AutoFormat choices based on the kind of document you are creating. The General AutoFormat is selected by default, but you can click the down arrow and choose Letter or Email instead.

Controlling AutoFormat

Depending on the nature of your document and how specialized your formats need to be, you may want to turn off some of the AutoFormat features so they aren't carried out automatically. Perhaps, for example, you don't want AutoFormat to turn your lists into bulleted lists. You can disable that setting so that Word still corrects formats for other items in your document but leaves your lists alone. Here's how to do that:

1 Display the AutoFormat dialog box by choosing AutoFormat from the Format menu.

2 Click Options.

3 In the Apply area of the AutoFormat tab, click Automatic Bulleted Lists to clear the check box and disable the option.

4 Review any other AutoFormat options you want to turn off; click the check box to clear it. Table 6-1 introduces you to the different Auto-Format options.

5 Click OK to accept your change, and then click OK again in the Auto-Format dialog box to return to your document.

Table 6-1   **AutoFormat Options**

Option	Description
Built-In Heading Styles	Applies the default headline styles for the current document
Automatic Bulleted Lists	Turns a list into a bulleted list automatically
List Styles	Applies list styles used in the current document
Other Paragraph Styles	Formats the paragraphs in your document according to styles in your current document
"Straight Quotes" With "Smart Quotes"	Replaces double-prime characters (quotations marks that are vertical) with open and close quotation marks, which are curly
Ordinals With Superscript	Formats ordinals to be superscript above and to the right of the number (1st, 2nd, 3rd)
Fractions (1/2) With Fraction Character (½)	Formats full-size fractions (2/3) to single-character size ($\frac{2}{3}$)
Hyphens (--) With Dash (—)	Replaces two hyphens in a row typed from the keyboard with a longer dash character
Bold And _italic_ With Real Formatting	Boldfaces text you type surrounded by asterisks and italicizes text you enclose in underscores
Internet And Network Paths With Hyper-links	Recognizes URLs and network paths and creates hyperlinks automatically
Preserve Styles	When the autoformat is done, keeps any styles applied in the current document
Plain Text Wordmail Documents	Causes any e-mail messages you open in Word to be displayed in an e-mail format

Try This!   We've been talking about the general AutoFormat options, but you can change additional formatting options by clicking the AutoFormat As You Type tab in the AutoCorrect dialog box. Here are the steps:

1   Choose AutoFormat from the Format menu.

2   Click Options.

3   Click the AutoFormat As You Type tab.

4   Scroll through the list to the Apply As You Type area.

5   Click Border Lines, and then click OK.

6   Back in your document, type three underscore characters (_), then press Enter. Word immediately replaces the three characters with a line drawn across the width of your document. If you want to erase the line, simply press Ctrl+Z or backspace.

Notice that you also can control styles, headings, lists, letter greetings and closings, and even tables and dates with AutoFormat.

Disabling AutoFormat

If you decide that you're really a do-it-yourself kind of person and you'd rather have AutoFormat turned off completely, you can disable the feature by following these steps:

1   Display the AutoFormat dialog box by choosing AutoFormat from the Format menu.

2   Click Options to display the AutoCorrect dialog box.

3   Click the AutoFormat tab. Go through the list and click all the boxes with checkmarks to clear them.

4   Click the AutoFormat As You Type tab. Repeat the process by clearing the check boxes.

5   Click OK, and then click OK in the AutoFormat dialog box.

Now AutoFormat won't make any formatting changes until you reverse the process by displaying the AutoFormat dialog box and choosing options you want Word to use.

Note   Even if you disable AutoFormat, there is another kind of AutoFormat that is available to you: Table AutoFormat. You'll learn more about that feature in the section entitled "Using Table AutoFormat," later in this chapter.

A Return to Themes

A *theme* in Microsoft Word is a design that is carried through your document and can be applied to other documents, your Web page, e-mail messages, and more. A theme applies design choices such as color selection, border style, list styles, text font and size, and line styles.

You apply themes to your documents (either before or after you create them) by following these steps:

1 Open the document to which you want to apply the theme (or begin a new document).

2 Choose Theme from the Format menu. In the Theme dialog box, click the theme style you'd like to see. Your document is shown in the pre-view window as it would appear if that theme were selected (see Figure 6-2).

Figure 6-2 Word includes themes that coordinate the heading, text, link, and list styles used in your documents.

3 When you find the one you want, click OK. The theme is applied to your document.

Changing Fonts, Font Styles, and Point Sizes

Similar to editing, which includes line-by-line editing and block (or paragraph) editing, in formatting you have the small, character-by-character changes and the larger, global paragraph or page changes. One of the more common format-ting changes you'll make involves choosing a different *typeface*, style, and size for the text in your documents.

Lingo   A *typeface* is a family of type that has a particular look and feel. Times Roman is an example of one typeface; Arial is another.

Word includes a set of tools on the Formatting toolbar (which you learned about in Chapter 4, "Creating a Simple Document") that help you make font changes quickly, as shown below.

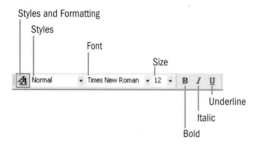

Note   Word actually uses the word *style* in two different ways. A *style* is a certain format that is typically saved in a document's template that controls the way the text to which it is applied is displayed. *Font style* is the phrase often used to refer to the type characteristics of a particular font. For example, *this text* is said to be in the *italic font style*. You will learn about the kind of styles you use to save format choices in the section entitled "Applying Styles and Templates," later in this chapter; this section introduces you to font style.

In addition to the tools on the Formatting toolbar, you can change these different type settings in the Font dialog box (shown in Figure 6-3). To display this dialog box, choose Font from the Formatting menu. You can then change the font, size, and style, as well as other text options, all at one time.

Figure 6-3   You can choose font, size, and style options all at once by using the Font dialog box.

> **Tip**   Word includes a number of "animated" text effects (such as Marching Red Ants and Sparkle Text) that can add some fun to the text in your more casual documents. To try some of these special text features, click the Text Effects tab in the Font dialog box.

Choosing a Font

The way in which you choose a font depends in part on what you're doing. If you're just beginning to enter text and want to choose a new font, simply position the cursor at the point in the document you want the new font to take effect and click the Font down arrow. Select the font you want from the displayed list. (Notice that Word displays the fonts as they will appear in the document, which helps you know what you're selecting.)

If you want to change the font of existing text, highlight the text before you click the Font down arrow and select the font you want. All selected text then appears in the new font.

> **Tip**   You can easily add new fonts to Office XP and make them available to all the programs in the suite. You'll find many font companies online (one I particularly like is Fonts.com). You can purchase and download fonts from the Web or arrange to have a CD sent to you—either way, the font manufacturer provides simple instructions on how to install the fonts in Windows XP and make them available to all your Office XP applications.

Changing Font Size

Choosing a new font size is so simple you might miss it. Ready? Again, to set the size for text you're about to enter, click in the document and then click the Font Size down arrow on the Formatting toolbar and choose the size you want. If you want to change the size of existing text, select the text before you choose the new size.

> **Tip**   Remember that if you don't like a change you make to existing text, you can undo the change quickly by pressing Ctrl+Z.

Selecting a New Font Style

You'll use different font styles when you want to make a word or phrase stand out from the text in some way. For example, you might want to italicize a defined term, boldface an important idea, or underline a Web address. To choose a new style for text in your document, follow these steps:

1   Select the text to which you want to apply the style change.

2   Click the style you want to apply.

The text is displayed in the font style you selected. Again, if you want to apply the style to text you're about to type, simply click the style to turn the feature on, type your text, and click the style a second time to disable it.

Note　Word displays only the most common font styles—bold, italic, and underline—on the Formatting toolbar. Some fonts also make the bold italic style available. Similarly, you can apply a number of special effects to text to further enhance the way it looks. In the Font dialog box (choose Format and then Font), you can select Strikethrough, Double Strikethrough, Superscript, Subscript, Shadow, Outline, Emboss, Engrave, Small Caps, All Caps, and Hidden as additional effects.

Changing Spacing

You may never have really noticed the spacing in a document until you began to create documents. If so, the spacing did its job, because you don't notice the spacing in an effective document. Chances are you have experienced trying to read a document with too many words and paragraphs crammed on a page—and, if you're like me, you tossed the document in the "read someday" pile instead of struggling through it.

Spacing in a document can make all the difference in the world, giving the readers' eyes a break; giving readers time to think; helping them understand, through use of white space and formatting, where they need to begin reading on a page and what the most important points are. Word gives you quite a bit of control over the spacing of your paragraphs and lines. These sections show you how to use space to arrange your text the way you want it.

Changing Indents

Many people rely simply on the paragraph indent to let readers know where one paragraph stops and another starts. For many documents this works fine. This is called setting a first-line indent, and here's how to do it:

1　Choose Paragraph from the Format menu.

2　In the Indentation area of the Paragraph dialog box, click the Special down arrow and choose First line. The value .5 appears in the By box. This tells Word to begin each new paragraph with an indent of one-half inch.

3　If you want to make the indent smaller or larger, decrease or increase the value shown. (*Note:* One-half inch is considered a standard indent for typical business formats.) The Preview window shows you how the text will look with the changes you have selected.

4　Click OK. Word saves the formatting changes.

The next time you press Enter to end one paragraph and begin another, Word will automatically indent the new paragraph for you.

Tip   You also can indent text and images by moving them in from the left and right margins. Enter the value by which you want to indent the text in the Left and Right boxes in the Indentation area of the Paragraph dialog box. Word will indent the text by the value you specify. If you enter .5 in the Right box, for example, the text you have selected (or the text you enter from the cursor position onward) will wrap to the next line when it gets to a point .5 inches before the right margin of the document.

Page Margins: A Different Matter   The indents you enter are added to the existing page margins for your document, which means that the text may be indented more than you expect. *Page margins* are the amount of white space around the edges of each page. You set the page margins for your document by choosing Page Setup from the File menu. By default, Word creates 1-inch margins for the top and bottom, and a 1.25-inch margin for the left and right edges. When you enter Left and Right indent values in the Paragraph dialog box, those values are added to the page margins displayed in the Page Setup dialog box.

Before and After Paragraphs

If you prefer not to use first-line indents to show the reader where your paragraphs begin and end, you can simply add extra space before and after paragraphs instead. Here are the steps for this approach:

1   Choose Paragraph from the Format menu.

2   Click the Before box in the Spacing area and increase the value to add space preceding the paragraph. Decrease the value to lessen the space before the first line of the paragraph.

3   Click the After box in the Spacing area and increase the value to add space after the paragraph. Decrease the value to lessen the space after the last line of the paragraph. The Preview window shows you the effects of both the Before and After changes.

4   Click OK to accept the changes and return to your document.

Note   Note that the values entered in the Before and After boxes show the characters pt. This is an abbreviation for *points*, which is a type measurement. To give you an idea of how much space 6 and 12 points really is, there are 72 points to an inch, and 12-point text is typically used for body text in a document.

Changing Line Spacing

Another important setting in the Paragraph dialog box you might want to use in your documents is the amount of vertical space between lines in your document. Word gives you the option of choosing Single, 1.5, Double, At Least, Exactly, or Multiple line spacing. The first three choices are standard—your document is single-spaced by default. The last three choices enable you to precisely control the line height, known as *leading*, by entering a specific value in the At box to cause the text to be placed at a desired measurement. To change the line spacing, click the Line Spacing down arrow and choose your selection from the list. If you select Exactly, At Least, or Multiple, enter the value for the line height in the At box.

Note   Once you get your paragraphs set up the way you like them, you can save them to a style so that you can format new paragraphs with a click of the mouse. For more about creating your own styles, see the section entitled "Creating a New Style," later in this chapter.

Setting Tabs

Tabs are those almost invisible little critters that control where and how your text lines up on the page. You set tabs using the horizontal ruler along the top edge of the Word window. If your ruler isn't visible, display it now by choosing Rulers from the View menu. The following graphic shows you the important elements of the ruler, so far as tabs are concerned:

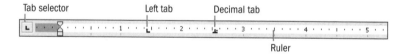

You can set tabs in two ways: by using the ruler or by working in the Tabs dialog box. Generally for documents in which precise measurement isn't important, I like to use the click-and-drag method in the ruler. Here's how to do it:

1   Click the tab selector on the far left side of the ruler until you see the tab you want (use Table 6-2 as a key).

2   Drag the tab to the place on the ruler bar you want it to appear. It's that simple.

Table 6-2 Word Tab Styles

Icon	Tab Name	Description
L	Left tab	Left-aligns text at this tab stop
⌐	Right tab	Right-aligns text at this tab stop
⊥	Center	Centers text at this tab stop
⊥⋅	Decimal tab	Creates a decimal tab so that numbers are aligned at their decimal points
I	Bar tab	Allows you to set a tab for bar characters

For more complicated tab-setting, you need the Tabs dialog box (shown in Figure 6-4). Display it by choosing Format and selecting Tabs. In the Tabs dialog box you have additional options, such as adding leaders (for example, a dotted line leading from one tab to the next, a technique often used in creating a table of contents).

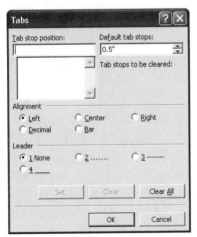

Figure 6-4   You can use the Tabs dialog box to set tabs at specific points in your document and add leaders.

To set tabs using the Tabs dialog box, click in the Tab Stop Position list box, type the location where you want to add the tab; choose the Alignment style (Left, Right, Center, or Decimal); click a Leader style if you want one; and then click OK. The tab is added in your document and applied to your text the next time you press Tab.

Tip   Tabs aren't retroactive, so they affect only the text in the current paragraph or the paragraphs you create after the current paragraph (when you press Enter, the tab entry travels with the cursor to the next paragraph). If you want to apply a tab to an entire existing document, press Ctrl+A to select all text before you display the Tabs dialog box or add a tab to the ruler.

When you want to clear tabs, you can use one of two super-simple methods:

- Select the tab you want to remove and drag it off the ruler. When you release the mouse button, the tab disappears.

- In the Tabs dialog box, click the tab you want to remove in the Tab Stop Position list and click the Clear button. If you want to remove all tabs in the selected text (or at the current cursor position), click Clear All.

Creating Bulleted and Numbered Lists

Bulleted and numbered lists are wonderful things. They give your readers' eyes a break; they help you make your points more clearly; they lead students through processes and confused gadget-builders through instruction manuals. Word makes it easy to create lists the way you want them. As you saw with AutoFormat, Word will even do it automatically for you if you want.

The easiest way to create a numbered or bulleted list is to use the Numbering or Bullets tools on the Formatting toolbar. Simply position the cursor at the point you want to begin the list and click one of those two tools. If you click Numbering, a number 1 is inserted in your document. If you click Bullets, a bullet character appears. Create your list by typing an item and pressing Enter; Word moves the cursor to the next line and adds another bullet or the next number, depending on what you have selected.

You can change the way Word handles bullets and numbers by choosing Bullets And Numbering from the Format menu. This displays the Bullets And Numbering dialog box, shown in Figure 6-5. To choose a different bullet or number style, click the tab you want and then click the example you like in the preview window. When you click OK, the new style is applied to your list and will be automatically used the next time you create a bulleted or numbered list.

You also can customize the bullet and number styles used in lists by clicking Customize in the Bullets And Numbering dialog box. This allows you to change the look, size, and position of the character as well as the spacing of the text and the color and style attributes.

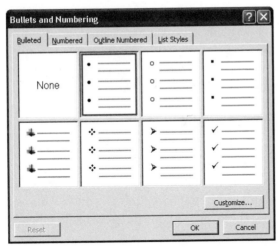

Figure 6-5   You can change the style of bullets and numbers Word uses in the lists you create.

Try This!   Word includes a set of fun, graphical bullets that you can use to spruce up your traditional bullet lists. Try inserting a colorful bullet style into your document by following these steps:

1   Position the cursor at the point you want to begin the list.

2   Choose Bullets And Numbering from the Format menu.

3   Click a bullet style in the preview window; the Customize button becomes available.

4   Click Customize.

5   In the Customize Bullet Style dialog box, click Picture.

6   The Picture Bullet palette appears. Click the bullet style you want to use or click Import to import a picture of your own you'd like to use.

Word adds the bullet style to the bullet selections in the Customize Bullet Style dialog box. Click OK to return to the Bullets And Numbering dialog box; then click OK to go back to your document. The new bullet style is entered at the cursor position.

Adding Tables

Tables, like bulleted and numbered lists, are another great quick-look feature that break up the long sections of text in your document and add visual interest to the page. A table can also be very useful in helping readers understand information quickly. Reading a detailed, four-page description about the new products in your spring catalog might be helpful for salespeople who have lots of time to kill and want to learn every subtle nuance of your latest line additions, but a table highlighting the key sales features, costs, and specifications of each of those items is a great way to help people grasp important information quickly.

Word makes it easy for you to create, format, and modify tables in your document. You begin in one of two ways: by using the Insert Table tool or by choosing Insert from the Table menu.

Creating a Table with the Insert Table Tool

The easiest way to create a table in Word is by clicking the Insert Table tool on the Formatting toolbar. When you click this tool, a drop-down grid appears, enabling you to select the number of rows and columns you want to create (as shown in Figure 6-6). Just drag the mouse to highlight the rows and columns you want; and then click the mouse button. Word adds the new blank table at the cursor position in your document.

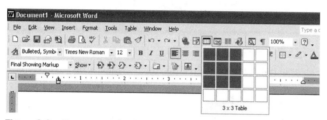

Figure 6-6   You can use the Insert Table tool to create a simple table quickly.

Using Insert Table to Create a Table

If you opt to create the table by choosing the Insert command, you need to position the cursor where you want to add the table, then open the Table menu and choose Insert and then Table. The Insert Table dialog box appears, as shown in Figure 6-7.

Insert Table

Table size
Number of columns: 5
Number of rows: 2

AutoFit behavior
- Fixed column width: Auto
- AutoFit to contents
- AutoFit to window

Table style: Table Grid   AutoFormat...

Remember dimensions for new tables

OK   Cancel

Figure 6-7   You can use the Insert Table dialog box to add a table with the size, fit, and format you want.

The first set of options in the Insert Table dialog box is predictable: You can enter the number of rows and columns you want to create in the table. The second set of options, AutoFit Behavior, controls how the table contents are arranged to fit within the cells of the table. The first option, Fixed Column Width, enables you to choose a specific size for each column; the second tells Word to automatically size the table to fit the contents you enter. When you select the last AutoFit option, AutoFit to Window, the table will be resized to fit a browser window when displayed in a Web browser.

Using Table AutoFormat

In the Insert Table dialog box, you can click the AutoFormat button to display and choose the format you want to apply to your new table. Figure 6-8 shows the Table AutoFormat dialog box.

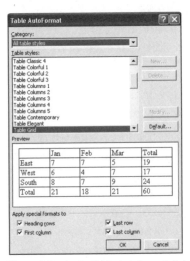

Figure 6-8   In the Table AutoFormat dialog box, you can choose the table style you want and add your own enhancements, if necessary.

Table AutoFormat gives you 45 different styles you can apply to the tables you create. Scroll through the list and watch the preview change. When you have selected the one you like, click Apply. Word formats your table accordingly.

Tip   You can customize the table format you've selected by clicking Modify in the Table Auto-Format dialog box. The Modify Table dialog box gives you all kinds of options, including changing the border style and width, content alignment, shading, and more. You can also save the modified table style as a new style if you choose.

Adding Table Data

Once you've added the table and applied the format you want to use, you're ready to enter data. The cells across the top of the table will most likely be your column headings—that is, the text labels that identify the values in the columns. You may also want to add row labels in the first column to identify the data being tracked.

To enter your data, simply click in the *cell* to which you want to add data, type the information, and press Tab. The cursor moves to the next cell, and you can continue entering data as needed.

Lingo   A *cell* is the rectangular area where you enter data in a table or spreadsheet. Each cell is the intersection of a column and a row.

Inserting and Deleting Table Columns and Rows

As your table grows, you will undoubtedly need to add rows and columns to accommodate the information. Here are the procedures for each of these simple tasks:

- ■ To add a row at the end of an existing table, click in the cell in the bottom right corner of the table and press Tab. A new row is added.

- ■ To add a row in the middle of an existing table, click just to the left of the first cell in the row above which you want to add the new row. The entire row should be selected. (If the row doesn't highlight automatically, drag to select the whole row.) Now choose Insert from the Table menu and select Rows Above to add the row. (As you can see, you can also add rows below the selected row if you choose.) If you want to add multiple rows, highlight however many rows you want to add before you select Insert Rows. When Word adds the rows, the number of rows you highlighted will be the number of rows inserted.

- ■ To add a column, position the pointer at the top edge of the column beside which you want to add the new column. When the pointer changes to an arrow, click to select the entire column. Now choose Insert from the Table menu and choose Columns To The Right or Columns To The Left, depending on where in the table you want to add the column. Word then inserts the column and the other columns are resized accordingly.

■ To delete columns and rows, begin by highlighting the columns or rows you want to delete. Then choose Delete from the Table menu and point to either Columns or Rows. Additionally, you can select and delete the entire table if you're ready to see it go.

Note Tables are a powerful Word feature and there are many, many things you can do with tables beyond these basics. You can use functions in your tables, sort data, use macros, create nested tables, and much more. For a fuller discussion on tables and the many things you can do with them, see *Microsoft Word Version 2002 Inside Out*, by Mary Millhollon and Katherine Murray, published by Microsoft Press.

Specifying Columns

Not all documents are made up of margin-to-margin text. Some have multiple columns, newsletter-style. In Word you can easily create multiple columns in your documents. To start the process, choose Columns from the Format menu, and the Columns dialog box appears (as shown in Figure 6-9).

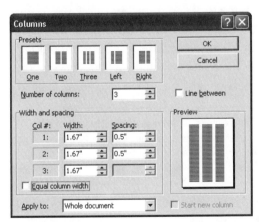

Figure 6-9 You can easily create multiple columns in your Word documents.

Where Do You Want Columns? You can create multiple columns for the entire document or you can choose columns for only a specific section, whichever you prefer. By default, Word applies the column change to the whole document. If you want to create columns in a section of your document, first highlight the text you want to format in columns. Next, display the Columns dialog box, click the Apply To: down arrow, and choose Selected Text. If you want to create columns from the current cursor position onward, select This Point Forward. Click OK to save your changes and close the Columns dialog box.

You use the settings in the Columns dialog box to control how many columns you have, how they are positioned, how much space you place between them, and whether they have a vertical line to separate them. Here are the specifics you can use to set up the columns in your document:

- In the Presets area, click the column style you want to create.

- In Number Of Columns, enter the number of columns.

- If you want a line to appear vertically between the columns, select the Line Between check box.

- In Width And Spacing, you can customize the widths of individual columns and control the amount of spacing between them. As you make these changes, Word displays the columns in the Preview window.

Tip   If you want the columns in your documents to be different sizes, click the Equal Column Width check box to clear it. You can then change the Width setting for each column to set individual values.

When you've got the column settings the way you want them, click OK to save the entries and create the columns. At first the only change you'll see in your document (unless you are applying the column change to selected text) is the addition of column markers in the horizontal ruler along the top of the document. As you enter text, you will see the text flow into the next column after the first column is filled.

Note   When you are working in Normal view, the columns you've created aren't visible. This can be confusing, so it's best to work in Print Layout view when you have a multicolumn document open on the screen. You'll also want to use Print Preview regularly to keep an eye on how your document will look when it is printed.

Applying Styles and Templates

All the formatting talk in this chapter has shown you how to control the look and feel of the text in your document. Wouldn't it be nice to be able to save all these settings for future use? That's what styles allow you to do. A *style* in Word is a preset format you apply to text in your document. By default, Word documents have the Normal template attached (this template includes the default styles for Heading 1, Heading 2, and so on). But you also can choose different styles, modify existing styles, or create your own styles, based on all the formatting changes you've learned to make in this chapter. And once you've created those styles, you may want to save them in your own template or add them to a template you already use.

At the far left end of the Formatting toolbar, you see a tool that looks like a double-A. This is the tool that displays the Styles And Formatting task pane (shown in Figure 6-10). It is here that you will do much of your work with styles.

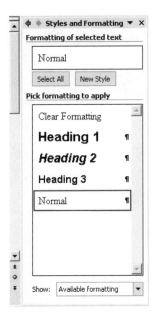

Figure 6-10 You'll use the Styles And Formatting task pane to work with styles in your document.

Choosing a Style

When you first open the Styles And Formatting task pane, Word shows you the style of the text at the current cursor position. The format is shown in the top entry box, and the list in the task pane displays all the available styles in the current document. To choose a different style, you simply scroll through the list and click it. The style is immediately applied to the text at the cursor position.

> **Tip** A faster way to choose styles, once you know the name of the style you're looking for, is to click the Style down arrow on the Formatting toolbar and choose the style from the list. Alternatively, if you know the name of the style, such as *quote*, you can click in the Style box on the toolbar, type the style name, and press Enter.

Creating a New Style

You can easily create your own style by formatting the text the way you want it and choosing the font, size, font style, spacing, and indent settings you want. After you've made your choices, follow these steps:

1 Highlight the text with the style you want to add.

2 Display the Styles And Formatting task pane by clicking the tool on the far left of the Formatting toolbar.

3 Click New Style.

4   In the New Style dialog box (shown in Figure 6-11), enter a name for the style, and then add any additional formatting changes you want to make.

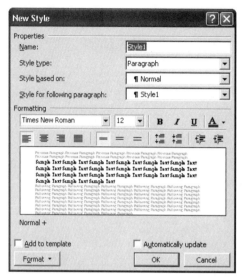

Figure 6-11   Choose additional style options and name your new style in the New Style dialog box.

5   If you want to add the style to the current template (which means this style will be made available to any document that uses this template in the future), click the Add To Template check box.

6   If you want the style to automatically update the text in the existing document, click Automatically Update.

7   Click OK to save the new style.

Replacing Styles Globally   If you decide that you *really* like this new style you created and you want to use it instead of other styles in your document, you can make the change easily. For example, suppose that you've created a style with a funky headline font you call Head1. You want to search for all the places in the document Word has used the Heading 1 (default) style and replace it with your cool Head1 style.

To do this, display the Styles And Formatting task pane, click the down arrow to the right of the style you want to change (in this case, Heading 1), and then click Select All *x* Instances (where *x* is the number of times that style appears in your document). Word highlights every occurrence of Heading 1 in your document. Now scroll through the style list in the center of the task pane until you see your style, Head1. Click it. Word automatically formats all the selected text using the style you selected.

Applying a Template

As you learned in Chapter 2, "Working with Programs," Word includes many (many!) preset templates you can use to build your documents. When you viewed a template file, you probably saw some nice design elements—an elegant fax cover memo, a sleek resume, a modern memo. But did you know that behind that nice design there were also formatting styles, saved and ready for you to use?

Each template file can include both the graphical elements you can use as the basis for your own designs and also the formatting styles for the look and feel of the text. As your experience with Word grows, you will become used to working with templates in more detail—adding templates that are standard for your company, for example, or creating your own templates that collect the styles you use in your work.

Creating Your Own Templates

When you've created and saved the styles you like, you can save the document as a template. This allows you to preserve the styles and apply them to other documents as well. To save a file as a template, follow these steps:

1 Complete your document with the styles the way you want them. (Refer to the section entitled "Creating a New Style," earlier in this chapter, if you need help saving custom styles.)

2 Choose Save As from the File menu.

3 Enter a name for the template.

4 Click the Save As Type down arrow and choose Document Template.

5 Click Save. Word saves your file as a template file in the folder you specified. You'll now be able to create new documents using this template and apply it to documents you've already created.

If you are creating this template based on a real document you are using for something else, don't forget to save the document as a regular document, too. If you close the document now without saving, any text changes you made during this work session will be lost.

Template File Cleanup   If you saved your regular document file as a template, you might want to do a few things to prepare the template to serve as a starting point for other documents:

- Delete long passages of text and leave only a sample paragraph of each style used in the template.

- Remove extra headings and leave only one heading showing each style.

- Be sure to preserve one of each special element that has its own style (notes, tips, quotes, bullet lists, and so on).

- Consider adding a list of elements used in the template, along with their names and a brief description so that other people using your template will know when to use each style.

After you make the modifications to the template file, save the template again by pressing Ctrl+S or by selecting Save from the File menu.

Attaching a New Template

Once you've created the new template, you need to attach it to other existing documents (or select it to start new ones). Starting a new document based on your template is the easiest route, so let's do that one first by performing the following steps:

1   Click the New Document tool on the Standard toolbar, or choose New from the File menu.

2   In the New Document task pane, click General Templates.

3   In the General tab, look for the template file you saved, click it, and then click OK. A new document opens, and you can create the document using the styles you previously saved.

To attach a template to an existing file so that you can apply the styles to the text in that document, follow these steps:

1   Begin with the document open on the screen.

2   Choose Templates And Add-Ins from the Tools menu.

3   In the Templates And Add-Ins dialog box, click Attach.

4   Navigate to the folder in which you saved the template file. When you find it, click the file and then click Open.

5 Back in the Templates And Add-Ins dialog box, click the Automatically Update check box.

6 Click OK. The template is now attached to the current document and the styles are automatically updated.

Note   Only those styles that have the same name as styles in your template file will be changed, however. For example, if the Normal text style in your current document is set to Times New Roman 12-point text and the Normal text style in your template is set to Garamond 10 point, the document will update to show Normal text as Garamond. To assign the new styles to the text in the document, you'll need to display the Styles And Formatting task pane, select the text you want to format, and click the style you want to use from the displayed Styles list. (If you're not sure how to do this, see the section entitled "Applying Styles," earlier in this chapter.)

Key Points

- Word includes many different formatting features to help you control the way your text looks and feels.

- AutoFormat catches formatting problems as you go and can help you automate lists, headings, and more.

- Themes give you a coordinated effect for your printed and electronic documents by establishing preset selections for colors, headings, links, and more.

- Changing the font, size, and font style is a simple matter of point-and-click on the Formatting toolbar.

- You adjust paragraph and line spacing and indents by using the features in the Paragraph dialog box.

- You can add tabs either by using the horizontal ruler or the Tabs dialog box.

- Tables enable you to show readers information quickly in a compare-and-contrast fashion. Word helps you add a professional touch to your table design with AutoFormat.

- Word allows you to create up to 11 columns in your document; you control the spacing, width, and flow of text in those columns.

- You can save your formatting choices as styles and use them again in other documents.

- The styles are saved in templates, and you can apply those templates to new or existing documents, which saves you time and formatting effort later.

Chapter 7

Special Features (and Challenges!) in Microsoft Word

By now you're probably getting the hang of dealing with basic documents in Microsoft Word. You know how to enter, edit, and format text to get the effects you want. Now we'll talk about some of the higher-end features—items you'll be more likely to include in longer documents. This chapter explains the basics of working with sections, adding art, drawing diagrams, inserting bookmarks, and creating hyperlinks. The final section rounds out this part of the book with a quick look at a few advanced features, such as generating a table of contents or an index and using macros. Ready to polish your Word knowledge? Let's get going.

Working with Sections

It's possible to have a long document and never need to work with sections. If you are preparing a long document of one-column text, you might never need to worry about sections at all. But if you want variety and flexibility in your formats, in your page orientation, and in your headers and footers, you'll need to learn how to create and work with sections.

A *section* serves as a kind of document within a document, allowing you to set formats for the different sections that do not affect the whole. Are you wondering when you'd want to do this? Here are a few examples:

- You've created a new product specification report that describes the research, development, audience, and projections for the new product your company is about to launch. Two-thirds of the way through the document, you need to insert a huge 14-column table that is currently in *landscape* mode. If you change the page orientation to *portrait* mode, the table will be messed up. What's the answer? Put the table in its own section in your longer document, and you can use the landscape orientation in the middle of the other portrait sections.

   Lingo   When a document is displayed or printed in 11-by-8.5-inch fashion (with the page horizontal rather than vertical), it is in *landscape* orientation. A document in traditional 8.5-by-11-inch format is said to be in *portrait* orientation.

- You are writing a training manual that will include 12 different modules. The page numbers, which will appear in the footer of each page, must reflect both the module number and the page number within the module. This means you need to create new footers for each module, yet keep the entire manual together in one document. How do you do that? Create a section for each module.

- Finally, suppose that you are writing a history of Allen County and you want to include summary sections at the end of each era that provide a timeline of events that occurred within that timeframe. You want the summary sections to have a different page design—with background elements and full page borders—but you don't want the format to affect the rest of the document. To handle this, you can create the summaries as—you guessed it—individual sections.

Inserting Section Breaks

The process of adding a section break is much easier to do than it is to explain. Here are the steps:

1 Position the cursor wherever you want to add the section break.

2 Choose Break from the Insert menu.

3 In the Break dialog box, choose the section break type you want to add (as shown in Figure 7-1). The following list gives you an idea of when you'll use the different types of section breaks:

- Next Page creates a section break that ends the current page and begins the next section on a fresh page.

- Continuous begins a new section but does not advance to the next page.

- Even Page begins the new section on the next even-numbered page.

- Odd Page starts the new section on the next odd-numbered page.

Figure 7-1 Word enables you to add a section break and start the new section wherever you like.

Note If you choose either Even Page or Odd Page, Word will leave the interim page blank, if necessary, to force the section start on the desired page.

4 Click OK to add the section break.

Depending on the view you are working in, you may not see anything at all after you add the section break. In Web Layout view and Print Layout view, no insert line is visible. If you are working in Normal view, you see a line that looks similar to the following:

Section Break (Continuous)

Now you can move the cursor after the section break and format to your heart's content. If you want to add different headers and footers, see the section entitled "Adding Headers and Footers," later in this chapter. If you're thinking about creating a multicolumn format, check out the section "Specifying Columns," in Chapter 6, "Formatting in Microsoft Word."

Removing Section Breaks

The basic task of deleting a section break is simple: You simply highlight the section break line (you need to be in Normal view or have paragraph marks turned on in other views to see it) and press Delete. However, the trick to removing section breaks is in remembering what happens to your document after you remove the dividers.

Because of the way Word keeps track of the formatting within sections, when you delete a section break, the format of the section that follows the break will be applied to the section that precedes the break. Let's look at an example to make this a little more clear. Suppose that you create a document in which:

- Section 1 has a one-column format;

- Section 2 has a two-column format; and

- Section 3 has a three-column format

When you delete the section break between Sections 2 and 3, the text in Section 2 takes on the three-column format. This isn't always a huge deal, but it's good to remember. Logic might tell us a section's format should continue until the next Section break occurs. But practical experience with Word will show you otherwise.

What this means is that before you delete a section break, take a good look at the formatting of the section following the break. Is that what you want applied to your text? If not, consider keeping the section break intact and making any necessary changes to the format within the section. If so, go ahead and press the Delete key.

Adding Headers and Footers

When you've read a book, you've seen headers and footers. You might think that *creating* them is a tougher deal. Actually, creating headers and footers is pretty simple in Word, even if you decide to use sections and want to vary the text from page to page.

What Will You Put in Headers and Footers? Typically, people use headers and footers to provide information about the document (such as the title, the page number, the date it was created, and the current section name) and the author or sponsoring company. Occasionally you will see copyright information or a Web address in a footer as well. You can use that space in whatever way makes sense to you or is standard for your company.

Inserting a Header or Footer

To insert a header or footer in your document, choose Header And Footer from the View menu. The text in your document appears gray and either a Header window appears at the top of your workspace or the Footer window appears at the bottom of the page. You'll also see the Header And Footer toolbar (as shown in Figure 7-2). Table 7-1 introduces you to the tools and tasks you'll manage while you're working with headers and footers.

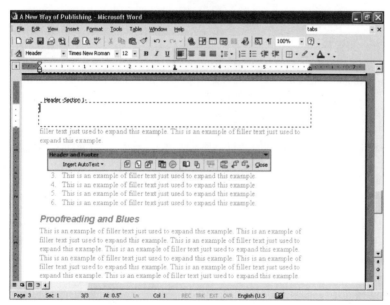

Figure 7-2   When you add a header, the Header And Footer toolbar appears and the cursor is positioned in the header area.

Table 7-1   Header and Footer Tools

Tool Icon	Name	Description
Insert AutoText ▾	Insert AutoText	Displays a drop-down list of items you can have Word insert in the header or footer
[#]	Insert Page Number	Inserts the current page number at the cursor position
[+]	Insert Number Of Pages	Displays at the cursor position the total number of pages
[#]	Format Page Number	Displays the Page Number Format dialog box so that you can enter page-numbering options
[z]	Insert Date	Inserts the current date in the form MM/DD/YYYY
⊘	Insert Time	Adds the current time
📖	Page Setup	Displays the Page Setup dialog box so that you can change header and footer options
[≡]	Show/Hide Document Text	Alternately hides and displays document text
[≡]	Same As Previous	Makes the selected header or footer the same as the previous one
[≡]	Switch Between Header And Footer	Moves the display from the header to the footer and back again
[≡]	Show Previous	If the header is selected, jumps to the previous header; if the footer is selected, jumps to previous footer
[≡]	Show Next	If the header is selected, jumps to the next header; if the footer is selected, jumps to next footer
Close	Close	Closes the Header and Footer toolbar

To add the header or footer, simply type in the window the text you want to appear. You can use AutoText if you choose, or insert the date, time, or page number using the appropriate Header And Footer tool. Note that you can apply any formatting considerations—a different font, a new point size, a special style, and so on—to the header text.

If you choose, you can create multiline headers and footers by pressing Enter at the end of the first line. This gives you room for more text.

When you've finished adding the text, click outside the header area. You are returned to the document and the header or footer is hidden. To see how the page will look when printed (headers, footers, and all), click the Print Preview button on the Standard toolbar.

Try This! You can use Word's drawing tools to add a line at the bottom of the header to separate it from the document text. Here are the steps:

1 Start by displaying the Drawing toolbar (open the View menu, choose Toolbars, and click Drawing).

2 Select the Line tool (use the ScreenTips to identify each tool if you need help finding the one you want); then position the pointer at the point you want the line to begin, press and hold Shift (which keeps the line straight), and drag the pointer to wherever you want the line to end.

3 Release the mouse and the Shift key and the line is put in place.

4 If you need to move the line, simply drag it as needed. The best place for header and footer lines is along the bottom edge of the header window. You'll need to remember to place lines on subsequent pages at the same location so your pages are consistent.

You can further customize the line by changing the line width, color, and style—just right-click the line and choose the item you want from the displayed menu.

Inserting Graphics

Not long ago, adding a photo to a document was a big deal. Cutting and pasting and rubber cement were part of the process. Today, you can add photos, charts, clip art, and diagrams easily to just about any document you create. If you have a digital camera or a scanner, you can import your own images directly into Word. If you have access to the Internet, you can download thousands of pictures to help you add visual appeal to the words on your pages.

Caution   Art abounds on the Internet, but you can't use it unless you are downloading clips from a free or shareware Web site or you have the permission of the artist to use the image you're copying. Copyright laws apply, even for pictures comprised only of colored electronic dots. To be safe, be sure to get the necessary permission before you use someone else's images in your documents.

Adding Clip Art

Let's say you want to add a piece of clip art from the collection that comes with Word. Open the Insert menu and choose Picture; then select Clip Art from the submenu. The Insert Clip Art task pane appears, as shown in Figure 7-3.

What kind of art do you want to add? If you're creating a document about your landscaping company's upcoming rose sale, you might want to search for *flowers*. Type the topic in the Search text line, then click Search. Word searches for art related to the item you entered and displays what it finds in the Results window. Click the image to place it in your document.

Figure 7-3   You can use the search feature in the Insert Clip Art task pane to find an illustration for your document.

Tip   If you don't find the art you want, click Modify to return to the Search options and start again.

You can work with the clip art you've found by clicking the bar to the right of the selected image. A context menu appears that allows you to copy the item to another collection, open it in your graphics program, edit the keywords Word uses to find the picture, or locate art created in a similar style (as shown in Figure 7-4).

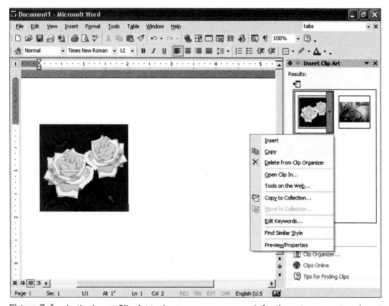

Figure 7-4   In the Insert Clip Art task pane, you can search for the art you want and customize it to your liking.

A Quick Look at the Microsoft Clip Organizer

When you work with clip art in any Microsoft Office XP application, you're using the Microsoft Clip Organizer, a media library that enables you to save, organize, and access picture, sound, and video files from a variety of sources. Some pictures and sounds are included with the program, but the biggest benefit of the Clip Organizer is its ability to help you catalog the files you create, import, or download from the Web.

You access the Microsoft Clip Organizer by clicking the Clip Organizer link at the bottom of the Insert Clip Art task pane. The first time you click this link, the Add Clips To Organizer dialog box tells you that it will scan your hard drive to collect and catalog all the image, sound, and video files already stored on your computer. Click Now to continue the cataloging. After a few moments, the Clip Organizer creates a Collection List and displays all the found media items in their various folders. To check out all the clip art included with Office XP, scroll down to the Office Collections folder and explore the subfolders (as shown in Figure 7-5).

Figure 7-5   The Microsoft Clip Organizer stores all kinds of clips—art, media, music, and more—and displays them in easy-to-use folders.

To close the Clip Organizer, click the Close box in the upper right corner of the window. You are then returned to the Word document window.

Tip   If you don't find the pictures you were hoping for, you can continue your search online. To begin the process, click Clips Online in the bottom of the Insert Clip Art task pane. If you are not currently connected to the Internet, the Connect dialog box appears so that you can establish the connection. Click Connect and you are taken to the Microsoft Office Design Gallery Live. The first time you visit, you are asked to review the end-user license agreement; after you click Accept, you are taken to a site that gives you a powerful search feature, articles on finding and using clips, and a wide selection of clips and tips-of-the-month that can help you in your work. It's a great resource! Check back often.

Importing Files

If you have a picture file that you'd like to use in your Word project, you can import it directly into the document you're working on. The steps are easy:

1   Open the Insert menu and choose Picture.

2   In the Insert Picture dialog box, navigate to the folder in which the images you want are stored.

3   Select the image, then click Insert. The picture is placed at the cursor position.

Once you import the picture, the Picture toolbar appears in your work area (as shown in Figure 7-6).

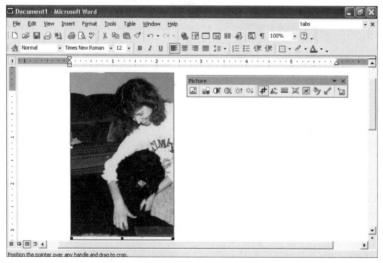

Figure 7-6   After you add a picture to your document, the Picture toolbar appears so that you can further work with the image.

You can work with the picture in a number of ways, using the buttons on the Picture toolbar. The buttons are listed in Table 7-2 in the order that they appear on the Picture toolbar, from left to right.

Table 7-2 Buttons on the Picture Toolbar

Button	Name	Description
	Insert Picture	Insert an image into a document
	Color	Change the color of the image
	More Contrast	Increase the contrast
	Less Contrast	Decrease the contrast
	More Brightness	Increase the brightness
	Less Brightness	Decrease the brightness
	Crop	Crop the image
	Rotate Left	Rotate the image to the left
	Line Style	Change the line style used to border the picture
	Compress Pictures	Compress the image to reduce its file size
	Text Wrapping	Control the way text wraps around the image
	Format Picture	Change the format of the picture
	Set Transparent Color	Makes the color you select transparent
	Reset Picture	Reset the picture to its original settings

Scanning Images Directly into Word

In today's age of digital everything, it's super easy to import your own photos into your Word document. If you have a digital camera, you can plug it right into your computer and use Word to download a photo from the camera to your document. If you still develop photos the old-fashioned way, that's okay, too. Just scan the photos directly into Word. Here's the simple five-step process:

1   Place the photo in your scanner or connect your digital camera to the computer.

2   Open the Insert menu and choose Pictures and then From Scanner Or Camera.

3   In the Insert Picture From Scanner Or Camera dialog box, first choose your scanner or camera in the device list (as shown in Figure 7-7).

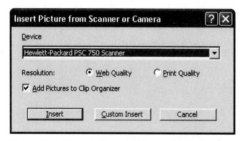

Figure 7-7   You can import pictures directly from your scanner or digital camera.

4   Choose either Web Quality (the default) or Print Quality. Web Quality imports the image at a lower resolution, which means it will require less space on your disk.

5   Click Insert if you want Word to scan the image or import the digital photo without any further action from you. If you want to display a dialog box for scanning or importing the digital image, click Custom Insert. The prompts on-screen will then walk you through the process of choosing the photo, scanning the image, or both.

The picture is then placed at the cursor position in your Word document. You can resize and edit the photo as you would any graphic image. And because the images were saved to the Microsoft Clip Organizer, you'll be able to use them in other Office XP documents you create.

Drawing Diagrams

If you use Word to write procedures and create flowcharts, you'll love the diagramming feature that is new in Word 2002. The built-in diagram tool enables you to create hierarchical diagrams in your document without ever leaving Word. Here are the steps:

1   Choose Diagram from the Insert menu.

2   In the Diagram Gallery (shown in Figure 7-8), click the type of chart you want to create. (If you're not sure which chart you need, click the different chart types to see a basic description of each.) After you've selected the diagram you want, click OK.

Figure 7-8   Word includes six types of diagrams you can create on the fly.

3   The diagram appears in your work area, along with the Diagram toolbar. In addition, blocks of text are marked with the prompt *Click to add text* to show you where to add your own information (as shown in Figure 7-9).

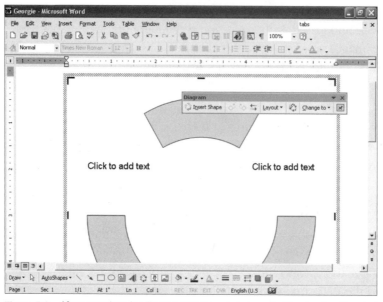

Figure 7-9   After you select the diagram type you want to create, Word makes the chart and displays both the Diagram toolbar and placeholder text you can replace with your own.

4   Use the tools on the Diagram toolbar to add shapes, move diagram elements, apply formatting settings, or change to a different type of diagram.

The Diagram feature includes a Diagram Style Gallery that lets you change the look of the shapes and colors in the diagram. To display the Style Gallery, click AutoFormat on the Diagram toolbar. Scroll through the Diagram Style list to find the look you want; then click Apply to apply the change to the diagram.

Tip   The final tool on the Diagram toolbar is the Text Wrapping tool. Click this tool to control how text flows around the diagram in your document. A drop-down menu appears, giving you a number of options that range from running text through the image to blocking out space above and below it to creating a custom border so text flows around the object just the way you want. Experiment with the Text Wrapping tool to get a feel for the best way to handle images in your documents.

Creating a Hyperlink

You can create links in your Word document so that readers who are viewing your document on the screen can move right to the sites and files you mention. In addition to linking to other Web pages and files, you can create e-mail links so that interested readers can e-mail you directly in response to your document. To create a hyperlink in your document, follow these steps:

1   Begin by selecting the item you want to link. If the item is a phrase of text or a Web address, highlight the text. If the item is a graphic image such as a button or photograph, click it to select it.

2   Press Ctrl+K (or choose Hyperlink from the Insert menu). The Insert Hyperlink dialog box appears, as shown in Figure 7-10.

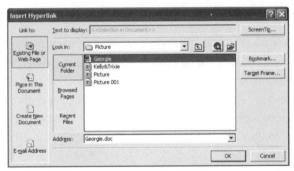

Figure 7-10   You can create hyperlinks for text and images in your Word documents using the Insert Hyperlink dialog box.

3   You can select whether you want to link to an existing Web page, a new document, or an e-mail address by clicking the Link To object in the far left side of the dialog box. The settings in the rest of the Insert Hyperlink dialog box change according to your choice.

4   Choose the file to which you want to link if you see it displayed in the Look In list, or enter the Web address in the Address line at the bottom of the dialog box.

   If you are creating an e-mail link, the Insert Hyperlink dialog box changes to allow you to enter the e-mail address, and any subject you want displayed in the Subject line. When a reader clicks the text you've used for the hyperlink, a new e-mail message will open in his or her e-mail program with your e-mail address and the Subject line filled in.

5   Click OK to create the hyperlink. When you return to the document, you will be able to see that the hyperlink has been generated because the pointer changes to a hand when you hold the mouse pointer over the link.

Tip   Office XP also allows you to create your own ScreenTips that pop up over links in your document. To create a ScreenTip, select the link to which you want to add the ScreenTip, and then press Ctrl+K to display the Edit Hyperlink dialog box. Click the ScreenTip button and enter the ScreenTip text in the Set Hyperlink ScreenTip dialog box that appears.

You can later remove hyperlinks by pressing Ctrl+K to display the Edit Hyperlink dialog box, clicking Remove Link, and clicking OK.

The High-End Stuff

Now you've been through many of the basic tasks you'll want to accomplish with Word. Rest assured, however, that there's much more to this powerful program—in fact, we could spend all week just talking about Word's features. There are just a few higher-end items I want you to know about before we end our Word discussion. These are elements you might want to explore as you get more comfortable and work with longer and more complex documents: the table of contents, the index, and macros.

Table of Contents

A table of contents is crucial when you are creating a document that people need to navigate easily. If you are leading a presentation based on a 50-page document you prepared, you don't want to be drowned out by the shuffling of pages when people have trouble finding the section you're referencing in the document. A table of contents will help them move right to the section they need—which makes things better for them (and for you).

Word creates the table of contents based on the headings you've entered in the document that use (or are based on) the default heading styles. To create a table of contents, follow these steps:

1   Position the cursor at the point in the document at which you want to create the table of contents.

2   Open the Insert menu and choose Reference. From the submenu, choose Index And Tables.

3   In the Index And Tables dialog box, select the Table Of Contents tab.

4   Review the format settings (the page numbers are right-aligned, with a dot tab leader). Change the settings to fit the needs of your project.

5   Click OK to generate the table of contents. The table is placed at the cursor position in your document.

If you change the headings later, you can easily update the table of contents by clicking in the table and pressing F9. A dialog box will appear, asking whether you want to update the page numbers only or the entire table. To make sure that you've got the most up-to-date TOC possible, select Update Entire Table and click OK.

Indexes

Indexes are a bit more complicated than tables of contents because you need to go through your document and mark the entries you want to include in your index; then you have Word compile the index into the traditional form that appears at the end of your favorite books. If you're a word-puzzle person and love crosswords and search-a-words, you'll enjoy creating indexes. Here's a quick overview of the process:

1   Beginning at the start of the document (so that you can review the entire document as you create entries), open the Insert menu, choose References, and click Index And Tables.

2   Click the Index tab. On this tab you see all the options you'll need to create your document index (as shown in Figure 7-11).

3   Begin by clicking Mark Entry. The Mark Index Entry dialog box opens. Here you will enter the entries and subentries for the index.

4   Move the cursor to the point you want to insert the first entry. (Word will insert an index code at the cursor position.) Type your first entry in the Main Entry box (for example, **Services**). Add a Subentry if desired (for example, **Layout**). Click Mark to add the code.

5   Continue moving the cursor and adding entries in the Mark Index Entry dialog box.

6   When you've finished, choose Cancel to close the dialog box.

7   Position the cursor at the end of the document (or wherever you want to generate the index). Choose Insert, Reference, and Index And Tables.

8   With the Index tab displayed, click OK. Word then compiles the index and places it at the cursor position.

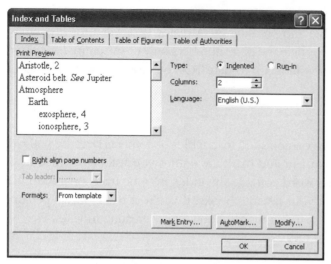

Figure 7-11   Word's indexing feature is a bit more complex than ordinary tasks, but worth the effort to learn.

If you find that you've misspelled an entry in the index or want to modify some of the page numbers listed, you can simply click in the index and edit it as you normally would.

Macros and More

And finally, we get to *macros*. You might create a macro for applying a certain format, adding a header you always use, searching and replacing an outdated style, or creating a table of contents.

> **Lingo**   A *macro* is simply a sequence of tasks that you record so that the steps can be automatically executed by Word next time.

A macro records the individual steps you take and then runs through them automatically when you play the macro later. This means that, in order to work with macros, you have to go through two stages: Creating the macro, and then running it.

To create a macro, position the cursor at the point you want to begin and choose Macro from the Tools menu. When the submenu appears, select Record New Macro. The Record Macro dialog box appears, as shown in Figure 7-12.

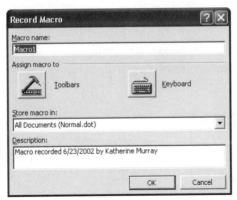

Figure 7-12   You can record a macro to automate tasks you find yourself performing over and over and over...

First, enter a name for the macro. Then choose whether you want to assign the macro to a tool or to either a shortcut key combination or an unused function key (for example, F12). You also need to tell Word whether you want to save the macro in the Normal template (the default) or save it in the current document only. Click OK to begin recording. A small palette containing two tools—Stop Recording and Pause Recording—appears over your Word work area.

Caution   When you're assigning a macro to a key, be sure to choose a key combination that isn't being used. Otherwise, you will overwrite the function of the existing key combination with the new macro you create.

The macro now records your every on-screen action. For example, suppose that you move the mouse to open the Insert menu, choose References, and click Index And Tables. You then click the Table Of Contents tab and click OK to generate a quick TOC. Now click Stop Recording. The macro is saved under the name you entered.

To play the macro, choose Macros from the Tools menu (you can also press Alt+F8). The Macros dialog box (shown in Figure 7-13) appears and you can click the macro you want to play and click Run. The macro is executed, automatically repeating the steps you saved.

As you can imagine, these last three features of Word are complex and offer real high-end power for those documents that warrant it. I hope you've enjoyed your trip through Word and feel sufficiently prepared—and challenged—to experiment with the many features you can use as you begin creating your own documents.

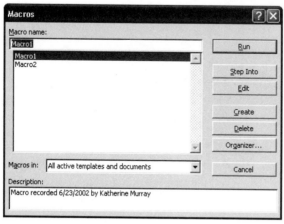

Figure 7-13   After you record the macro, play it back by choosing it from the list and clicking Run.

Key Points

- Creating sections in longer documents enables you to vary the format from section to section.

- You can add many different items to headers and footers in your Word documents.

- The Microsoft Clip Organizer stores your picture, sound, and video files so that you can use them with all your Office XP documents.

- If you have a scanner or digital camera, you can import your images directly into your Word document—and save them in the Microsoft Clip Organizer at the same time.

- Word includes a built-in diagramming feature that offers you six types of diagrams, from mapping process to relationships to flowcharts.

- Creating hyperlinks for documents, Web pages, e-mail, buttons, and more is simple with Ctrl+K in Word.

- You can use Word for high-end tasks such as generating a table of contents or index for your long document. Additionally, you can record macros to automatically step through tasks that used to be repetitive chores.

Part III

Excel the Easy Way

If you thought number-crunching was boring, think again. The features, new and old, in Microsoft Excel 2002 allow you to do things with data you never could have done with a calculator and an accountant's pad. Create a simple spreadsheet? Sure, but then you can publish it on the Web in such a way that it provides an interactive worksheet for Web visitors to use. Enter data easily and then plug in stock quotes by using smart tags. Generate professional-looking reports, charts, and forms with a few simple clicks and rely on wizard technology to lead you through the process.

In this part of the book, you'll look at the most common tasks you'll need in order to get up to speed quickly with Excel 2002. Chapter 8, "Creating and Saving a Spreadsheet," shows you around the Excel window and walks you through starting a new spreadsheet, entering data, adding simple functions, and saving the worksheet.

Once you create a spreadsheet, you can work on improving, enhancing, and printing it in Chapter 9, "Editing, Formatting, and Printing Spreadsheets." In this chapter, you'll learn to make simple data changes, work with ranges, insert and delete rows, change the appearance of text, borders, and backgrounds, and change data format and alignment. When you get to Chapter 10, "Charting Spreadsheet Data," you'll be ready to create charts that illustrate the trends you see in your spreadsheet data. Excel includes 14 standard chart types—and a virtually unlimited number of custom chart types that you can create yourself.

Chapter 8

Creating and Saving a Spreadsheet

Microsoft Excel makes it easy—even for those of us who weren't math majors—to do sophisticated things with numbers. Want to create an amortization table for that new home you're thinking about? Need to create a professional-looking balance sheet to give potential investors a good sense of what they're putting their money into? Preparing a sales analysis for the corporate meeting that compares the results in each of your eight sales regions?

Whatever your intent, if your project has something to do with numbers, Excel can help you create it. This chapter explains spreadsheet basics and shows you how to master the tasks of creating the spreadsheet, entering data, and saving the spreadsheet in the form you want.

What Can You Do with Microsoft Excel?

Although Excel is a full-featured program that offers everything from simple math calculations to complex and sophisticated operations, you might find that you start using Excel to solve a simple problem or create a project. From there, as your familiarity with Excel grows, you'll be likely to try using it for other operations as well. Here are just a few ideas of tasks you can try in Excel:

- Track the accounts receivable and payable for your small business.
- Create and track sales projections and results.
- Create and maintain a donor list for your small nonprofit organization.
- Handle all your standard business documents, including income statements, balance sheets, cash-flow reports, and more.
- Develop budgets for the various departments in your company.
- Produce cost-analysis reports.
- Publish financial information to the Web.

Note   If you haven't yet started Excel, do so now. Click Start and choose All Programs; then click Microsoft Excel. For more information on starting programs, see Chapter 1, "Getting to Know Microsoft Office XP."

Learning the Language   If you're unfamiliar with spreadsheets—or simply new to spreadsheets in Excel—knowing common terms will help you get up to speed faster. Here is a quick overview of terms you'll see often:

The *worksheet*, a grid of columns and rows in the center of the window, is the primary workspace in Excel. The worksheet extends off the viewing area of the window, to the column lettered IV (which is a total of 220 columns) and the row numbered 65,536 (now that's a large worksheet!) The columns and rows are lettered and numbered.

The intersection of each column and row is called a *cell*, and each cell has a unique address, which is a combination of the column letter and row number (for example, cell B7 is the cell at the intersection of column B and row 7). A *range* is a group of selected cells. You use ranges when you work with multiple cells in formulas, copy and move operations, chart creation, and so on.

A *workbook* in Excel is a collection of worksheets organized by a common topic or function. For example, you might create a workbook to track your company's sales and create four different worksheets (each occupying one tab in the workbook) to record sales of each of your four regions. Every worksheet is saved in a workbook (even when there's only one worksheet in use).

A Walk Around the Excel Window

Right off, you'll notice some elements of the Excel window are similar to items you saw in Microsoft Word—and you'll notice that some things are completely different. The Excel window has a familiar look and feel in the menus, the task pane, and the status bar. Beyond that, there are many differences. Figure 8-1 highlights the important aspects of the Excel window.

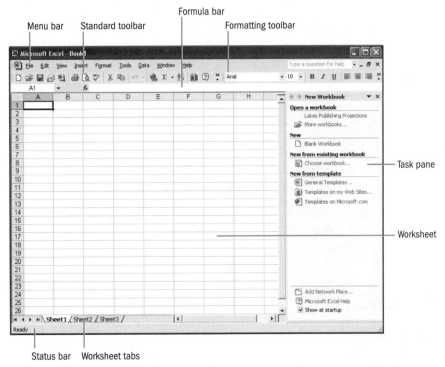

Figure 8-1   The Excel window brings the tools, menus, and options within easy reach of the mouse.

Excel Menus

At first glance, the menus in Excel appear similar to the menus in Word. In fact, they are organized around similar concepts—all the commands you need for dealing with files are on the File menu, the commands for inserting objects into the spreadsheet are found on the Insert menu, and so on. As you begin to explore the menus, however, you'll see that there are several differences. Excel includes its own unique features, commands, and extra tools. Table 8-1 gives you an introduction to the menus and provides a brief description of each one.

Table 8-1   Excel Menus

Menu	Shortcut Key	Description
File	Alt+F	Contains commands for anything related to working with Excel documents—opening, saving, printing, importing, setting up, and previewing documents.
Edit	Alt+E	Includes everything you need for selecting, finding, cutting, copying, pasting, and clearing text. In addition, you can undo and redo recent operations using the commands from this menu.

Table 8-1   Excel Menus   *(continued)*

Menu	Shortcut Key	Description
View	Alt+V	Lets you choose the different ways in which you view your Excel documents; also allows you to choose customized views you create and select the toolbars and screen elements you want to display.
Insert	Alt+I	Enables you to insert rows, columns, other worksheets, charts, pictures, functions, and more into your spreadsheets.
Format	Alt+O	Controls the way your spreadsheet looks—from individual cells to rows, columns, and even entire worksheets. You also can use the AutoFormat feature, apply styles, and set up conditional formatting, which is applied only when certain conditions are present.
Tools	Alt+T	Gives you access to all the add-on tools you can use to enhance and extend the functionality of your spreadsheet. You can check for spelling and errors, track changes, create scenarios, control online collaboration, protect your worksheet, audit formulas, and set options.
Data	Alt+D	Lets you work with data in your spreadsheet by sorting, filtering, or subtotaling it. You also can convert text to columns, perform group editing, work with data tables and PivotCharts, and more.
Window	Alt+W	Enables you to arrange, split, hide, and freeze worksheets or select a different open workbook that is displayed in the menu list.
Help	Alt+H	Displays the Help menu options you can choose to find out more about your current task.

Changes in the Toolbar

The Excel toolbar is an amalgam of the Standard and Formatting toolbars. You'll find the Standard tools on the left end of the toolbar and the Formatting tools on the right. Use the following graphic to learn where the different tools are:

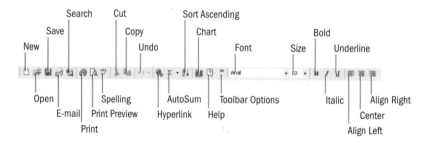

Tip   You can divide the Standard and Formatting toolbars into two rows if you prefer. Simply click Toolbar Options in the center of the toolbar; then choose Show Buttons On Two Rows. The Standard and Formatting toolbars are then separated and the Formatting toolbar is placed below the Standard toolbar, just above the Formula bar in the Excel window.

Similar to the tools in Word, the Excel tools give you the means to work with Excel files: You can copy, cut, and paste information, as well as changing the look of the spreadsheet data you enter. Excel tools also enable you to create hyperlinks and charts, apply common functions, sort spreadsheet data, and more.

You can display additional tools for both the Standard and the Formatting toolbars by clicking one of the two Toolbar Options buttons, located at the left end of both sets of tools. Simply click the tool you want to use. After you use the tool, Excel adds it to the left end of the toolbar so that you can choose it again easily later.

Note   If your tools appear in a different order than what you see here, don't worry—you can rearrange tools and customize the look of the toolbars in a number of ways. The most important thing is that you have all the tools you need to do the work you want to do. If you don't see a tool you need on the displayed toolbar, click Toolbar Options to select the tool from the menu.

Checking Out the Formula Bar

You'll use the formula bar as you enter and edit Excel formulas and functions. The following graphic shows you the different parts of the bar:

The Name box displays the location of the cell that's currently selected. You can use the Name box to move to other cells or select named ranges. The Cancel and Enter buttons abandon or accept the function you've entered, and the Insert Function button displays the Insert Function dialog box so that you can insert it in the function box.

See Also   For more about using simple functions in Excel, see the section entitled "Working with Functions," later in this chapter. For more about using the Name box, see the section entitled "Naming and Moving to Ranges," later in this chapter.

Exploring the Workspace

The grid in the center of the workspace is the worksheet on which you'll do all your calculating tasks in Excel. Along the bottom and right sides of the worksheet area are two scroll bars—one vertical and one horizontal. You will use these to scroll to different areas of your worksheet when it gets too large to display on one screen.

At the bottom of the left side of the work area, you see the worksheet tabs, which enable you move from sheet to sheet when you have created more than one worksheet in your Excel workbook. To move to a different worksheet, simply click the worksheet tab of the sheet you want to view. In addition, you can rename worksheets by right-clicking the tab to display a context menu (as shown in Figure 8-2).

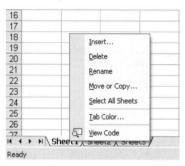

Figure 8-2   Right-clicking a worksheet tab displays a context menu you can use to customize the worksheet tabs to your liking.

When you first start Excel, the New Workbook task pane also appears on the right side of the workspace, enabling you to open an existing workbook or start a new one from scratch or from a template. You can close the task pane to give you more room on the screen by clicking the Close box in the upper right corner of the task pane.

Creating a Simple Spreadsheet

Now that you know your way around the spreadsheet window, you're ready to create a simple spreadsheet. You might be surprised to find out how easy it is— even if numbers aren't your favorite things.

When you first start Excel, a blank worksheet opens automatically and the task pane appears on the right side of the window. (If the task pane does not open automatically on your system, press Ctrl+N to display it.) If you want to open an existing worksheet instead of creating a new one, choose the worksheet you want to use from the Open A Workbook area. If you don't see the file you want in the task pane, click More Workbooks to display the Open dialog box so that you can navigate to the folder in which the file you want is stored.

Most worksheets commonly include these familiar elements:

- **Column and row labels.**   A huge page of numbers won't make much sense unless you know what the numbers represent—and that's where column and row labels come in. Common labels might be months, sales regions, product names, or the names of personnel.

- **Data.**   The data is the numeric (or text, date, and time) information you are recording in the spreadsheet.

- **Formulas.**   A formula is an equation performed on the data in the worksheet. For example, a formula might add the values of two cells, as in =A4+D5. A formula usually includes a *function*, which performs a common operation on the data, as in =SUM(A4:D5).

Depending on the goal of your particular worksheet, you might also include charts to show trends in data and formatting enhancements, such as pictures, lines, and boxes, to help add visual interest to the page. For the most basic worksheets, you need only a few numbers, a couple of labels, and maybe a simple function. That's the approach we'll take in the last few sections of this chapter.

Try This! Microsoft Excel also includes professionally designed templates you can use as the basis for your worksheets. This is a great help, especially if you are unfamiliar with the traditional forms of common financial documents such as balance sheets or a sales invoice. To start a worksheet from an Excel template, follow these steps:

1   Choose New from the File menu.

2   In the task pane, click General Templates.

3   Click the Spreadsheet Solutions tab, and click the icon of the template you want to see. An example of the spreadsheet appears in the preview window.

4   When you find the template you want, click OK.

Excel displays the worksheet in the workspace, and you can click in the sheet and fill in your own data as needed.

Adding Column and Row Labels

The column and row labels you use in your spreadsheet tell others (and remind you) what the data in the cells means. There's no hard and fast rule for what types of labels you use—your own projects will determine that. Generally, how-ever, many people create row labels that refer to the data being tracked (for example, Region 1, Region 2, Region 3), and the column labels refer to the period of time used to track the data for each of the regions (Quarter 1, Quarter 2, Quarter 3, and so on).

Another way to organize your spreadsheet involves using columns to display the items you want to compare (such as profit margin by month, new hires by district, or expenses per employee). Then the rows would include the detail of each of those comparisons. Figure 8-3 shows an example of a spreadsheet used to track employee expenses by category. Notice that the columns list individual employees, and the rows break down the costs by category.

	Akers, K.	Barnhill, J.	Charney, N.	Dixon, A.	Nayberg, A.
Lakes Publishing					
Employee Expense Reporting Quarter 1					
Office Expenses					
Supply purchases	$230.00	$175.00	$30.00	$25.00	$20.00
Cell phone	$230.00	$250.00	$200.00	$310.00	$175.00
Reference materials	$0.00	$130.00	$0.00	$0.00	$125.00
Shipping	$0.00	$50.00	$35.00	$0.00	$35.00
Training	$0.00	$0.00	$0.00	$250.00	$0.00
Total Office Expenses	$460.00	$605.00	$265.00	$585.00	$355.00
Travel					
Lodging	$245.00	$0.00	$280.00	$280.00	$0.00
Airfare	$0.00	$0.00	$290.00	$390.00	$0.00
Mileage	$25.00	$0.00	$0.00	$0.00	$67.00
Phone use	$33.00	$0.00	$45.00	$145.00	$20.00
Client meals	$125.00	$0.00	$158.00	$250.00	$45.00
Miscellaneous	$30.00	$45.00	$25.00	$35.00	$15.00
Total Travel Expenses	$458.00	$45.00	$798.00	$1,100.00	$147.00

Figure 8-3   The columns in this spreadsheet display the items to be compared; the rows list the individual data items being tracked.

Okay, enough theory. The best way to figure out how to organize your spreadsheet data is to get in there and do it. When you're ready to enter the column and row labels for your worksheet, follow these steps:

1   Click the cell where you want to enter the first label.

2   Type the label and press the Tab key if you're entering column labels (this moves the highlight to the next cell) or Enter to move to the next row.

3   Type the next label and repeat to enter all the column or row labels you need.

If you are entering a common series of labels, such as *January*, *February*, *March* or *Quarter 1*, *Quarter 2*, *Quarter 3*, you can have Excel enter the labels for you. Type the first label and then click the small box in the bottom right corner of the selected cell. Drag the cell to encompass the entire area for you which want to add labels. A ScreenTip appears to show you the entered labels as you drag (as shown in Figure 8-4). Release the mouse button and the labels are entered automatically.

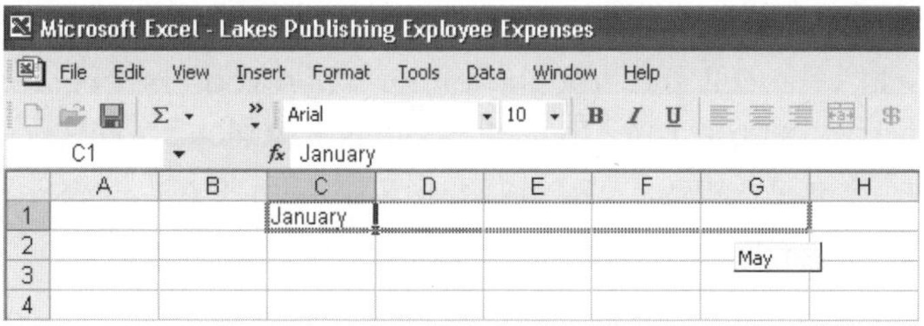

Figure 8-4 You can have Excel enter common labels for you by dragging over the columns or rows.

Note Begin your column or row labels a few rows down from the top of the document to leave space for important identifying information, such as the worksheet title and subtitle, your name, the department number, and so on. Of course, you can easily add rows any time you want by clicking the point where you want to add a row and choosing Rows from the Insert menu.

Entering Data

Entering data is another simple process that Excel is glad to help you with. Again, it's just a matter of clicking a cell and typing the data. What kind of data can you enter? Here's the list:

- **Numbers.** This is the most common type of data, and you can format numbers in several different ways, including General (303), Number (303.00), and Currency ($303.00). In addition, you can use the Accounting format to align the numbers by their decimal points and currency symbols.

- **Date.** You also can store date values in your worksheet, which is important for tracking information over time, dating reports, sorting according to date, and more. Once you enter date information, you can apply a wide range of date formats to the date.

See Also For more about formatting dates, see Chapter 10, "Charting Spreadsheet Data."

- **Time.**   Time also is an important value for many items you'll be tracking in your worksheets. You can format time values in a number of different ways in Excel.

- **Text.**   Not only can you enter text as row and column labels in your worksheet, but you can also track names, addresses, and product IDs; enter serial numbers or product codes, and add comments to your entries. Text data is formatted as text and can be sorted alphabetically in ascending or descending order.

To enter the data, click the cell and type the value. When you first begin entering information, the default format of the cell is General, which applies no particular format to the information you type. Let's try an example just to get some data entry practice:

1   Click cell C3.

2   Type **3456** and press Enter.

3   Type **practice** and press Enter.

4   Type **45.00** and press Enter.

Notice that each of these entries caused something different to happen. When you type a number in General format, even if the number should have a comma separating the thousands place, Excel displays the number as you entered it. The second entry was left-aligned in the cell because Excel recognized it as text data. The third entry removed the decimal places and rounded to the whole number because General format is in control. In Chapter 10, you'll learn more about your formatting choices and when to apply them both to individual cells and groups of cells.

Try This!   Want to have your computer read back that last column of numbers so you can make sure you got it right? Excel can read the data to you by using Speech playback. To play back your data, follow these steps:

1   Highlight the column or row of data you want to hear. (If you were following along in the preceding section, highlight the values in cells C3 through C5 you entered.)

2   Choose Speech from the Tools menu and select Show Text To Speech Toolbar.

3   On the Text To Speech toolbar, click Speak Cells.

A computer-generated voice reads the values beginning at the top of the column or the left end of the row. If you want to have Excel read you each entry after you enter it, select Speak On Enter at the right end of the Text To Speech toolbar.

AutoFilling Cells

In addition to simply clicking and typing, you can use the Fill feature of Excel to fill spreadsheet cells with data. You might use this, for example, when you are entering sequential check numbers in a row. To autofill the cells, follow these steps:

1   Click the cell and enter the starting value.

2   Click the small rectangle in the lower right corner of the cell and drag across the row or down the column.

3   At the end of the area you want to fill, release the mouse button. The area fills with a copy of the value you entered in the initial cell.

4   Click AutoFill and a list of choices appears (as shown in Figure 8.5). To create a sequential series, click Fill Series.

$33.00	$0.00	$45.00	$145.00	$20.00	
$125.00	$0.00	$158.00	$250.00	$45.00	
$30.00	$45.00	$25.00	$35.00		
				○ Copy Cells	
$458.00	$45.00	$798.00	$1,100.00	⊙ Fill Series	
				○ Fill Formatting Only	
$838.00	$650.00	$1,063.00	$1,685.00	○ Fill Without Formatting	
1312	1313	1314	1315		

Figure 8-5   You can use the AutoFill button to fill data in a sequential series.

Note   The choices on your AutoFill button list will vary depending on the type of data you are using. The choices here allow you to simply copy the cells in the selected range, apply only the formatting of the cell to the other cells, or add only the data without copying the formatting.

Importing Data

You have another option for entering data in your worksheet: You can use data you have stored in other programs. To import data from another program (or from another Excel workbook), follow these steps:

1   Select the sheet onto which you want to import the data by clicking the worksheet tab.

2   Click the cell you want to serve as the upper left corner for the imported data.

3   Choose Import External Data from the Data menu and choose Import Data.

4   In the Select Data Source dialog box, navigate to the folder storing the data file you want to import.

5   Click the Files Of Type down arrow and select the program type from the list.

6 Locate the file in the list, click it, and then click Import.

7 Depending on the type of program from which you're importing, options will appear asking you to select the table you want to use. Click the table choice, and then click OK.

8 The Import Data dialog box appears, asking where you want to add the data. (You've already positioned the cell pointer in a new work-sheet, which takes care of this step.) Click OK.

9 The data is then displayed in the worksheet.

You might need to do a little formatting to display the data the way you like it, but by importing an existing file, you've saved yourself the time and trouble of re-entering information, and you've reduced your margin for error at the same time.

Can We Talk? You also can use Speech Recognition to enter data in the cells of your work-sheet. To do this, click the cell where you want to add the first value and choose Speech and then Speech Recognition from the Tools menu. The Language Bar appears. When the word *Listening* appears on the bar, speak clearly into your microphone.

This feature is great in theory, but you should be aware that teaching Excel to recognize your intonations and voice patterns reliably requires you to do a considerable amount of training. Click the Tools button on the Language bar and choose Options. In the Recognition Profiles area of the Speech Recognition tab, click Train Profile and then follow the on-screen instructions to teach Excel how to recognize and interpret your dictation. Plan to spend about 30 minutes talking to your computer s...l...o...w...l...y as you teach it to understand your words, numbers, and commands.

Moving Around and Selecting Cells

Now that you've gotten the hang of entering information in your worksheet, you'll need to know how to navigate the worksheet and select the cells you want to use for various operations. Let's tackle the navigation part first. Table 8-2 gives you a quick overview of the important keys for moving around on the worksheet.

Table 8-2   **Keys for Navigating the Excel Worksheet**

Press This Key	To Move Here
Enter	Next cell down
Tab	Next cell to the right
Shift+Tab	Next cell to the left
Any arrow key	One cell in the direction of the arrow

Table 8-2   Keys for Navigating the Excel Worksheet

Press This Key	To Move Here
Home	Column A
Ctrl+Home	Cell A1
Ctrl+End	The last cell in your worksheet
Page Down	Down one screen
Page Up	Up one screen
Alt+Page Down	Right one screen
Alt+Page Up	Left one screen

Tip   Two quick ways to move to the cell you want: Click in the Name box, type the cell address or range name, and click Enter; or press F5 to display the Go To dialog box, type the destination cell or range, and then click OK.

Selecting Cells

Once you get to where you're going on the worksheet, you need to know how to select cells. Here are some of the different ways in which you'll select the cells you want to work with:

- To select a single cell, either click the cell or type the cell address (for example, B7) in the Name box in the left side of the Formula bar and press Enter. The highlight moves to that cell.

- To select a range of cells, click the first cell and drag to the last cell in the block. The area highlights as you drag the mouse. When the range is the size you want, release the mouse button.

- To select noncontiguous (that is, not touching) ranges or cells, select the first cell or range as just described. Then press and hold Ctrl while selecting subsequent cells or ranges. When you've selected all the cells you want, release Ctrl and perform your task as needed.

- To select the entire worksheet, press Ctrl+A. The entire area is highlighted.

Naming and Moving to Ranges

Once you know how to select a group of cells, you can save those cells as a range that you use in common operations. For example, suppose that you often use the yearly sales figures for each salesperson (cells F5 to F20) in worksheets and reports that you create. You can name that range so that you can refer to it by name in other operations, and Excel will automatically know to which cells you're referring. To create a range, follow these steps:

1   Highlight the area you want to name as a range.

2   Click the Name box on the Formula bar on the right side of the worksheet.

3   Type the name you want to assign to the range (in this case, Year-Sales); then press Enter.

> **Tip**   Be sure to start range names with letters, and don't use spaces (use under-scores to separate words instead). Otherwise, Excel won't know what to do with the name and will display an error box asking you to enter a valid name.

Now you can move right to that range by typing **YearSales** in the Name box or by clicking the Name box down arrow and selecting it from the displayed list.

> **Tip**   If you prefer, you can press Ctrl+F3 to display the Define Names dialog box. Then simply type the name for the range, and then click OK to save it.

Working with Functions and Formulas

Functions in Excel do most of the heavy work when it comes to complicated operations. Luckily, you can put away your trigonometric calculator and relax, because Excel has the know-how you need and the support to help you use it.

Deconstructing Formulas

A *formula* is an equation that carries out a particular operation on specified values. You'll use formulas to calculate sales projections, estimate taxes, average your expenses, total your income, and tally your inventory, among other things. A *function* is a preset formula that carries out a specific kind of operation. For example, you use the =SUM function to add a column of numbers; you use =AVERAGE to display the average of a group of cell values. Excel functions always appear in this form:

=FUNCTION (argument, argument)

Does that look strange? It's really pretty simple, and here's a step-by-step explanation:

■   The equals sign (=) tells Excel that what follows is a function. You always need to use the equals sign or Excel won't know what to do with the data you enter and will display an error.

■ The word *FUNCTION* above is where the actual name of the function appears. The function might be SUM, AVERAGE, IF, COUNT, MAX, or something else.

■ The (*argument, argument*) text represents the part of the formula in which you tell Excel which values to use. Cell addresses are commonly used as arguments, but you can also use text, TRUE or FALSE, or numbers. For cases in which you'll need complex formulas (which is beyond our intention here), you can create *nested formulas* by including other formulas and functions as the arguments.

Entering a Formula

To create a simple formula that uses a function, follow these steps:

1 Enter the following four values in a blank worksheet:

      In cell C4, type **230**
      In cell C5, type **450**
      In cell C6, type **120**
      In cell C7, type **580**

2 Click cell C9 to select it.

3 Click the Insert Function tool in the Formula bar. The Insert Function dialog box appears (as shown in Figure 8-6).

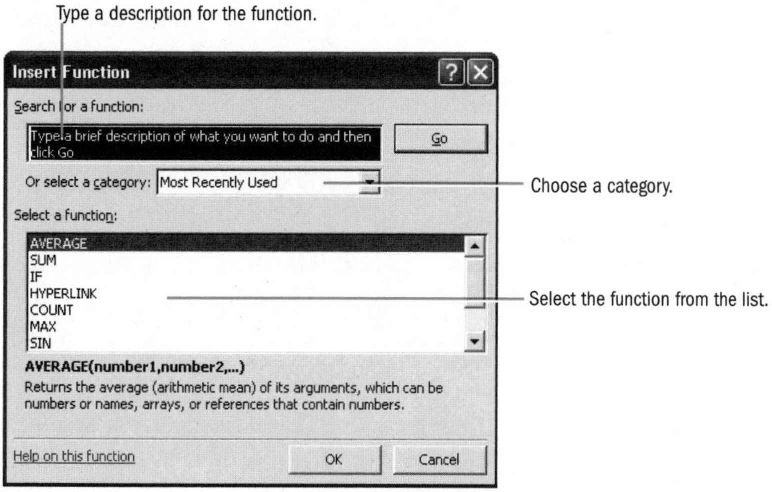

Figure 8-6   The Insert Function dialog box gives you three ways to find the function you need.

4 Click AVERAGE in the Select A Function list.

5 Click OK.

Excel adds the equals sign in the formula bar and inserts both the AVERAGE function and its best guess at the arguments you wanted to use. In addition, Excel displays the Function Arguments dialog box so that you can change the arguments included. For this example, no change is needed—click OK to return to the worksheet.

Note   New changes in Excel make using functions easier than ever. As you saw in Figure 8-6, you can find your function in three different ways: by typing a description of what it does and clicking Go (Excel calls this feature the Function Wizard), by choosing the category to which it belongs (which narrows the displayed list and makes it easier for you to find), or by clicking the function in the function list. Each time you click a function in the Insert Function dialog box, a description of the function appears beneath the list. And if you feel you need still more information about that function before choosing it, you can click the Help On This Function link in the bottom of the dialog box to see what the Help system has to say about it.

Special Formula Features

As your experience with Excel and with formulas begins to grow, there are a few features that will help you ensure that your formulas work as you want them to. Remember to try the following features when you find yourself building more complex operations:

■   The AutoSum tool (available on the Standard toolbar) allows you to enter common functions by selecting them from the AutoSum menu. You can choose Sum, Average, Count, Max, or Min, or click More Functions to display the Insert Function dialog box and use the Function Wizard to find the function you need.

■   You can have Excel check your formulas for you to make sure there are no mistakes. To start the checker, choose Error Checking from the Tools menu. Excel will display any errors found in the formulas in your worksheet, and you can make corrections as needed in the formula bar.

■   Whenever an error occurs in a formula in the spreadsheet, the Trace Error button appears beside the formula in the cell. You can click the Trace Error button to choose options that will help you run down and fix the error in the formula.

■   You can watch a formula and keep an eye on its results by using the new Watch Window feature. Start by selecting the cells with the formulas you want to watch, and then point to Formula Auditing on the Tools menu and choose Show Watch Window. Next, click Add Watch, and then click Add to save the selected cells as the range you want to watch. You can then reposition and resize the Watch Window to keep it open in your workspace while you continue to work with the current worksheet. When any of the values or formulas in the watch range change, the value change is reflected in the watch window.

Saving the Spreadsheet

Now that you've been through the whole process of entering spreadsheet labels and data and entering simple formulas, you're ready to save the spreadsheet. Excel gives you three primary ways to save the worksheets you create:

- Choose Save from the File menu
- Press Ctrl+S
- Select the Save tool on the Standard toolbar

Each of these methods displays the Save As dialog box. To save the worksheet, simply navigate to the folder in which you want to save the file, enter a file name, and click Save.

Saving Options

When you save your Excel worksheet, you can choose to save the file in a number of different popular formats. The list is amazing: You can save your worksheet as a Web page, as a Web archive, or as an XML spreadsheet. You can choose to save the file as a template (so that you can use it to create other worksheets), or you can save it as Text or Unicode Text. Additionally, you can save the file in formats supported by older versions of Excel, Lotus 1-2-3, Quattro Pro, and dBASE (versions II through IV). If you've got the program, chances are that Excel supports it. That's good to know when you need to transfer data among multiple computers and programs—you can get the most out of your data and still have the latest features at your disposal.

Key Points

- Excel is a full-featured program that you can use to do simple or complex math operations.
- Excel toolbars and menus are similar to those found in other Office XP applications; however, you'll also find new tools specifically designed for working with cell values and formulas.
- A *workbook* is a collection of worksheets in Excel. A *worksheet* is the page on which you perform mathematical operations. A *cell* is the intersection of a column and row and stores one data value.

■   You add data to the worksheet—including number, text, date, and time values—by clicking a cell and typing the information.

■   You can use Excel's AutoFill feature to fill data cells quickly.

■   You can use a number of shortcut keys to move around the worksheet window.

■   A *range* is a selected group of cells in a worksheet. You can name ranges that you work with regularly to find and reference them more easily.

■   Excel includes a number of preset functions you can include in formulas to execute common operations. Excel provides a number of features to help you find the right function and ensure that your formulas are correct.

■   Excel allows you to save your worksheets in a number of different file formats, including Web pages, XML Spreadsheets, text files, and files supported by other popular spreadsheet and database programs.

Chapter 9

Editing, Formatting, and Printing Spreadsheets

Entering and saving worksheet data is only a fraction of what you can do with Microsoft Excel. First, you need to make sure your worksheet is as accurate as it can be; then you can spruce it up with new fonts, colors, pictures, and more. And finally, when everything looks good and you've got the worksheet the way you want it, you can preview it to make sure the page breaks occur in the right places and choose your favorite options before you print.

Editing Spreadsheet Data

Especially if you are new to using spreadsheets, it may take you a while to get comfortable with creating worksheets that make sense. Which information would be best for the columns? What should your row labels be? As you gain experience creating worksheets you like, you may want to go back and change some of your earlier efforts. Perhaps you've thought of better labels, a clearer arrangement, or an easier way to deploy the information to make it easier to understand. Or perhaps Ms. Jones in Accounting pointed out (again) that you've got your numbers reversed (again) in the yearly totals of your spreadsheet report. It's time to revisit your worksheet (again) and correct the typos you inadvertently entered.

All such tasks are editing operations. This section discusses the various ways you can make changes to your Excel spreadsheets.

The Old-Fashioned Change: Click and Type

The easiest way to make an editing change in an Excel worksheet it to click the cell you need to change and type the correct information. The process actually involves four simple steps:

1   Open the worksheet that includes the data you need to change.

2   Select the cell.

3   Click in the Formula bar, backspace through the data, and type the correct entry.

4   Press Enter to accept the change.

Tip   If you want to edit quickly in the cell without typing in the Formula bar, double-click the cell (or press F2 to turn on Edit mode), delete the errant data, and type the correct information; then click outside the cell or press Enter.

Figure 9-1 shows a worksheet being edited. Notice that the active cell, D7, shows the cursor in the cell (indicating that I've double-clicked the cell to edit it). The value also appears in the Formula bar, and the status bar shows that the worksheet is in Edit mode.

Tip   If you don't like the change you just made, you can undo it by pressing Ctrl+Z.

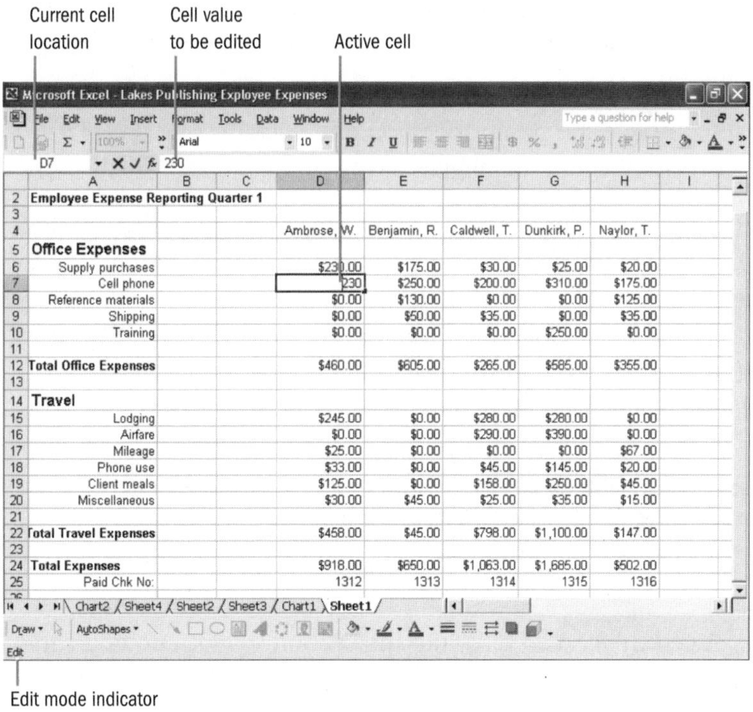

Current cell location   Cell value to be edited   Active cell

Edit mode indicator

Figure 9-1 You can edit individual cells by changing their values in the cell or in the Formula bar.

Copying and Pasting Cells and Ranges

At times you may need to make bigger edits—the kind that require highlighting a range of cells and then copying, cutting, pasting, or dragging them to another location. Suppose that after reviewing your worksheet, your boss wants to see the travel expenses displayed on a different worksheet. That's simple to do, because your current workbook includes three worksheets by default. First, you'll want to make a copy of the data, then you'll paste it into Sheet2, and finally, you'll go back and delete the information on Sheet1. Here are the steps:

1 Select the area you want to move to the new sheet. If you have previously named the range, choose the range name in the Name box to select it. If you have not saved the area as a range, drag to select the area.

2 Copy the cells by pressing Ctrl+C. (You can also choose Copy from the Edit menu or click the Copy tool on the Standard toolbar.) This places a copy of the selected range on the Office Clipboard. A dotted outline (often called *marching ants*) appears around the perimeter of the range.

3 Click the Sheet2 worksheet tab. The blank worksheet appears.

4   Click in the cell where you want the data to be placed. Press Ctrl+V to paste the cells. (You also can choose Paste from the Edit menu or click the Paste tool on the Standard toolbar.)

5   Press Enter to complete the paste operation and click outside the selected range to remove the highlight.

Notice that the copied data brings with it any formats you previously applied; however, the cell widths on the new sheet appear at their default setting. If you want to retain the column width and row height settings when you paste cells in your worksheet, click the Paste Options button that appears beneath and to the right of the pasted cells. Click the Keep Source Column Widths option; Excel then preserves the column widths with the pasted information.

Caution   Be sure that you are pasting data into a clear area, because the incoming information will overwrite the data in existing cells without any warning from Excel.

Clearing Data

Now that you've placed the copied data into the second worksheet, you can clear the information from the first worksheet. To do that, follow these steps:

1   Click the Sheet1 worksheet tab. The information you previously high-lighted is still selected.

2   Choose Clear from the Edit menu and then select All (as shown in Figure 9-2). The cell contents are cleared.

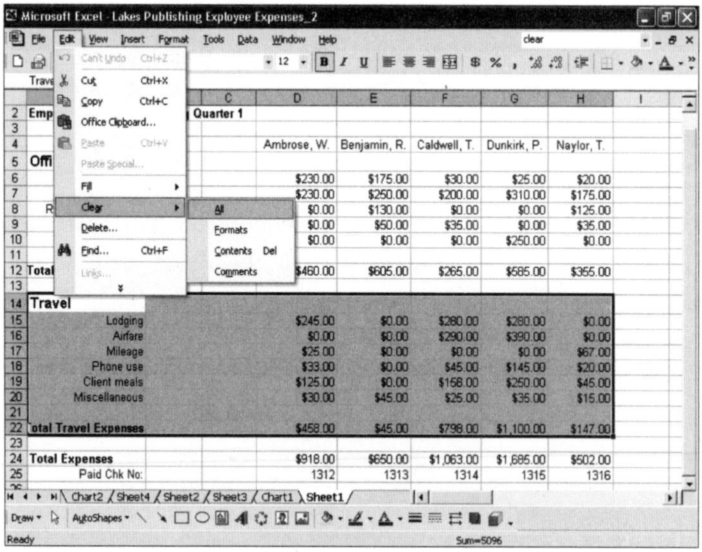

Figure 9-2   Clear All removes the data and format assigned to selected cells.

3   Click outside the highlighted area to deselect it.

There's another way to handle this copy-paste-and-clear operation: You can select the information on the first worksheet, choose Cut from the Edit menu (or press Ctrl+X), move to the new worksheet, click the area where you want the data to go, and press Ctrl+V (or Enter) to paste. This removes the data and places it in the new worksheet in one process; you don't need to go back and clear the data later. Note that when you use Cut to remove data, the format and cell contents are cleared and the blank cells are preserved in the worksheet.

Clearing vs. Deleting Data   At first glance, it may not be obvious why we need two commands that seem to remove data from a worksheet. There's a subtle difference between clearing and deleting data, however.

When you clear data by using the Clear command in the Edit menu, you are telling Excel to wipe the cell clean of all contents, formats, and comments. The cells remain intact but now they are simply empty.

When you use the Delete command from the Edit menu, you are actually removing the selected cells from the worksheet. The other cells in the worksheet are moved to close that void, which means that the cell references in your formulas are automatically updated.

When you highlight a range and then press your Delete key or use the Backspace key to delete data, you are removing the data only; the format of the cell remains in place. For that reason, when you want to remove all data and formats within a given range, use the Clear command when you intend to plug other data into the blank space you've created; use Delete when you want to condense the amount of space on your worksheet and remove the unnecessary rows or columns.

Working with Rows and Columns

Some of the rearranging you need to do might involve changing the width or height of columns and rows. By default, Excel's columns are set wide enough to display 8.43 characters (yes, it's an odd number), and the rows are set to 12.75 points, or slightly more than 1/6 of an inch in height, since 72 points equals1 inch.

When you want to make a change to a column or row, you need to begin by selecting the one you want to work with. To select an entire column, click the column label. To select an entire row, click the row label. Then use the following steps to make the changes you want to make:

■   To change the width of a column, choose Column from the Format menu and select Width. In the Column Width dialog box, type a new width for the column and click OK.

■ To set the width of a column or the height of a row automatically to accommodate the largest data entry, use AutoFit. Choose Column from the Format menu and then select AutoFit Selection to resize a column automatically; choose Row from the Format menu and click AutoFit to resize a row.

■ To change the height of a row, select Row from the Format menu and choose Height. In the Row Height dialog box, type a new value in the text box and click OK.

Tip   You also can resize columns and rows by selecting the divider line in the column or row label area and dragging the divider in the direction you want. Dragging a divider line down in the row labels increases the row height; dragging a divider line to the right in the column labels widens the column. All other rows and columns are moved accordingly to allow for the size change.

■ To insert columns and rows, select the column or row beside which you want to add another column or row. Then, depending on what you've selected, choose Rows (or Columns) from the Insert menu. If you add a row, the new row is added above the selected row; if you add a column, the new column is added to the left of the selected column.

Tip   If you want to insert multiple rows or columns, highlight the number of columns or rows you want to add before you choose Rows or Columns from the Insert menu. Excel will add as many rows or columns as you have highlighted.

■ To hide columns and rows, you can again choose Row or Column from the Format menu and choose Hide (or, alternately, Unhide). But there's also another way: Right-click the column or row you want to hide. A context menu of row or column options appears and you can choose Hide to hide the selected column or row.

Tip   How do you select a hidden column to "Unhide" it? Simple. If you have hidden column C, for example, select columns B and D and then right-click the column label area. Choose Unhide from the context menu, and column C reappears.

Try This! If you're the lucky person who is reviewing another's work, you will find the Comment feature comes in handy. You can add your thoughts and suggestions in little pop-up boxes without adding information in the worksheet itself. To add a comment, follow these steps:

1   Click the cell to which you want to add the comment.

2   Choose Comment from the Insert menu. (If you prefer, you can right-click the cell and select Insert Comment from the context menu.) A little message box appears, connected to a comment tag in the cell.

3   Type your comment in the box and click outside the cell.

To display the note, simply position the pointer on the red comment tag. The comment box appears, looking something like this:

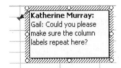

To remove the comment later, select the cell with the comment attached, open the Edit menu, and choose first Clear and then Comments. If you want to remove all comments in the entire worksheet, press Ctrl+A to select the worksheet contents and then choose Clear Comments from the Edit menu.

Formatting Spreadsheets

Now that you know how to take care of simple editing errors and work with blocks of cells on your worksheet, you're ready to focus on making your worksheet look good. Adding special formats, cool fonts, attention-getting graphics, and lines and borders isn't necessary—they are the add-ons of the visually pleasing spreadsheet. But adding these extra touches can help you make sure that people don't go to sleep reading your numbers. And, if you use them well, the added design elements will help readers clearly understand which elements are most important in the worksheet.

Tip   Here's a new design feature that can help make your worksheet easier to use: Color-code your worksheet tabs so that people viewing the workbook can understand what the different tabs mean. To set the color of a tab, right-click the tab, choose Tab Color, and select the color you want from the Format Tab Color palette.

Formatting the Easy Way

If you want a quick-and-easy spreadsheet that looks professional and will get at least a few appreciative blinks from the crowd, try AutoFormat. Excel's AutoFormat is a set of worksheet formats you can apply to your data. To use AutoFormat, follow these steps:

1 Begin by selecting the area of the worksheet to which you want to apply the format. If you want to apply the format to the entire worksheet, click Ctrl+A.

2 Choose AutoFormat from the Tools menu.

3 Scroll through the list of formats in the AutoFormat dialog box. Click the format you want and click OK.

By default, AutoFormat applies its own format for number, border, font, pattern, alignment, and width/height settings. If you want to turn off the automatic formatting for any of those items, click the Options button in the AutoFormat dialog box and click the check box of the item you want to clear. Then click OK to apply the format to your worksheet.

Tip Excel also includes a feature called Conditional Formatting, which enables you to apply formats to data based on certain conditions. For example, you could specify that a cell highlight in red if its value falls below a certain level—this would be good for an inventory tracking worksheet or spreadsheet that monitors your cash flow. To use this feature, choose Conditional Formatting from the Format menu.

Choosing Data Formats

The most common formatting task you'll do in Excel is formatting the data you enter. When you first type numbers, text, dates, and times, they are placed in a generic format based on the data type Excel recognizes. (For more about this, see Chapter 8, "Creating and Saving a Spreadsheet.") As you work with your worksheets, you will need to know how to display data in the necessary format. To set the format of cell data, follow these steps:

1 Select the cell you want to format. (You can also choose a range, column, or row if you want to apply the same format to multiple cells.)

2 Right-click the selected cell(s). Choose Format Cells from the context menu.

3 The Number tab is displayed by default. Click the format you want in the Category list on the left. Each time you choose a different format, options related to that format, as well as a general description of the format, appear on the tab (as shown in Figure 9-3).

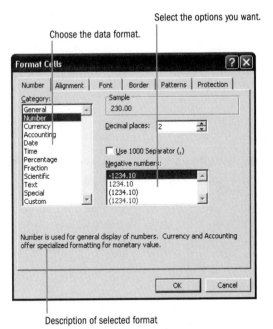

Figure 9-3   You can control all kinds of formatting tasks in the Format Cells dialog box.

4   Select the format you want, specify any options you need, and then click OK.

Tip   This section shows you how to use the Format Cells dialog box to apply different formats to the data in your worksheet, but remember that you can apply many format changes quickly by selecting the cells and clicking the appropriate formatting tool on the Formatting toolbar. You can change font, style, alignment, and color by using tools on the toolbar. Additionally, you can change common number formats, add borders and lines, and fill worksheet areas with a color of your choosing. If you're not sure which formatting tool is which, position your pointer over the tool and a ScreenTip will display the tool's name. For a refresher of the various tools on the Formatting toolbar, see Chapter 8, "Creating and Saving a Spreadsheet."

Changing Alignment, Font, Style, and Size

As you can see, the Format Cells dialog box is a one-stop shop for all your Excel formatting needs. The various tabs in the dialog box contain options related to a specific task. You'll use the options in the Alignment tab to control how the data appears in the cells of the selected area. And the Font tab—well, that's obvious isn't it?—allows you to choose a different font, style, size, and color for the data in your worksheet.

To set the alignment for your data, display the Format Cells dialog box by right-clicking in the selected cell and choosing Format Cells. Then click the Alignment tab and change any necessary settings. You may not use Alignment much for ordinary worksheets, but it does come in handy when you want to create special effects, such as vertical or skewed text labels or worksheet titles.

To change the font, style, size, and color of your data, follow these steps:

1 Display the Format Cells dialog box and click the Font tab.

2 Scroll through the Font list to find a typeface you like. Click one you'd like to see and an example is displayed in the Preview window (as shown in Figure 9-4).

3 Choose the Font Style and Size you want by selecting the items from their lists.

4 If you want to change the color of data, click the Color down arrow and click the color you want from the displayed palette.

5 Set other options and effects as needed; then click OK. The text changes are applied to the selected cells.

Tip   The settings shown in Figure 9-4 have been changed from the default font, style, and size. If you want to return your settings to their default values, select the Normal font check box to return the text to Arial, Regular, 10-point text.

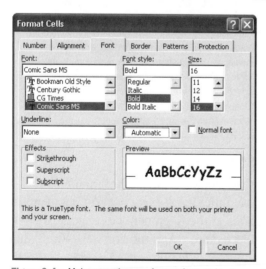

Figure 9-4   Make your changes for text font, style, size, and color on the Font tab of the Format Cells dialog box.

Adding Borders and Shading

Once you've mastered the formatting of cells and labels, you'll start thinking about sprucing up your worksheet in new ways. Borders can add a professional look and give you more flexibility than simply drawing boxes around worksheet areas or charts. You can use Excel's Border feature to add horizontal or vertical lines, grid lines, surrounding borders, or specialty lines. You can work with borders three ways:

- Select the area to which you want to apply the border, and then click the Borders tool, shown below, to display the Borders palette and select the tool you want.

- Display the Borders toolbar, shown below, by clicking the Borders tool and choosing Draw Borders. You can then select the cells you want to border, select the Draw Border tool, choose your line style and color, and draw the border by dragging the pencil tool in the areas you want to draw. Press Esc to turn off border drawing.

- Select the cells you want to border and then right-click the selection and choose Format Cells. Click the Borders tab in the Format Cells dialog box and choose one of the Presets or click one of the Border lines to create a custom border. Choose the line style and color you want and click OK. The border is applied to the selected cells.

Try This! Another feature that goes hand-in-hand with bordering your worksheet cells is coloriz-
ing them. You can change the background color and pattern of cell areas using the Patterns tab in
the Format Cells dialog box. You might want to change the background color of column labels or row
labels, for example, or perhaps highlight an area of your worksheet that you want to stand out in a
unique way. To change the color of your worksheet cells, follow these steps:

1   Select the cells you want to change.

2   Right-click the selection and choose Format Cells.

3   Click the Patterns tab in the Format Cells dialog box. Click the color you want in the Cell
Shading area. The Pattern selection becomes available.

4   Click the Pattern drop-down arrow, producing a palette that offers you additional patterns you can apply in the color you selected, as shown below.

5   Click the pattern you want and then click OK. The colored pattern is applied to the
selected cells.

Tip   If you want to apply color to cells without opening the Format Cells dialog box, you can simply select the cells you want to color and then click Fill Color on the Formatting toolbar. This
applies the currently selected color to the highlighted cells. If you want to use a different color,
click the Fill Color down arrow and choose the color you want from the displayed palette.

Printing Spreadsheets

Once you get your worksheet looking just the way you want it, you will probably want to print a copy. Even if your goal is to send the file over the Internet
or post it on the Web, having a printout to stick in a file somewhere is a good
idea for very important documents. The process of printing a spreadsheet in
Excel is basically this: Choose what you want to print, and print it.

Getting a Fast Print

If you know that you want the default settings of Excel to apply to your print
job, the fastest way to print your spreadsheet is to display your worksheet and
click the Print button on the Standard toolbar. A quick status box appears, telling
you that the file is being sent to the printer and then—voilà!—there it is. Fast
and easy.

Choosing a Print Area

If you regularly print a selected area of your worksheet (for example, you might turn in a selected portion of the payroll worksheet with your departmental reports each week), you can save the area as a print area. To set a print area, begin by selecting the cells you want to include. Then choose Print Area from the File menu and select Set Print Area. A dotted outline surrounds the range, indicating that it is now marked as a print area.

Tip   Clear the print area you've selected by choosing Print Area from the File menu and choosing Clear Print Area.

Look Before You Print

To see how the selected print area—or the entire worksheet—will look before you print it, choose Print Preview from the File menu or click the Print Preview tool on the Standard toolbar. The print area you selected appears in the preview window, showing the orientation, margins, and the header and footer of your worksheet.

Tip   If you want to add a header and footer or change the margins for your worksheet before you print it, display the worksheet in Print Preview mode (click the Print Preview tool on the Standard toolbar) and click the Setup button at the top of the Preview window. In the Page Setup dialog box, click the Margins tab to set margins and the Header/Footer tab to enter a header and footer for the worksheet. After you make your changes, click OK to return to Preview mode.

Setting Print Options

Your last stop before you print—whether you're viewing your worksheet in Print Preview or Normal view—is the Print dialog box. When you click Print in Print Preview or select Print from the File menu, the Print dialog box appears.

In this dialog box, choose the printer you want to use (if you have more than one connected to your system). You can also choose whether you want to print the entire document or selected pages. In addition, you can enter the number of copies and choose whether you want the pages collated (arranged in order) or printed with like pages together. Finally, you can determine whether you want to print only the current selection, the current worksheet, or the entire workbook. After you've selected your options, click OK to print. Excel sends the file to the printer and in seconds you should be able to hold a copy of the worksheet you've been working so hard to finish.

Key Points

- The most basic editing task in Excel is so simple you might miss it: Click the cell you want to correct and type in the new data.

- You can copy, cut, and paste cells by first marking them as a block or a range and then using the commands on the Edit menu or the appropriate tools on the Standard toolbar.

- When you clear cells, all data and formats are removed and the blank cells remain; when you delete cells, the data *and* the cells are removed from the worksheet.

- You can use Excel's AutoFormat feature to apply professional designs to the worksheet quickly.

- The Format Cells dialog box (available when you right-click selected cells) contains all the options you need for controlling the format of cells on your worksheet.

- You can add borders by clicking the Borders tool or working with the Draw Borders toolbar.

- Protect your finished worksheet to guard against accidental or unauthorized deletions by choosing Protect Sheet from the Tools menu.

- Print your worksheet or selected worksheet area quickly by clicking Print on the Standard toolbar or by selecting Print from the File menu and choosing your print options. To make sure that the pages will break correctly in your printed worksheet, choose Page Break Preview from the View menu.

Chapter 10

Charting Spreadsheet Data

Now that you know how to create a basic spreadsheet and how to edit, format, and print worksheet information, you may be interested to learn another way of displaying your work: using *charts*. Charts are great for helping people quickly grasp what you're trying to present. If you want to show people that your product outperforms the competition, for example, you can align two sets of data that show test results on your product and test results of the competitor's product. A bar chart enables you to put data items side by side and convince everyone that your product is the one to bank on.

Lingo A *chart* is a graphical representation of your data that's designed to show readers at a glance the trends that your data suggests.

Microsoft Excel enables you to create a number of different charts and even gives you a Chart Wizard to lead you quickly through the process. Along the way, you have the option of creating associated details as you want them—adding chart titles and labels, displaying a legend, coloring the chart, and more. This chapter shows you how to make the most of Excel's charting feature in the shortest time. You're just a few clicks away from a few good-looking charts.

Charting 101: Just the Basics

At its most basic level, a chart is a picture of the data in your worksheet. You simply specify the data that you want Excel to illustrate by choosing your chart type, and then Excel does the rest. You'll see the following elements commonly used in charts (shown in Figure 10-1):

- **Data series.**   The data series is the data you are tracking. The column or row labels are used as the labels in the chart legend.

- **Data marker.**   The data marker is the item used to represent your data graphically. In Figure 10-1, the data marker is a bar. In a pie chart, the data marker is a pie slice; in a line chart, the data marker is a point on the line for an individual data series.

- **Axes.**   The horizontal and vertical lines along the left and bottom sides of some charts (including bar, line, and area charts) are known as *axes*. The x-axis is the horizontal bar and the y-axis is the vertical bar. The data values in the chart are plotted in relation to the categories shown on the x-axis and y-axis.

- **Gridlines.**   The gridlines extend by default off the y-axis in some charts, giving you a visual clue about the value of individual data items. You can add gridlines and customize the ones already there by changing the increment between them or hiding them completely.

- **Chart title and axis titles.**   The title of the chart typically appears at the top of the chart. Subtitles appear along the x-axis and y-axis as applicable.

- **Legend.**   The legend advises how to read the data markers that readers see in your charts. The legend labels are taken from the data series row or column labels you select.

Note   Note that not all Excel charts use all these elements. A radar chart, for example, is created using only a y-axis, and pie and doughnut charts do not use either an x-axis or a y-axis. You will add titles and axis titles and change the gridlines and legend as necessary as you create the chart using the Chart Wizard.

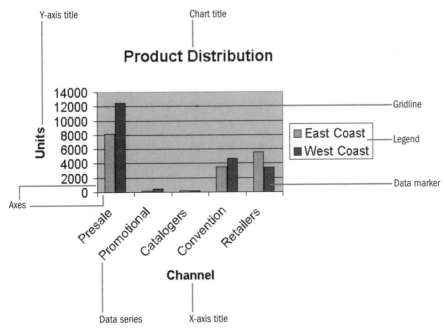

Figure 10-1   The most common chart types share these traditional chart elements.

What Makes a Good Chart?

The best charts are clear, colorful, and easy to understand, giving readers the information they need and helping them grasp it quickly. Charts also add visual interest to pages of mind-numbing numbers and give readers' eyes a break. Here are some suggestions for ensuring that your charts accomplish what you intend:

- **Choose a chart type that will be easy for your readers to understand.**   The most common chart types—the ones everybody is used to seeing—are bar, line, pie, and area charts. (It might just be me, but I always have to scratch my head and puzzle a bit over area charts, even when I know what they are supposed to portray.) The chart types available in Excel are described in detail in the section entitled "Choosing a Chart Type," later in this chapter.

- **Make sure your chart shows something worthwhile.**   Don't waste your audience's time depicting data that won't mean much to them. Use charts to highlight the important comparisons you want to make and use them sparingly to maximize their effectiveness.

- **Choose the right chart for the job.**   Resist the temptation to use bar charts to show everything—from sales results to inventory to personnel hires to vacation time. There are two problems with this blanket approach: First, there will be times when other chart types will better represent what you're trying to show (a chart about new hires in your department as a percentage of total company hires would be best rendered as a pie chart, for example). Second, your audience members are likely to think they already know what you're getting at (or worse, they'll mistakenly think they've already seen that chart) and skip over it, missing your point entirely.

■ **Create clear titles and labels for your chart.**   Don't leave your readers guessing about what the data items represent. Use an easy-to-read font and a comfortable font size so that people who might see the chart online or in a slide presentation can make out the items without straining.

■ **Test new charts with others before you finalize them.**   A quick review by friends or coworkers can reveal where your chart is hard to understand or where you need to make an aesthetic change so that readers won't stumble on their way to your message.

Creating a Chart

Excel employs the Chart Wizard to help you build the chart that best portrays your data. First highlight the row or column labels and the data you want to include in the chart. Then start the wizard in one of two ways:

■ Choose Chart from the Insert menu.

■ Click the Chart Wizard tool on the Standard toolbar.

Either way, the Chart Wizard dialog box appears, ready to lead you through the four steps of creating a chart in Excel:

1 Choose a chart type.

2 Choose the data series you want to use.

3 Add chart options, including a title, legend, gridlines, and more.

4 Specify where you want to put the chart.

The following sections take you through the process. If you want to follow along and create your own chart, highlight your worksheet data and click Chart Wizard on the Standard toolbar.

Choosing a Chart Type

The first page of the Chart Wizard shows you the library of chart types from which you can choose. Excel offers 14 chart types that portray data relationships. The following list introduces you to the various charts and explains when you might use each one:

■ **Column.**   The column chart enables you to compare data in different categories. For example, you might create a column chart that compares the number of proposals your consulting firm presented in 2002 with the number of new accounts that resulted from those proposals.

■ **Bar.**   This type of chart is great for showing comparisons among your data. If you want to compare the sales of apples, oranges, and mangoes during the first three months of the year, for example, the different colored bars tell the story at a glance (as shown in Figure 10-2).

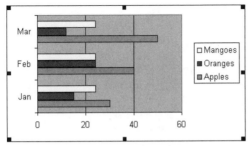

Figure 10-2   A bar chart is an easy way to compare two or more sets of data.

■ **Line.**   A line chart is another often-used type that is good for showing how data changes over time. You might track the number of hits on your Web site, the number of books signed, or the new donors added to your donor list during a specific period.

■ **Pie.**   The pie chart is commonly used to show how each individual data item (or slice) relates to the whole pie. You might use a pie chart to show how your department's expenses relate to company-wide expenses.

■ **XY (Scatter).**   A scatter chart enables you to compare pairs of data values. For example, you might depict a comparison of foreign and domestic sales of your product in relation to sales during a specific period.

■ **Area.**   This type of chart shows how each of the data items relates to the whole (what percentage they represent) over time or by category.

■ **Doughnut.**   The doughnut chart shows how data items relate to the whole (similar to a pie chart), but it can also track multiple data series.

■ **Radar.**   The radar chart plots data points along intersecting x and y axes.

■ **Surface.**   A surface chart is similar to an area chart, showing relationships and trends in data over time.

■ **Bubble.**   A bubble chart can compare three sets of data. The bubbles are sized according to the data values, giving readers a strong visual impression of which items in the chart have the highest value.

■ **Stock.**   Stock charts are also known as *high-low-close* charts. These items track data series that include three distinct values. For example, if you are following a specific stock offering, you could use the stock chart to show the highest value, the lowest value, and the market closing value for a specific stock. You also could use this chart to show wholesale, retail, and discount prices on merchandise.

■ **Cylinder, Cone, and Pyramid.**   These chart styles are simply different designs based on the Column chart type, which enables you to compare values in different series.

Note   For each chart type, Excel offers additional subtypes that allow you to choose different looks and designs for the primary chart. For example, when you choose a column chart, you can then select from the following subtypes: clustered column, stacked column, 100% stacked column, 3-D clustered column, 3-D stacked column, 3-D 100% stacked column, and 3-D column.

To find the chart type that's right for you, follow these steps:

1   Click the chart type you want to see in the Chart Type list on the left side of the Chart Wizard dialog box.

2   Click a subtype (each time you click a different subtype, a description of it appears below the Subtypes window).

3   Click Press And Hold To View Sample. The wizard shows you how your data will appear in the kind of chart you selected.

4   If you don't like what you see, select a different chart type. If you're happy with the chart, click Next.

In addition to the standard chart types and subtypes, Excel gives you several custom chart types that are more difficult to categorize. Some of these charts have cool special designs and are ready to place right into a presentation or on the Web. Click the Custom Types tab to see the additional charts. Click through the sample types and find one you like. (I'm partial to Columns With Depth, but that's just me.)

Specifying the Data Range and Series

The next step in the Chart Wizard enables you to specify whether you want the data series to be taken from the rows or columns in the worksheet. When you choose Columns, the data displayed in the columns is assigned to the data markers in the chart. In my example, I'm comparing the East and West Coast distribution of a new product. The two columns show East Coast and West Coast, respectively. The chart is created to answer the question: "Are we doing better with our East Coast or West Coast distribution?" The row items show the categories through which these two data items are tracked—Presale, Promotional, Catalogers, Convention, and Retailers. Figure 10-1, shows an example of this chart.

If I wanted to answer a different question with this information, such as, "How are our different distribution methods working in the different sales regions?," I could flip the data series so that Excel uses the rows instead of columns as the basis for the chart (as shown in Figure 10-3). To make that change, simply click Rows from the Series In area of the Data Range tab. When you're happy with the way the data is shown in the preview window, click Next.

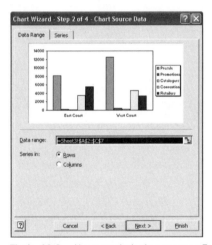

Figure 10-3   You control whether you want Excel to use columns or rows as the data series to be charted.

Tip   To further customize how Excel uses data series, you can click the Series tab in Step 2 of the Chart Wizard. This tab offers you a number of different settings that allow you to add or remove new data series; move to the worksheet to choose a different name or value selection; or choose different axis labels. For simple charts, you probably won't need these items, but it's nice to know where to find them, just in case.

Setting Chart Options

The next step in the Chart Wizard lets you choose all the options you want for your chart. You set the various options by clicking the tab you want to change and choosing the options you want to use. Table 10-1 explains the various choices available to you.

Table 10-1   Working with Chart Options

Tab	Description
Titles	Lets you add a chart title or titles to the x-axis or y-axis.
Axes	Helps you hide or display the x-axis or y-axis. You also can choose whether you want the x-axis to be selected automatically by Excel or to be preset as a category or time-scale axis.
Gridlines	Enables you to choose whether you want to display or hide major and minor gridlines on both axes.
Legend	Lets you choose whether to display or hide a legend. If you want to show a legend, you also need to choose where the legend will be displayed in relation to the chart.
Data Labels	You can have Excel display the series names, category names, and values on the individual data markers to help your viewers understand your chart. (Note: Use this feature sparingly, however, because too many labels can make your chart difficult to read.)
Data Table	If you click Show Data Table on the Data Table tab, Excel will display a table of the data values used to create the chart beneath it.

Each time you make a change in the Chart Options dialog box, the preview window changes to show you the effect of your selection. When you're satisfied with the options you've added, click Next to move to the last page of the wizard.

Choosing the Chart Location

The final step in the Chart Wizard involves specifying where you want the chart to reside. (You also can choose where to place a chart by selecting it and then choosing Location from the Chart menu.) You can place the charts you create directly in your worksheet or you can create a chart sheet to store only the new chart. By default, after you select the worksheet data and create your chart, the chart is placed on the current worksheet. If you want the chart to be placed on a sheet of its own, click As New Sheet in the Chart Location dialog box.

Are you ready to see your new chart? Click Finish. Excel creates the chart and places it in the location you specified.

Tip   If your chart labels overlap, fix the problem this way: Double-click the scrunched text. In the Format Axis dialog box, click the Font tab. Choose a smaller size for the text (8 points often works well) or click the Alignment tab and, in the Orientation area, click the small red marker in the rotation diagram and drag the marker to angle the text labels. This places the labels at an angle in your chart so that the labels can be seen in their entirety.

Editing a Chart

Once you click Finish and the completed chart is placed on your worksheet, it is treated just like any other inserted graphic or picture. This means that when you click the chart, handles appear, and you can drag the mouse to resize, move, or rearrange the chart as you would any object.

> **Tip** If you really don't like the chart and want to start again, simply click the chart and press Delete. Be sure to click outside the main chart area and away from the legend, however, or, instead of deleting the chart, you will simply select one of the chart elements for editing.

The Appearance of the Chart Menu

Once you've created a chart using the Chart Wizard, Excel changes the Data menu (which is normally in the menu bar at the top of the window) to the Chart menu whenever you click a chart to select it. The Chart menu contains all the commands you need to change settings you selected in the Chart Wizard. Depending on the type of chart you're working with, you may also see the 3-D View option, which enables you to change the current chart type into a 3-D display of the same chart type.

> **Tip** If you don't like the background color of your chart, double-click the chart background. In the Area section of the Format Walls dialog box, click the color you want to apply to the background; and then click OK.

Working with the Chart Toolbar

Excel gives you a handy Chart toolbar to use as you work on your charts. The toolbar is not displayed automatically, however; you'll need to look for it. To display the Chart toolbar, choose Toolbars from the View menu, and then select Chart. The Chart toolbar then pops up on your work area and you can dock it along with other toolbars or leave it floating over your workspace while you work. The Chart toolbar looks like this:

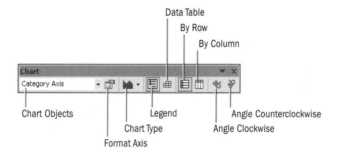

Tip   You can right-click any element in the chart to see a context menu of editing options for that item. For example, when you right-click a data marker, options appear that enable you to change any of the settings you entered in the Chart Wizard. You also can add a trendline or clear the element you selected.

Key Points

■   Excel includes 14 basic chart types—plus numerous subtypes and custom types—that you can use to help others understand your information.

■   Use the Chart Wizard to go through the four-step process of creating charts.

■   You can easily modify charts you create by using the Chart toolbar or right-clicking an individual chart element you want to change.

■   Everything on a chart—titles, background, data items, labels, and more—can be customized by modifying the Chart Options.

■   The Chart menu, which is available only when a chart is selected on your worksheet, contains all the commands you need to edit your charts.

Part IV:

Simply PowerPoint

This next part of the book will be fast and furious fun. Hold on to your hat! Microsoft PowerPoint is a great presentation graphics tool—and one of my all-time favorite programs—that lets you create slides, handouts, and full-blown presentations complete with audio, video, and interactive features. PowerPoint makes it easy for you to make your point clearly and professionally, in a way that's interesting and (hopefully) entertaining for your viewing audience.

In Chapter 11, "Creating a Presentation—From Start to Finish," you'll learn everything you need to know about preparing that first slide show. We won't go into all the bells and whistles here (I save that for Chapter 13), but you'll learn enough from Chapter 11 to put together your first presentation in 30 minutes or less.

Chapter 12, "Animating and Timing Your Presentation," focuses on some of the more important aspects of creating a slide show—how your slides appear, act, and fade one into another, as well as the amount of time you allow viewers to read what you've displayed on the screen. This chapter guides you through the process of controlling the animations, timing, and transitions for individual slides as well as for entire presentations.

We get to pull out all the stops in Chapter 13, "Enhancing Your Presentation," in which we discuss adding movies and sound to your presentations, recording narrations, and even broadcasting your presentation live to an audience. Fun stuff, eh?

Chapter 11

Creating a Presentation— From Start to Finish

Some people are natural-born presenters. They just *love* getting in front of a crowd. They don't sweat it if they drop their note cards at the last minute; they're not stressed when the audiovisual equipment they need isn't there; and they don't swoon when they look out at the audience and see 350 people instead of the 30 they expected.

I'm not one of those people. Are you?

Microsoft PowerPoint helps you prepare presentations that are easy, smooth, and professional, whether you're a seasoned veteran or a novice quaking in your boots. To those who would rather do just about anything other than give a presentation, PowerPoint provides all kinds of help—professional designs, easy-to-use special effects, and even a wizard to help you with content. To experienced presenters, PowerPoint offers convenience, interesting effects, and the ability to take the presentation to people, to desktop, or to the Web. This chapter covers all the basics you need to know to put together a solid, professional presentation in PowerPoint. Maybe you'll be so excited about the result that you won't even notice those butterflies.

What Can You Do with PowerPoint?

Any situation—business or otherwise—that calls for acetate sheets, a flip chart, blackboard scribbling, or a slide project or can be improved with PowerPoint. PowerPoint is a program that mixes all kinds of presentation tools to help you create effective, impressive, and professional-quality presentations. How can PowerPoint help you present your ideas? Here are a few examples:

■ Present your next report to the board in a 10-slide PowerPoint presentation, complete with printed handouts.

■ Use a PowerPoint presentation instead of overheads in the next English Lit class you teach; print the slides as handouts for students so they can spend more time discussing your topic and less time taking notes.

■ Use PowerPoint (with embedded spreadsheets from Microsoft Excel) to show potential investors why your company is worth a closer look.

■ Prepare a PowerPoint presentation to walk your new technicians through the process of repairing copper tubing.

■ Design a PowerPoint presentation to show the group how the project workflow will be handled.

■ Use a PowerPoint presentation to give a multimedia annual report at your next stockholders meeting.

■ Prepare a PowerPoint presentation to introduce your top 50 donors, live and online, to your organization's new giving program.

These are only a few of the more traditional business uses for PowerPoint. But if you're feeling artsy, you can use PowerPoint to create a digital short film, mixing audio and video clips with still photos. Or you could produce a low-budget commercial for online broadcast. Or create a Web page that launches your annual report and gives visitors control over which elements they want to see and when they want to see them.

The list goes on and on. PowerPoint has the functionality to handle any level of creativity you can throw at it. And once you create the presentation, you can display it in a number of ways:

■ Run it on a desktop computer as a welcome-to-our-company orientation for new trainees.

- Display it on a movie screen (run from your laptop computer) at the front of the lecture hall.

- Package it to run on a kiosk in the mall.

- Burn it to a CD with an auto-running utility so that clients who don't have PowerPoint can view your presentation as soon as they pop the CD into their computers.

- Save the presentation as a Web page so that visitors to your Web site can view the presentation interactively online.

- Broadcast the presentation live, online, to a group of invited clients.

Enough inspiration? Ready to start the perspiration part? Let's move on to a tour of the PowerPoint window.

A Walk Around the PowerPoint Window

Similar to the other Office XP programs, PowerPoint brings the tools you'll need to use and displays them within easy reach in the PowerPoint window (as shown in Figure 11-1).

Figure 11-1 The PowerPoint window displays familiar toolbars but a much different window design.

Right off the bat, you'll notice the familiar Standard and Formatting tool-bars, as well as the task pane. You'll see two new tools on the Formatting tool-bar that are particularly worth mentioning:

- The Design tool lets you choose a design for your presentation.

- The New Slide tool displays the Slide Layout task pane so that you can add slides to your presentation.

In addition to the familiar items, you'll find a screen separated into different areas, each providing a different look at the current slide.

The largest area you'll see as you start a new presentation is the slide view, in the center of the workspace. This is where you'll do the majority of your work as you're adding text and placing graphics. The onscreen text *Click to add title* and *Click to add subtitle* are placeholders that will be replaced by the text you type.

On the left of the slide area is the thumbnail pane, which shows you a small representation of the current slide. As you add slides to your presentation, these will fill the column. This column also has a second tab, Outline, which enables you to see the slide headings and text items in your presentation.

Beneath the slide area is a small section where you can enter notes related to the slide displayed. To add a note, simply click in the *Click to add notes* area and type whatever information you want to add. The text you type will stay with the slide but will not appear in a presentation or on presentation handouts, unless you specifically choose to print the slide while showing all notes.

Understanding the PowerPoint Views

When you first start PowerPoint, the application automatically displays Normal view. Normal view includes a number of panes that enable you to work with different aspects of your presentation. PowerPoint includes three different views that you'll use, depending on the tasks you're trying to accomplish. The View controls, located in the bottom left side of the PowerPoint window (in the Outline And Slides pane) enable you to switch to these different views quickly. Table 11-1 introduces the different views you'll use in PowerPoint and tells you a little bit about each one.

Table 11-1   PowerPoint Views

Button	View Name	Use When...
	Normal View	You want to work on individual slides or add notes to your slides.
	Slide Sorter View	You are organizing, reviewing, rearranging, or setting timing and transitions for your slides.
	Slide Show	You want to display a slide show based on the open presentation, starting with the currently selected slide.

You also can display the current slide in Notes Pages view, which displays a small version of the current slide atop a large notes area.

To Master or Not To Master   If you're simply planning to create a quick and easy presentation, you might not want to worry about master pages. A *master page* is a page that works in the background of the slide, controlling such details as the format of headers and footers, the placement of slide numbers, the selection of a color scheme, background images or graphics used throughout the presentation, and so on. If your presentation is short and sweet and doesn't include such special design considerations as footers or whatnot, you won't need to bother with master pages. For longer presentations or presentation styles you plan to use again, however, master pages can be great time-savers.

PowerPoint offers you three kinds of masters: A Slide Master, which controls format settings for individual slides; a Handout Master, which sets up the format of the handouts you create and print; and a Notes Master, which tracks the styles in effect for notes included with your presentation.

To create any of these masters, choose Master from the View menu, and then click the type of master you want to create. You are taken to the master page, where you can change the text style, insert a new master page, change the master layout, and modify the slide number, date, and footer information. You'll learn more about making modifications and formatting changes later in this chapter.

Starting with the End in Mind: Setting Up the Show

Because PowerPoint is so flexible that you can give the presentation in a variety of different ways, it's important that the first question you ask when you start a new presentation is: How will my presentation be delivered?

The answer to this question will determine some of the considerations you'll need to keep in mind as you create the presentation. You answer that initial question in the Page Setup dialog box, shown in Figure 11-2.

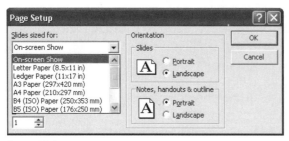

Figure 11-2   You use the Page Setup dialog box to tell PowerPoint how you plan to deliver the presentation.

To display the Page Setup dialog box, choose Page Setup from the File menu. You can then prepare your presentation by following these steps:

1   Click the Slides Sized For down arrow to display the list of available options. On-Screen Show is the default setting, but you can also choose a number of paper sizes, 35mm Slides, Overhead, Banner, and Custom.

2   If you want to change the width and height of the slides, click in the Width and Height boxes, respectively, and change those values either by clicking the up and down arrows or by typing a new value.

3   Enter the number you want PowerPoint to use as the first page number in the Number Slides From box.

4   By default, the Slides orientation is set to Landscape (horizontal, 11 × 8 1/2 mode). For most purposes, you should be able to leave this setting as is. The Notes, Handouts And Outline orientation setting is Portrait (vertical, 8 1/2 × 11-inch mode). This is a traditional orientation for the printed page, so this, too, should be fine as it appears.

5   Click OK to save your settings. You're now ready to begin creating your presentation.

Tip   Before you start working on the presentation, close the task pane if it's still visible by clicking the close box in the upper-right corner of the pane. This gives you more room to work with your slide on the screen.

Creating a Presentation

When you first start PowerPoint, a blank presentation opens on your screen. Along the right side of the window you see the familiar task pane. You can use the task pane to start a presentation in any of the following ways:

■   Click Blank Presentation to open a new blank document on your screen. (There's no need to choose this option right now, however, because you've already got a blank document displayed on the screen.)

■   Click From Design Template to display a collection of design templates in
     the task pane (as shown in Figure 11-3). These design templates are
     great—experiment with them to see whether one fits your vision for your
     presentation. The templates include background designs, color schemes,
     and text settings that work together to provide a pleasing, interesting
     look. In the task pane, scroll to the design you like and click it; Power-
     Point then displays a new presentation based on the design template
     you've selected. Your next task is to add text and images to make it yours.

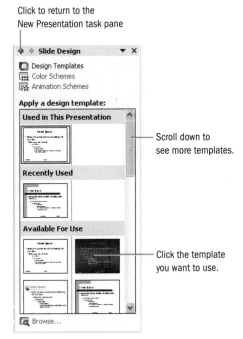

Figure 11-3   When you choose From Design Template, a collection of templates appears in the
task pane.

■   Click From AutoContent Wizard to start a wizard that helps you pull
     together the content for your presentation. The next section takes you
     through the process of using the AutoContent Wizard.

Using the AutoContent Wizard

When you click From AutoContent Wizard in the task pane, PowerPoint starts
the wizard immediately, displaying it in a pop-up box in front of the PowerPoint
work area, as shown in Figure 11-4.

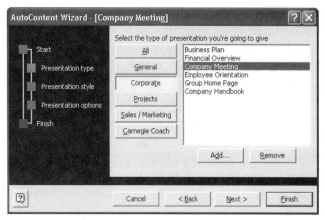

Figure 11-4   The AutoContent Wizard walks you through the process of creating basic text for your presentation.

Click Next on the first page of the wizard. This automated helper then leads you through the following four steps:

1   The first step asks you to choose the category of presentation you want to create (General, Corporate, Projects, Sales/Marketing, or Carnegie Coach). When you click one of the choices, a list of specific presentations appears. Click the one closest to the presentation goal you are trying to achieve, and then click Next.

> **Tip**   If you want to see all the types of presentations the AutoContent Wizard has to offer, simply click the All button to display the entire list. Click the one you want and then click Next.

2   In the next step, the AutoContent Wizard asks what kind of output you will use for your presentation. Click your choice (for most presentations, you will likely use either On-Screen Presentation or Web Presentation); and then click Next.

3   Enter a title for your presentation and, if you want to include a footer (which might include your company or department name), type it in the Footer box. If you want the date and slide number to appear in the footer line, leave the options checked; otherwise, click the boxes to clear them and disable the options. Click Next.

4   Click Finish on the last page. The presentation is created and placed in the work area (as shown in Figure 11-5), ready for you to modify to your heart's content.

Text in individual slides   Current slide

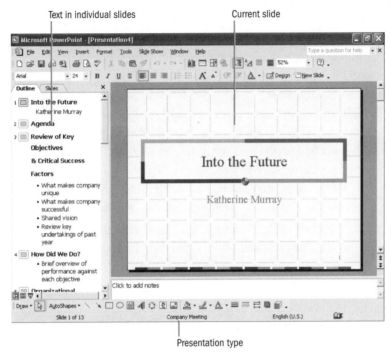

Presentation type

Figure 11-5   When you create a presentation with the AutoContent Wizard, PowerPoint creates an entire presentation for you, providing text prompts for the type of information to include.

Try This!   One thing the AutoContent Wizard doesn't allow you to do is choose the design you want to work with. Luckily, PowerPoint is extremely flexible, and you can go back and change a design at any time as you work on the presentation. When you want to choose a different design for your presentation, follow these steps:

1   Open the presentation you want to change.

2   Click the Design button on the Formatting toolbar. The Slide Design task pane appears with the various design templates displayed.

3   Find a design you like and click it. PowerPoint applies the design to the entire presentation, and that old presentation design is gone, gone, *gone*.

If you don't like the change, you can return the presentation to its earlier design by pressing Ctrl+Z immediately.

Adding and Editing Your Own Text

When you start with a blank presentation or choose a design template, the text prompts within individual slides say such things as *Click to add title* or *Click to add text*. To add text, simply click in the box and type whatever you want to add. Click outside the box to accept the addition.

If you've used our friend, the AutoContent Wizard, to start the presentation, you've got all kinds of text in your presentation. The topics that are already there are prompts that are intended to spark your ideas for the information you need to provide. You shouldn't feel roped into what the AutoContent Wizard does for you, of course—your presentation should have its own flavor and approach. (But why reinvent the wheel if the one you've got is working fine?)

You can change the text in the presentation two ways:

- On the slide, you can click the text you want to change. The text box highlights and the cursor appears. You can then highlight the text you want to replace and type the new text. The AutoContent text is replaced as you type.

- When all the text for that slide is highlighted in the Outline pane, begin typing. This replaces all the text in that slide.

Tip   If you accidentally erase more information than you intended, press Ctrl+Z and PowerPoint will undo your last action.

Adding Pages

Although the AutoContent Wizard fills up your presentation with pages of its choosing, if you have created a blank presentation or started with a design template, it's up to you to add your own pages. Here's how to do it:

1   Display the page before which you want to add the page.

2   Click New Slide on the Formatting toolbar. The Slide Layout task pane appears, offering you a collection of different text and content layouts (as shown in Figure 11-6). Scroll to the slide layout you want to use and click it.

The new slide is added in the format you selected. Now you can plug in new text or add objects as needed.

Changing Page Layout You also can apply a new slide layout to slides you've already got in your presentation. This is helpful as you go through and edit your AutoContent-generated presentation to convey the information that is important to you. To change the page layout using the Slide Layout task pane, simply display the slide you want to change and choose Slide Layout from the Format menu. When the Slide Layout task pane appears, click the layout you want to apply.

Figure 11-6 Choose a layout for the new slide in the Slide Layout task pane.

Creating a Chart

Charts can be particularly helpful in presentations because they show data trends and concepts in simple, graphical ways. A picture is worth at least a dozen words, you know. When you want to add a chart to your presentation, begin by choosing a page that has a chart placeholder in it. If you don't have such a chart in your presentation, add one by following these steps:

1   Display the page before which you want to add the slide with the chart.

2   Click the New Slide button on the Formatting toolbar. The task pane appears.

3   Scroll to the Other Layouts section of the Slide Layout task pane and click the Title, Text, or Chart layout. The new slide in the layout you selected is displayed in the work area.

4   Now, double-click the chart area to begin the chart-creation process. A bar chart is drawn by default and a sample datasheet appears with dummy data already inserted.

5   Replace the data in the datasheet with your own information. You can edit these cells the way you edit cells in Excel: Click the cell and type the new information. Like an Excel spreadsheet, the column and row labels are used as the axis labels and the legend on the chart (as shown in Figure 11-7).

6   After you've replaced the data, click the datasheet's close box to hide the datasheet and give yourself more room to work.

7   If you want to change the type of chart used to portray your data, click the Chart Type tool on the Standard toolbar. A palette of chart styles appears, and you can simply click the chart type you want to use.

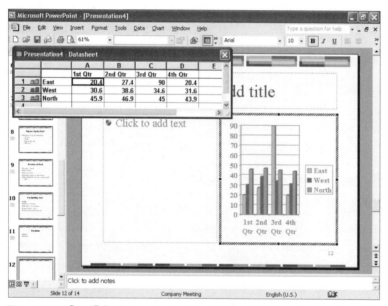

Figure 11-7   PowerPoint draws a bar chart by default and displays dummy values in the datasheet.

Note   Notice that the PowerPoint Standard toolbar and menu bar change when you are working with charts. The new Chart menu is added to the menu bar; in this menu you'll find all kinds of options for customizing and enhancing charts. Also on the Standard toolbar you'll find chart tools that are identical to those you used with Excel charts. (See Chapter 10, "Charting Spreadsheet Data," to learn more about using chart tools.)

Importing Chart Data PowerPoint allows you to import data into the datasheet if you want to use information you've created in another program. Just click Import File on the Standard toolbar and PowerPoint displays the Import File dialog box. Navigate to the folder storing the file you want to import, click the file, and then click Open.

In the Import Data Options dialog box, select the sheet you want to import; then tell Power-Point whether you want to import the entire sheet or only a selected range. (If you want to specify a range, enter it in the Range box.) Finally, if you want the incoming data to replace the existing data in the datasheet, leave the Overwrite Existing Cells check box selected. Click OK to import the data and have PowerPoint redraw the chart.

Inserting Graphics

There are other types of visual aids you might want to add to your presentation. How about that caricature of the CEO? What about the architect's drawing of the new office? Or perhaps some clip art or a few photos would help.

Some people make the mistake of creating presentations that are pages and pages of text. But think about it: Just as you need something now and then to break the monotony of reading page after page of this book, your audience will need a picture, a photo, or a splash of color every so often to give their eyes a rest and help them pause a minute before they focus again on your words.

Inserting graphics in PowerPoint is simple. And PowerPoint makes it even easier for you by providing ready-made clip art that you can use. The process starts with adding a slide to your presentation, as follows:

1 Select the slide before which you'd like to add the slide that will include the graphics.

2 Click New Slide on the Formatting toolbar.

3 Scroll down to the Text And Content Layouts portion of the Slide Layout task pane.

4 Choose a layout that gives you the ability to add objects.

5 Click the Insert Clip Art tool in the *Click icon to add content* area of the slide. (If you're not sure which tool is the Insert Clip Art tool, position the mouse pointer over each tool until the name appears.)

Adding Objects the Easy Way PowerPoint understands that there are many kinds of things you want to add to your presentation. The toolset that appears in the *Click icon to add content* field of some slide layouts gives you a palette of tools from which to choose, as shown below:

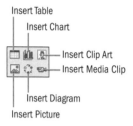

Insert Table
Insert Chart
Insert Clip Art
Insert Media Clip
Insert Diagram
Insert Picture

The tools work as follows:

- When you click Insert Table, the Insert Table dialog box appears and you can specify the number of columns and rows you want and then click OK to create the table.

- Insert Chart displays a default bar chart and a dummy datasheet so that you can enter your chart information.

- Insert Clip Art displays the Select Picture dialog box so that you can choose the art you want to add. Click the art, and then click OK to insert it.

- Insert Picture displays the Insert Picture dialog box so that you can navigate to the folder storing the picture or photo you want to add. When you find the picture you want, select it and click Insert to add it to your slide.

- Insert Diagram or Organizational Chart displays the Diagram Gallery so that you can choose one of six diagram types to include on your slide. Click the type you want and then click OK.

- Insert Media Clip displays the Media Clip dialog box with a collection of animated pictures and sounds. Click the clip you want and then click OK.

If you aren't happy with the object you added, delete it by clicking it and pressing Delete. The palette of object tools reappears and you can choose to add a different object or change the layout of the slide to remove the object area by choosing Slide Layout from the Format menu.

Now that you have added the type of slide you need to add graphics, click Insert Clip Art. The Select Picture dialog box appears, showing the art available in PowerPoint. Simply click the picture you want to use and PowerPoint adds it to the slide.

Tip   If you want to look for pictures that show something specific—such as people, animals, or trees—you can enter the topic in the Search text box and click Search. PowerPoint then displays all the clip art related to your subject, and you can place the art by clicking it and then clicking OK.

Formatting Slides

For the most part, the formatting of your PowerPoint slides is already done for you. When you click a text box and type your information, PowerPoint puts the text in a font, size, and style that matches the rest of the presentation.

Pretty much everything in PowerPoint is changeable, however, and you can alter the look and placement of text to match whatever you envision. You'll make formatting changes using these methods:

- You can choose a tool on the Formatting toolbar that enables you to make the change you want quickly.
- You can select the command you need from the Format menu.
- You can right-click the object you want to change and choose the formatting command you want from the object's context menu.

Making Simple Formatting Changes

What kind of formatting changes will you want to make? Some are simple, requiring only the change of a word or two; others are farther-reaching and can affect each slide in your presentation. Here are a few of the simple formatting changes you'll commonly make:

- **Italicizing or boldfacing a few words for emphasis.** Select the text you want to change and click Bold or Italic on the Formatting toolbar. You also can press Ctrl+B to boldface the selected work or Ctrl+I to italicize it.

> **Tip** To select one word quickly, simply click in it. The formatting change will be applied to the word at the cursor position. To select a line of text (such as a single bullet item or a slide title), triple-click in the line.

- **Changing the color of a title.** Highlight the text and click the down arrow to the right of the Font Color tool on the Formatting toolbar. Click the color your want from the displayed palette.
- **Changing the bullet characters on a bullet list.** Right-click in the list you want to change and select Bullets And Numbering from the context menu. In the Bullets And Numbering dialog box, click one of the alternate bullet styles or click Customize to display the Symbol dialog box. Click the character you want to use as a bullet and then click OK.

> **Tip** If you don't see a character you like, you might want to see what other fonts have to offer. Click the Font down arrow and choose a different font. The standard symbol fonts included in Office XP are Webdings, Wingdings, Wingdings 2, Wingdings 3, and Symbol, but your system may have others as well.

- **Changing the alignment of text.**   The easiest way to change the way text is aligned is to select it and then click Align Left, Center, or Align Right on the Formatting toolbar. You also can press Ctrl+L, Ctrl+E, or Ctrl+R, respectively, to make these changes.

- **Modifying indent levels.**   If you want to increase or decrease the indent of text on the current slide, you can use the Increase Indent or Decrease Indent tools. You also can change indents by clicking the text you want to change and pressing Alt+Shift+Right-arrow to increase the indent and Alt+Shift+Left-arrow to decrease it.

Try This! Depending on the design you selected (*if* you selected a design template), you might want to add more color or an image to the background of your slides. Not only can you choose a color or pattern for your slides, but you can also add your own pictures (Perhaps a company logo? A beautiful sunrise? A picture of your dog?). Here's how to do it:

1   Open the presentation to which you want to add the background picture.

2   Choose Background from the Format menu.

3   Click the down arrow in the color bar beneath the Background fill window in the Background dialog box to display the pull-down menu, as shown below.

4   Click Fill Effects, and then click the Picture tab in the Fill Effects dialog box.

5   Click Select Picture. This brings up the Select Picture dialog box so that you can navigate to the folder where the picture you want is stored. Click the picture and then click Insert.

6   Click OK to close the Fill Effects dialog box.

7   Back in the Background dialog box, check the change by clicking Preview. The current slide shows the background change behind the Background dialog box.

8   Click Apply to add the background image to the current slide only, or click Apply To All to update all the slides in your presentation. Of course, if you'd rather abandon the change, you can simply click Cancel.

Selecting a Different Font

The fastest way to change the font of selected text is to click the Font down arrow on the Formatting toolbar and choose a new font. You can also use the Font dialog box to make the change by performing the following steps:

1   Select your text and then select Font from the Format menu. The Font dialog box appears.

2   Scroll through the Font list and select the font you want.

3   In the Font style box, click the style you want to apply to the text.

4   Click the new size in the Size box.

5   Add any special text effects you want by clicking the appropriate checkboxes.

6   If you want to choose a new color for the font, click the Color down arrow and click your choice from the palette. If you don't see one you want, click More Colors to see additional choices.

7   When you're finished entering font settings, click OK.

Applying Text Changes Globally   When you want to make a font change that is applied throughout your presentation, you need to work on the master that applies to that slide type. Choose Slide Master from the View menu and then make the changes—font, size, style, color, and alignment—that you want to make. When you're finished making changes, click Close Master View on the Slide Master View toolbar, as shown below.

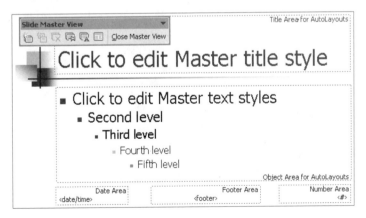

Note   When you change a master, the new settings affect only the current presentation.

Changing Color Scheme

Perhaps you like the look of the presentation design but you're not crazy about the colors. You can easily change that. Here are the steps:

1   Open the presentation you want to change.

2   Choose Slide Design from the Format menu.

3   In the Slide Design task pane, click Color Schemes. A selection of color schemes appears in the task pane.

4   Point to the one you like and a down arrow appears. Click it and choose whether you want to apply the change to all slides or the selected slide. After you make your choice, the color change is made.

From Color to Grayscale   With a click of the mouse, you can see how your presentation would appear in black and white. This is helpful for projects in which you'll be printing handouts on a monochrome printer and want to see how your slides will look on the printed page. Click the Color/ Grayscale tool on the Standard toolbar and a drop-down menu appears, giving you the choice of Color, Grayscale, or Pure Black And White. Click your choice and the change is applied to the current slide. The Grayscale View toolbar appears so that you can choose additional settings, or click Close Grayscale View when you're finished.

Arranging Slides

After you've created the slides you need (complete with text, charts, and pictures) and edited and formatted the slides the way you want them, you're ready to move up to the level of presentation producer. Now you need to take a look at the way your presentation flows from one slide to the next. Are your ideas arranged in a logical order? Should this slide come before that one? Perhaps that slide should be moved to the end of the presentation, just before the review.

You use Slide Sorter view to make these kinds of changes in your presentation. You can display this view using one of two methods:

■   Choose Slide Sorter from the View menu.

■   Click the Slide Sorter View tool in the view controls in the lower left portion of the PowerPoint window.

Slide Sorter view displays all the slides in your presentation in a thumbnail view (as shown in Figure 11-8). You can easily review the different slides in this view and make choices about the order in which they are arranged. If you want to rearrange the slides, simply click the one you want to move and drag it to the new location. An insertion bar moves with the slide as you drag it to show you where the slide will be positioned when you release the mouse button. You can reverse a change you make by pressing Ctrl+Z.

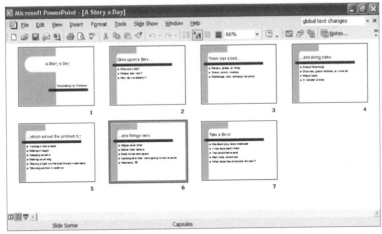

Figure 11-8 You can rearrange your slides easily in Slide Sorter view.

See Also *Slide Sorter view is the place where you add slide transitions and set the timing of your presentation. You'll learn more about those tasks in Chapter 12. "Animating and Timing Your Presentation."*

Take One: Running the Presentation

Are you ready to take a test drive with your new presentation? Okay, then press F5. The presentation starts, displaying the first slide in full-screen view. Advance to the next slide by clicking the left mouse button or pressing Enter, the right-arrow key, or the spacebar. If you want to return to a previous slide, press the left-arrow key. When the presentation is finished, PowerPoint displays the message *End of slide show, click to exit.* Click the prompt or press Esc and you are returned to the view you were using before you pressed F5.

Tip You also can start a presentation from any view by choosing Slide Show from the View menu or by clicking Slide Show View in the view controls in the bottom-left part of the screen.

Saving Your Presentation

Congratulations! In one short chapter, you've learned to create and run a simple presentation. The next two chapters continue to use the presentation you've created, so you'll want to save it for later. Here are the steps for saving your file:

1 Press Ctrl+S to display the Save As dialog box.

2 Navigate to the folder in which you want to store the file.

3 Enter a name for the presentation in the File Name box.

4 Click Save.

Saving in Other Formats

Your PowerPoint presentations can be more than simple slide shows; you can use them to create Web pages, add-ins, templates, and more. You also can save your PowerPoint files in a variety of graphics formats and formats supported by previous versions of the program. To save the presentation in a format other than the default Presentation style, click the Save As Type down arrow and choose the format from the list. When you click Save, PowerPoint saves the file in the format you specified.

Previewing for the Web

How quickly can you make a Web page? As fast as you can create a PowerPoint presentation. Once you've finished your presentation, choose Web Page Preview from the File menu. PowerPoint displays the presentation as it would appear on the Web (as shown in Figure 11-9).

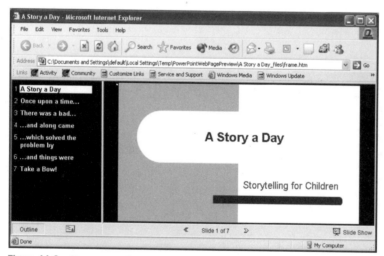

Figure 11-9   The presentation displayed as a Web page.

The presentation is created using frames to provide users with the links they need to get to other pages. The first page of the presentation appears in the right pane; on the left you see the titles of the other slides in your presentation. To go to another page, simply click the title.

Things to Watch for in Web Preview As you're taking a look at your Web page in Web Preview, ask yourself the following questions:

- Is the text easy to read?

- Will visitors understand how to move from page to page?

- Have you used standard colors that can be displayed by most browsers?

- Are your charts large enough? Are they clearly labeled?

Click the browser's close box to close the Web Preview and return to the presentation. Make any changes that are needed, and then save the file in Web format.

Saving as a Web Page

To save your presentation as a Web page, simply click Save As Web Page from the File menu. The Save As dialog box appears with some special Web options (as shown in Figure 11-15).

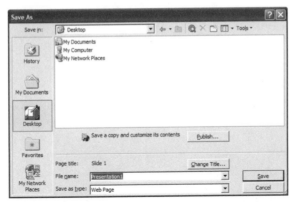

Figure 11-10   The Save As dialog box has a few additional options for Web pages.

Beneath the file list in the Save As dialog box, click Publish to set further options, such as whether to save the entire presentation or a selected range, whether to include speaker notes, which browsers you want to support, and the title and folder for the saved Web page. Click the Open Published Web page in the browser check box if you want to see the page after it has been saved. Click Publish to complete the process.

Printing Handouts

As you learned in Chapter 2, "Working with Programs," common tasks such as opening, saving, and printing files are almost identical in all Office XP applications. Each application has its own unique considerations when it comes to printing, however. In PowerPoint, although the basic process is the same, you also have the opportunity to print handouts, outlines, and more.

To begin printing in PowerPoint, choose Print from the File menu. In the Print dialog box, set all your options as you would in any other Office application. When you get down to the Print What box, click the down arrow and choose the setting you want from the displayed list, as shown in Figure 11-16.

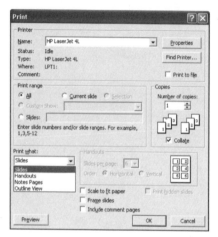

Figure 11-11   You can choose to print handouts, outlines, and speaker notes in PowerPoint.

Before you print your document, click Preview to look at what you're printing. Then, when you're ready, click Print and then OK to print your file.

Key Points

- PowerPoint is a presentation graphics program that makes it easy for you to create professional-quality presentations.

- You can start a presentation by selecting a blank page, working with a design template, or using the AutoContent Wizard to suggest content based on the topic you select.

- Add pages easily by clicking the New Slide button on the Formatting toolbar.

- Changing the layout of a slide is a simple matter: Choose Slide Layout from the Format menu and choose the layout you want from the thumbnails displayed in the task pane.

- PowerPoint includes layout templates that make it easy for you to add charts, clip art, tables, pictures, diagrams, and media clips.

- You use the tools on the Formatting toolbar to make simple changes; additional options are available on the Format menu and on individual objects' context menus.

- Click Design on the Formatting toolbar to display the Slide Design task pane; then choose Color Schemes to choose a different color set for your presentation. You can also see how the presentation will look in black and white by clicking the Color/Grayscale tool on the Standard toolbar.

- You will use Slide Sorter view to rearrange the slides in your presentation.

- Run your presentation by pressing F5, and advance the slides by clicking the left mouse button or pressing the right-arrow key, Enter, or spacebar. Return to a previous slide by pressing the left-arrow key.

- You can save your PowerPoint presentation as a Web page. Choose Save As Web Page from the File menu to save a browser-ready version of your presentation.

- In PowerPoint you can choose to print handouts of your slides, your entire presentation, the presentation outline, or speaker notes.

Chapter 12

Animating and Timing Your Presentation

Now that you know the tricks of creating, editing, and formatting your Microsoft PowerPoint presentations, you're ready to add the polish that turns it into a real show. You'll work in Slide Sorter view to control how your presentation behaves, adding such items as:

■ Special setup options that determine whether your slides are advanced automatically or manually and whether your show loops continually or plays once and then stops.

■ Animation schemes that give your slides extra impact by adding special effects to the text and objects on your slides.

■ Transitional effects—fades, wipes, dissolves, sound effects, and more—which control how slides appear and disappear.

■ Speaker notes that give other presenters clues about how to handle certain slides

■ Settings that hide certain slides for some presentations, enabling you to customize the effect for different audiences.

■   Setting that control the timing of your slides, determining the amount of time the slides appear on the screen in a slide show that advances automatically.

By the time you finish this chapter, you'll have a fully functioning presentation with professional-quality transitional effects. Along the way, we'll throw in some tips for choosing the effects that are best suited to your audience.

Working in Slide Sorter View

You got a brief look at Slide Sorter view in Chapter 11, "Creating a Presentation—From Start to Finish," when you learned to rearrange the slides in your presentation. But let's take a closer look at this feature now. To get started, display Slide Sorter view by clicking the Slide Sorter view tool in the lower-left portion of the PowerPoint window. (You also can select Slide Sorter from the View menu.) Figure 12-1 shows you Slide Sorter view and highlights the important tools you'll be using here.

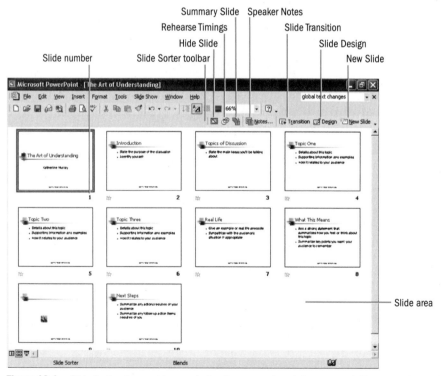

Figure 12-1   Slide Sorter view enables you to fine-tune your almost-done presentation.

You'll use the tools on the Slide Sorter toolbar to perform the following tasks:

- Hide Slide alternately hides and then displays slides.

- Rehearse Timings starts a slide show and adds a timer so that you can go through the presentation and set the duration for individual slides.

- Summary Slide adds a summary slide for the segment of the presentation immediately preceding it.

- Speaker Notes displays a Speaker Notes dialog box in which you can add notes for a particular slide.

- Slide Transition enables you to set the transition effects for individual slides or for the entire presentation.

- Slide Design displays the task pane so that you can change the presentation design.

- New Slide enables you to add a new slide in a layout you choose.

In addition to the tools on the Slide Sorter toolbar, you'll use the options on the Slide Show menu to work with various aspects of your presentation.

The options on the Slide Show menu enable you to work with your presentation as a whole. Here you'll find what you need to set up the show, do an online broadcast, add animation effects, set *transitions*, hide and display slides, and create custom shows. Many of these options have counterparts on the Slide Sorter toolbar.

Lingo A *transition* is the effect applied to a slide as it is replaced by the next slide. Transitions can include animation, sound, and special effects like fades, wipes, and dissolves.

Setting Up the Show

Before we go any further, let's look at the basic setup for the slide show you're producing. Choose Set Up Show from the Slide Show menu. The Set Up Show dialog box shown in Figure 12-2 appears.

In the Show Type area, choose the form in which you'll be giving the presentation. Will you be presenting in front of an audience? Will someone be sitting at a computer, viewing the presentation on a monitor? Will the presentation be running on a terminal in a training room at your corporate office? Each of the options in the Show Type area adds unique features to the presentation, depending on what you're trying to do. The first option is the default selection—this is the normal, full-screen view. The second option, Browsed By An Individual, adds commands and navigational tools to help people move through the presentation in a way that's most comfortable for them. The third option, Browsed At A Kiosk, creates the presentation as a continuous loop that restarts automatically after five minutes of inactivity. Click the option that best fits how your presentation will be used.

Figure 12-2   You make some basic choices for the way your presentation will operate in the Set Up Show dialog box.

The Show Options area enables you to control whether your presentation loops continuously or goes from start to finish and then ends. If you want the presentation to loop, click the check box to enable the feature. Additionally, you can choose to run the presentation without narration or animation, if you're trying to keep the file sizes small and the special effects to a minimum. Finally, the Show Options area allows you to set the Pen color (click the down arrow and choose the on-screen color you want). You'll use the pen to draw on the screen while you present the slide show, circling or underlining important concepts.

In the Show Slides and Advance Slides areas, you specify which slides will be included in your presentation and how they will advance from one to the next. If you want the slides to change automatically, leave Using Timings, If Present selected (this is the default setting). If you want to give the user the ability to move on to the next slide by clicking a button or pressing a key, select the Manually option.

The final options in the Set Up Show dialog box enable you to display the show on multiple monitors and improve system performance. If you have multiple monitors set up on your system, you can click the Show Presenter View check box to display a toolbar of Presenter tools, which enable you to display slide thumbnails, navigation tools, and speaker notes. If you have a graphics accelerator card in your system, clicking the Use hardware graphics acceleration check box may accelerate the display of slides in your slide show. Once you're finished setting up the show, click OK to close the dialog box and return to Slide Sorter view.

Note   Many of the discussions in this chapter—including setting slide transitions and rehearing timings—are based on the idea that you have elected to advance the slides automatically. If you choose the manual method, the slide show's users will control when the pages advance.

Using Animation Schemes

Now that you've entered all the information on your slides, you can do cool things with them. You can add *animation schemes* globally (which means the scheme is applied to all slides in your presentation) or you can apply different schemes to different slides. Here's how to add animation schemes to your slides:

1   Begin by opening the presentation in which you want to insert animations.

2   Click each slide to which you want to apply the animation.

3   Choose Animation Scheme from the Slide Show menu. The Slide Design task pane appears, displaying a list of animation schemes you can choose to apply to the current slide (as shown in Figure 12-3).

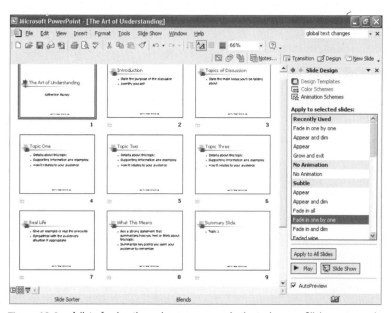

Figure 12-3   A list of animation schemes appears in the task pane. Click one to see its effect—the selected slide shows the result.

Lingo   *Animation schemes* enable you to apply animation—that is, movement and special effects—to individual objects on your slides.

Note   Notice that the animation schemes are organized by the kind of effect they produce. You can choose from Subtle, Moderate, or Exciting animation effects—or, of course, you can leave the slide set to the default of No Animation.

PowerPoint plays the animation effect on the current slide as soon as you click it, but if you want to see it again, click the Play button at the bottom of the task pane. If you want to see how the effect will look in the slide show, click Slide Show. And if you want to apply that animation scheme to all the slides in the presentation, click Apply To All Slides.

To apply a different animation scheme to another slide, click that slide and choose the scheme you want. You also can apply animation schemes to multiple slides by first selecting the group (press and hold Ctrl as you click additional slides) and then selecting the scheme you want to use.

Adding Transitions to Slides

In addition to adding special effects to individual slides, you can control the way the slides appear and disappear on their way through the presentation. These appearances and disappearances are known as *transitions*, and they can add a solid sense of professionalism to even the simplest presentation.

When you want to add transitions to your slides, follow these steps:

1   Display the presentation you want to work with in Slide Sorter view.

2   Click the first slide to which you want to add a transition.

3   Click the Transition tool on the Slide Sorter toolbar.

4   In the Slide Transition task pane, click the transition effect you want to see (as shown in Figure 12-4). The effect is applied immediately to the selected slide.

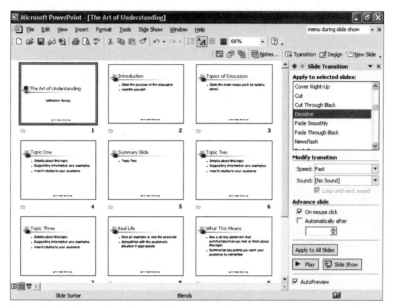

Figure 12-4   Choose the slide transition you want from the displayed list and watch the selected slide to see the effect.

Tip   You may need to experiment with a number of transitions before you find the one that you want for a particular slide. Test the different effects by going through the list and making note of your favorites. For the best results, don't overdo it by using too many effects, but don't bore your audience to tears by using the same transition for every slide, either.

Changing Transition Speed

When you first select a transition for your slide, its Speed setting is set to Fast. This means that you might have trouble seeing the transition if you blink while you're working. To slow the transition speed, click the Speed down arrow in the Modify transition area of the task pane and click either Slow or Medium. Test them both to see which you like best for individual transitions.

Adding Sound Effects

You can also add sound effects to the transitions on your slides. By default, PowerPoint sets the transition to No Sound, but you can easily remedy that by clicking the Sound down arrow and choosing the sound you want from the displayed list. Again, play around with the sounds to find the ones you like best, and remember to use them sparingly. If you want the same sound effect to be applied to the transition of each slide until you select a different sound (or choose Stop Previous Sound in the Sound list), click the Loop Until Next Sound check box.

Controlling Slide Display

If you've set up your presentation to advance automatically from slide to slide, you must specify the amount of time you want each slide to be displayed so PowerPoint knows how long you want it to be visible. By default, PowerPoint sets up your presentation so that the slides will advance only when you click the mouse or press the right-arrow key. You can change this in the Slide Transition task pane by choosing to advance your slides automatically. Follow these steps to advance your slides automatically and specify the length of time each slide is displayed:

1   Set any transition and sound effects for the current slide.

2   In the Advance Slide area of the Slide Transition task pane, click the Automatically After check box. The timing *00:00* appears in the box beneath the option.

> **Tip**   You can choose to leave both options selected in the Slide Transition task pane so that users have a choice of clicking to advance the slide or waiting for the timing to play out. If you want viewers to just relax and watch, disable the On Mouse Click option so that the slide will not advance when someone clicks the mouse button.

3   Use the arrow to increase the time, or click in the box and type a new value. After you click outside the slide, the timing value will be displayed beneath the slide.

> **Tip**   Because clicking the Apply To All Slides button applies all the transition effects to all the slides in your presentation, you need to use this button carefully. If you want to apply the same timing to all the slides, but you want to set individual transitions and sound effects, set the Advance Slide settings first and then click Apply To All Slides. This will apply the same time to all slides (you'll see the small time indicator under the lower-left corner of each slide in Slide Sorter view). Then you can go back and set transitions and sounds (and modify individual timings, if needed) without losing the unique effects of each slide.

Rehearsing Your Timings

Another way you can record the ideal timing for your slides is to use the Rehearse Timings feature. This feature enables you to go through your presentation as a slide show, manually advancing each slide after you've had enough time to read and digest everything displayed and making a record of the time amounts. Start the rehearsal by clicking the Rehearse Timings button on the Slide Sorter toolbar. Your presentation begins and a small Rehearsal toolbar appears in the upper-left corner of your screen, as shown below.

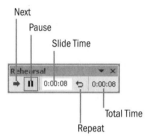

The Slide Time value begins immediately as it tracks the seconds you want the slide to display. Click to advance to the next slide and PowerPoint will record the time value and set the Slide Time value back to 00:00 for the next slide.

Caution   Here's something tricky about the Rehearse Timings feature: If you have added Animation Schemes to an individual slide, each of the elements on that slide—such as the title, the bullet text, and any charts or graphics—might have individual animation effects applied. For those slides, you need to click Next on the Rehearsal toolbar to play the animated effect, and you might need to click Next several times before moving on to the next slide. Don't sit and wait an inordinately long time for an element to show up on an animated slide—PowerPoint is waiting for you to click Next, and those waiting periods will distort your timings.

At the end of the show, PowerPoint tells you how long the presentation is and asks whether you'd like to keep the timings as you rehearsed them. If you click Yes, the timings you rehearsed will override any timings you entered in the Advance Slide area of the Slide Transition task pane. If you click No, the timings you entered manually will be retained.

Working with a Manual Show

If you decide that the Automatic-Advance method is not right for your audience, you can leave all the slides set to Manual Advance (or, if you've already changed a few of them, you can change them back to On Mouse Click or click Apply To All Slides if you haven't applied transition effects).

When you run the slide show, a button appears in the lower-left corner of the presentation window. When you (or your users) click the button, the menu shown in Figure 12-5 appears.

Figure 12-5   You can use this menu to move to different points in the presentation, add notes, enter meeting information, or change pointer and pen options.

To jump to another slide in the presentation, click Go and select the slide you want to view from the displayed list. If you want to change the way the mouse pointer works—including turning it into an on-screen pen that you can use to draw diagrams and circle important items—choose the Pointer Options command. You also can add Speaker Notes, add information for Meeting Minder, get help, or end the show from this menu.

First Things First   There's yet one more consideration when you begin putting together slides with multiple objects. Which one do you want to play first? And then what? To control the order in which your objects appear, rotate, play, and fade, you need to work with Custom Animations on the Slide Show menu. When you choose Custom Animations, the following task pane appears:

To change the order in which the objects play, click the item you want to move and click one of the Re-Order buttons to move it. You also can set additional options for individual objects by clicking the object's down arrow and choosing what you want to change from the displayed list.

> **Tip**   Meeting Minder is a feature shared by all Microsoft Office XP applications that you can use
> to make notes for meetings about the project at hand. You can also enter Action Items based on
> the current project and even coordinate the action items with your Outlook Schedule.

Notes for the Speaker

If you will be giving the presentation yourself, you'll probably remember that
you need to leave extra time in slide 9 to accommodate the slower readers in
your audience, or that you want to put in an optional question or two for particularly responsive audiences. But if someone else will be giving your presentation, you need some way of giving others the information about how to
deliver individual slides. The answer to that problem is the Speaker Notes feature of PowerPoint.

You can add notes to individual slides that only the person giving the presentation—or reading the handouts you've printed for their use—will see. To
add speaker notes, click the Speaker Notes tool on the Slide Sorter toolbar. The
Speaker Notes dialog box appears, as shown in Figure 12-6.

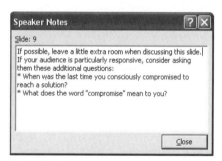

Figure 12-6   Speaker Notes enable you to add presentation suggestions and comments for others who might
be giving your presentation.

To add your notes, simply type them in the available space. When you're
finished adding notes, click Close. Or, if you want to add notes to another slide,
click that slide and the Speaker Notes dialog box for that slide is displayed.

> **Tip**   Once you make all your animation, transition, and timing changes, you'll want to go through
> the presentation from start to finish and see how everything looks. (And be prepared to modify the
> presentation a few times to get it to run as smoothly as possible.)

Key Points

- PowerPoint includes a number of features for animating and automating your slides.

- Slide Sorter view enables you to organize your slides and add transition, animation, and timing effects.

- You use the Animation Schemes feature to apply animation features to the text and objects on individual slides.

- The Slide Transition task pane contains everything you need for controlling the way one slide disappears and the next appears.

- You can add sound effects to your slide transitions by choosing the sound you want from the Sounds list in the Slide Transition task pane.

- If you want to advance slides by clicking a button in PowerPoint, leave On Mouse Click selected for your slides. If you want to have slides advance automatically after the amount of time you specify, click the Automatically After check box and enter the amount of time you want the slide to be displayed.

- Click Rehearse Timings to go through the slide show and record the time used to display animated elements and advance to the next slide. You have the option of accepting these settings over any you entered on the Slide Transition task pane.

- Add Speaker Notes to help others who might be giving your presentation know how to present certain slides. (Of course, you may also find this helpful if you have a long presentation or tend to get nervous—Speaker Notes can prompt you if your mind goes blank.)

Chapter 13

Enhancing Your Presentations

Your presentation should be looking good by now. You've learned to create and save a simple presentation in Microsoft PowerPoint. You've learned to edit, format, and arrange the presentation, as well as coordinate its animation effects, slide transitions, and timing. You're probably eager to jump up in front of that group and wow the audience. Well, almost.

The features of PowerPoint go on and on—in fact, an entire book could be (and has been) written about using all the aspects of the program to create high-quality, imaginative presentations. But this section of the book wouldn't be complete without at least a quick look at some of the high-end effects you can achieve with PowerPoint. The tasks covered here may be reserved for special presentations—effects that include video, adding music, and broadcasting your presentation online.

See Also   For extensive details about working with PowerPoint, see Microsoft PowerPoint Version 2002 Step by Step, by Perspection, Inc., also from Microsoft Press.

What Kind of Enhancements Will You Use?

Now that you've had a chance to go through a presentation from start to finish and prepare it to run as you like, you may want to think about a "wish" list of additional features. Some great ideas might be a bit too much for your budget or schedule—a custom video showing interviews with all your top salespeople might be a great inspiration for your regional sales staff, but it would also cost a small truckload of money and take months to complete. But there are some enhancements you can easily add that will make your presentation more interesting, more enjoyable, and easier for viewers to navigate. Here are a few of the possibilities:

- **Movie clips.**   Add two or three quick video segments to your presentation at strategic times—perhaps showing your animated company logo, walking up the steps of your new building, a few smiling faces, and so on.

- **Narration.**   You can add voice-over narration to your PowerPoint presentation, welcoming your audience, giving directions on how to use the presentation, or inviting visitors to your Web site.

- **Music clips.**   The music you add to your presentation can be anything from a simple logo jingle to a full-score musical arrangement that plays while your presentation continues on the screen.

Tip   You can get clips, templates, and more online by choosing Tools On The Web from the Tools menu. This takes you to the Microsoft Office XP site, where you can browse the latest utilities and download files that fit what you're looking for.

Adding Movies and Animations

Just a few years ago, it wasn't possible to add real, moving pictures to your presentation without paying for an elaborate and expensive custom video produced by a production company that did the whole thing. Adding video wasn't simply a matter of inserting a video file wherever you want it to play in your presentation. Today it is almost that easy. If you've got a digital video camera or know where to find and download animations or video clips, you can add *movies* to your presentation.

Tip   Remember that movies aren't your only choice if you want movement in your presentation. By using the Custom Animation feature (on the Slide Show menu), you can animate objects on your slides. The transitions you select also add movement, so think carefully about what movies will add to your presentation before you set about finding them.

Lingo   A *movie* is a digital film of any length, complete with audio and video. An *animation*, on the other hand, is an illustration that moves.

PowerPoint makes it easy for you to work with video and sound files by tucking all the options you need in the Movies And Sounds command on the

Insert menu. When you choose this command, a submenu appears, as shown below, giving you the following choices for adding movies:

Tip   As you learned in Chapter 12, "Animating and Timing Your Presentation," you also can add objects to your slides by choosing a slide layout that includes a Content box. The Content box displays icons for adding six objects—tables, charts, clip art, pictures, diagrams, or media clips. To add a movie, click the Insert Media Clip icon.

Inserting a Movie Clip

To add a movie clip to a slide in your presentation, begin by displaying the slide you want to use. Then choose Movies And Sounds from the Insert menu and select Movie From Clip Organizer. The Insert Clip Art task pane appears so that you can choose the movie clip you want from the displayed list (as shown in Figure 13-1).

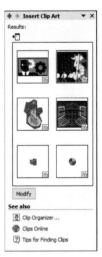

Figure 13-1   You can choose the clip you want to add by clicking it in the Insert Clip Art task pane.

When you click the movie, it is added as an object in the center of your slide. PowerPoint asks whether you'd like the movie to play automatically when the slide is displayed in a slide show or wait until the mouse is clicked. Click Yes to have the movie play automatically; otherwise, click No.

Tip   If you want to use a digital file you've captured or you have a video clip you've downloaded from the Web, you use the Movie From File option to add the file. Choose the option from the Insert menu; the Insert Movie dialog box appears. Navigate to the folder storing the movie you want to add, click it, and then click OK.

Capturing Your Own Movies If the digital film producer in you is just dying to work some original video into your presentation, go ahead and use that QuickCam or Sony digital camcorder. You can then use your camera's software to download the video file so that you can clean it up in a digital editing program, such as Adobe Premiere, and then place it as a media object in PowerPoint. Once your original file is ready for your presentation, just add it to a slide by choosing Movies And Sounds from the Insert menu and selecting Movie from the File menu; then choose your file in the Insert Movie dialog box and click OK.

Alternately, you can add the movie to the Clip Organizer and then place it in your presentation. Start with a slide that includes the content prompt (the small palette containing the object icons), and click the Insert Media Clip icon to display the Media Clip palette. Click Import and navigate to the folder in which your file is saved; then select your file and click OK. The clip is added to the Clip Organizer and you can now select it as usual and click OK.

Searching for Movies Online

If you are looking for just the right movie or animation and the Clip Organizer doesn't quite cut it, you can go online to the Microsoft Office Design Gallery Live and see what you can find there. To find movies or animations online, follow these steps:

1   Connect to the Internet.

2   Choose Movies And Sounds from the Insert menu; then click Movie From Clip Organizer.

3   In the Insert Clip Art task pane, click Clips Online.

4   On the Design Gallery Live page, in the Search For box, enter a word or phrase that describes the content you'd like to see.

5   If you want to isolate the search to a specific category (such as Emotions, Cartoons, Office, and so on), click the Search On: down arrow and choose the category from the displayed list.

6   Click the Results Should Be: down arrow and choose the type of file you want to find (in this case, Motion, which covers both movie and animation clips).

7   Click the Order By down arrow and choose the item that's most important to you. Do you want the files to be listed with newest files first, by a certain style, showing those with the smallest file sizes first, or by length?

8   Click Go to start the search. After a moment, the Design Gallery will display all the files that meet the criteria you entered.

9   Click the check box of a file you want to download.

10   Click the download button to start the process. The File Download dialog box appears momentarily, and then the Microsoft Clip Organizer reappears. The file is copied to the Clip Organizer automatically. The Collections List panel on the left side of the organizer shows where the file was placed.

Tip   Once you get the movie file placed where you want it to be played, choose Custom Animation from the Slide Show menu to display the Custom Animation task pane. Then verify that the objects on the slide appear in the order in which you want them—for example, suppose that you want the slide title to appear, then you want the movie to begin, and finally you want the text box to rotate in at the bottom of the slide. Make sure that each item appears when it should in the Animations list in the center of the task pane. If you need to change the order of the items, click the Re-Order buttons to do so.

Adding Sounds and Music

Do you want your presentations to sing? Were you hoping to have a cricket chirping through your new presentation about the nature center? Did the board think it would be nice to have the board members say their names at the introduction to the new staffing video? Did you want to have Frank Sinatra singing "Fly Me to the Moon" behind your new junior high school presentation about the effects of gravity? Whatever your intentions for sound and music, you can add the objects easily—and have them play automatically—in PowerPoint.

When you're ready to insert a sound object on your slide, follow these steps:

1   Display the slide on which you want to add the sound.

2   Choose Sound From Clip Organizer after you choose Insert and then Movies And Sounds. The Insert Clip Art task pane reappears along the right side of your PowerPoint window, this time showing all the sound files stored in the Clip Organizer.

3   Click the sound you want to add it to the slide. PowerPoint will ask you whether you want the sound to play automatically during your slide show. If you do, click Yes; otherwise, click No.

Tip   If you're unsure whether you've got the right sound clip, you can play it by clicking the button on the right side of the file icon. Click the Open Clip In option and Office opens the Windows Media Player so that you can listen to the clip before you place it. You can also play a sound object after you add it to the slide by right-clicking the sound icon and selecting Play Sound.

Recording and Playing Sound Effects

Most of us, if we're being honest, will admit that we like to hear the sound of our own voices. We might not have the vocal quality to do voice-overs for movie trailers or the creative wherewithal to generate funny or interesting noises for special sound effects, but including your voice—or the voices of your kids or the sounds of your pets—can be a fun and interesting addition to a more casual presentation.

If you want to record a sound for your presentation, display the slide you want to add the object to and then choose Record Sound from the Movies And Sounds submenu. The Record Sound dialog box appears. Type the name you want to assign to the sound and click the circle to begin recording (as shown in Figure 13-3). Speak, say, sing, hiccup, bark, ring a bell, whatever—and Power-Point records it. After you've recorded your sound (I *couldn't* get my puppy to bark at just the right time, darn it), click the square button to stop recording.

PowerPoint adds the sound object to your slide and makes the sound available in the Sounds list in the Slide Transition and Custom Animation task panes so that you can add the custom sound to other slides as well.

Tip   Use the Record Sound option when you want to add short sounds—bells and whistles, nature sounds, office sounds, and more. When you want to make a voice-over narration, use Record Narration in the Slide Show menu. For more about this option, see the section entitled "Recording Narration," later in this chapter.

Adding Background Music

So what about Frank Sinatra singing "Fly Me to the Moon"? You can play a CD track (or an entire CD, for that matter) by using the Play CD Audio Track option in the Movies And Sounds submenu. Here's how:

1   Display the slide on which you want to add the object. If you want the CD track to play for the duration of your presentation, display slide 1.

2   Choose Movies And Sounds from the Insert menu and then click Play CD Audio Track. The Movie And Sound Options dialog box appears (as shown in Figure 13-2).

Figure 13-2   Choose the CD track you want to play; then click OK.

3   In the Start area, choose the number of the track you want to start with (the At value will be filled in automatically according to the Track you select). Choose the number of the final track in the End area.

4   If the CD track is shorter than your presentation, you can make the track repeat by clicking the Loop Until Stopped check box.

5   Click OK to add the CD track to the slide.

6   Play your presentation by pressing F5.

Tip   Again, order is everything, so you might need to choose Custom Animation from the Slide Show menu and check to be sure that the CD track object executes where you want it to on the slide. If necessary, click the Re-Order buttons to change the order of the objects. Then click Slide Show to see the effects.

Recording Narration

Here's another opportunity to do a little vocal work. Suppose that your CEO is a very gregarious guy. People like him. He inspires trust. The board decides he's the one to deliver the news to shareholders that earnings were down 15 percent in the last quarter. The vehicle for this message-delivery will be the presentation you're working on this afternoon.

Adding narration, at least in theory, isn't any more difficult than speaking into the microphone attached to your computer. But similar to the speech-recognition features we discussed in Part I of this book, narration still has a long way to go before it is fully, no-fuss functional. To start narrating your presentation, follow these steps:

1 Display the slide on which you want to add the narration. (You can add narration to more than one slide.)

2 Choose Record Narration from the Slide Show menu. The Record Narration dialog box lists the amount of room you've got on your hard drive for recorded voice (as shown in Figure 13-3). Sound files take up massive amounts of space, remember.

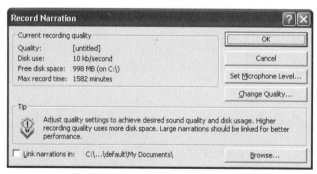

Figure 13-3 The Record Narration box provides everything you need for setting up and recording narrations.

3 Click OK to begin narrating. As your presentation begins running in a slide show, begin your narration.

4 When the slide show finishes (or you press Esc), PowerPoint displays a message box asking whether you want to save the slide timings and the narrations on each slide. Click Save if you do; otherwise, click Don't Save.

5 Press F5 to display your presentation and listen to the narration.

> **Tip** You can keep your presentation file relatively small by linking—rather than embedding—the narration file. Linking causes the narration to be stored on your hard drive (which means you must have the source file available at presentation time); embedding saves the narration as part of the presentation file, which makes the file huge. To link the narration, click the Link Narrations In check box in the Record Narration dialog box and click Browse to navigate to the folder in which you want to store the file.
>
> High-quality sound files, which are enormous, are especially likely to cause a space problem. That's why PowerPoint automatically defaults to the lowest-quality sound available. If you feel you can afford the space and want to go with the higher-quality sound, click the Change Quality button and click the Name down arrow. You can choose from CD Quality (44.100 kHz, 16-Bit, Stereo sound—the highest quality), Radio Quality (22.050 kHz, 8-Bit, Mono sound), and Telephone Quality (11.025 kHz, 8-Bit, Mono sound—the default selection). You can click the Attributes down arrow to choose other configurations for the sound quality you select. Click OK to close the Sound Selection box and return to the Record Narration dialog box.

If, after hearing the narration, you decide you liked the presentation better without it, simply display the slides in Slide view and delete the sound icons in the lower-right corner. This removes the narrations attached to the slides.

> **Note** If you have other sounds on your slides, the narration overrides those sounds and they will not play. This does not affect any sounds applied as part of slide transitions, however.

Broadcasting Your Presentation

Suppose that you've just finished the prototype of your new sports sack and, as your first self-marketing effort, you found the e-mail addresses for the buyers from 15 of the largest sports equipment manufacturers worldwide. You've used PowerPoint to create a stellar, three-minute presentation that shows how the sports sack is made, what kind of research went into it, why it's different, and how it can be used. You hope to capture the interest of at least one or two of these major-league buyers. You want to use an online broadcast—a novel idea you hope will capture someone's attention—as a means of getting recognition for your invention. This section shows you how to prepare and broadcast your presentation.

> **Tip** You can either give a presentation live or record it and save it to your hard disk for delivery later. This section covers the steps for a live broadcast, but to record a broadcast, choose Online Broadcast from the Slide Show menu and then choose Record and Save a Live Broadcast.

Setting Up a Broadcast

Start the process by choosing Online Broadcast from the Slide Show menu. Choose Settings from the submenu. In the Broadcast Settings dialog box, you choose how you want the presentation to appear to your viewers (as shown in Figure 13-4).

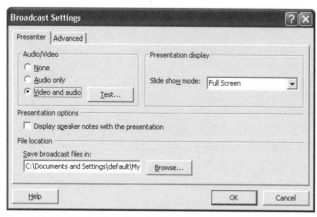

Figure 13-4   Use the Broadcast Settings dialog box to specify what you want to display and how you want to display it.

Transmitting Video and Audio with the Presentation Broadcasts let you send live video and audio data with the presentation. This means that you can use a video camera and a microphone to be "present" with your viewers in much the same way you could if you were in the same room with them. If you want to set up video and audio transmission, leave the default set to Video And Audio. Click Test to check your microphone and video settings. If the Microphone Check dialog box pops up, speak into the microphone to test it. As you read the suggested sentence, PowerPoint adjusts the volume level of your microphone if needed. After you click OK, the Video Source dialog box opens, enabling you to check the settings for your camera. If you make any changes, click Apply; then click OK to go to the Camera Check dialog box. After you have a good look at yourself (or your product), click OK to close the dialog box.

In the Presenter tab, make your choices about the following details:

■ Sending additional audio/video transmission, audio only, or no additional data

■ Presenting the show in full-screen or resizable screen mode

■ Displaying speaker notes along with the presentation

■ The location on your hard drive where the broadcast files are stored

After you enter your settings, click the Advanced tab. On this tab, you tell PowerPoint where the presentation will be given. If you are hosting a small meeting (fewer than 10 people), you don't need a server—you can simply broadcast the presentation from a shared folder on your computer. If you are giving a larger presentation and aren't sure what to enter here, click Use A Third Party Windows Media Service Provider and you will be directed online to providers for more information. Click OK to save your settings. Now you're ready to schedule the broadcast.

Tip   If you work on a networked system, be sure to talk with your system administrator while you are setting up your broadcast. Your company might have access to a Windows Media Server, which will eliminate the need for outside services.

Scheduling a Broadcast

When you're ready to schedule the broadcast, choose Online Broadcast from the Slide Show menu and choose Schedule a Live Broadcast. A window showing the data for your presentation appears (this will be displayed on the first page of your presentation). Review the information, make any necessary changes, and click Schedule. PowerPoint schedules the meeting and displays a confirmation message. Click OK to close the message box.

Inviting Your Audience and Broadcasting the Presentation

When you're ready to broadcast the presentation, choose Start Live Broadcast Now from the Online Broadcast submenu. In the Live Presentation Broadcast dialog box, select the name of the broadcast you want to give; then click Broadcast. This returns you to the Live Presentation Broadcast dialog box, but this time there's an additional button: Invite Audience. Click that button and your e-mail program starts. You can then send e-mail messages to the audience members you want to invite.

Running Your Online Broadcast

When you click the Start button, the Broadcast Presentation dialog box appears. Click Preview Lobby Page to see what your audience members will see when they join the presentation. After PowerPoint performs its necessary preparations, a green arrow flashes beside a message telling you to click Start when you're ready to begin the presentation. When you click Start, the presentation begins and your guests are able to watch it and participate.

Collaborating Online Note that hosting and giving a presentation online is different from having an online broadcast. A broadcast is a time in which you give your presentation to an invited audience. An online collaboration, however, is a group who comes together to work cooperatively on the project at hand. To collaborate with others online, choose Online Collaboration from the Tools menu and then select Meet Now, Schedule a Meeting, or Web Discussion. The feature works with Microsoft NetMeeting to access a shared server in which you and others can meet and discuss the project. PowerPoint displays an Online Collaboration toolbar for you to use while you're working with others.

Key Points

- For special presentations, you can easily add animations, movies, music, and more to your slides.

- You can add a movie clip in two ways: By choosing Movies And Sounds from the Insert menu and selecting Movie From Clip Organizer or Movie From File, or by clicking the Insert Movie Clip icon in the content palette on selected slides.

- Use the Clips Online link (found in the Clip Organizer and in the Insert Clip Art task pane) to find and download animations, movies, and sounds from the Web.

- You can record your own sound effects and save them in the Slide Transition task pane by choosing Record Sound from the Movies And Sounds submenu.

- PowerPoint allows you to add narration for your presentations by using the Record Narration command on the Slide Show menu. You can then link the file to the presentation (which helps you limit the file size) or embed the narration file in your presentation, whichever you prefer.

- PowerPoint gives you the ability to broadcast your presentations on the Web or on your company local area network (LAN) by using the Online Broadcast feature. This way, you can give your presentation to a selected group at a specified time, and add your own live video and voice-over, if you like.

Part V

Organize with Microsoft Outlook

Are you the type of person who has a day planner, a Pocket PC personal digital assistant (PDA), a Rolodex, and a to-do list—and you never use any of them consistently? Welcome to the majority of the human race. We have so many tools to help us get organized, but who has the time to do it religiously?

If only we'd remember that we have almost everything we need to be organized right there on our desktops, in the unassuming icon of Microsoft Outlook. This multitalented program includes not only a full-featured e-mail utility (which is what it's best known for), but also a calendar, a journal, a task scheduler, a notepad, and a contact manager. And the best thing is that it works seamlessly with all the other Microsoft Office XP programs.

Chapter 14, "E-mailing with Microsoft Outlook," introduces you to the Outlook window and shows you the basics of setting up e-mail accounts and sending and receiving, printing, and deleting e-mail. Chapter 15, "Organizing with Microsoft Outlook," shows you how to weed out your junk mail, track and manage your contacts, add ideas to your journal, and work with tasks and notes. And in Chapter 16, "Scheduling with Microsoft Outlook," you'll learn to use Outlook to organize your day, scheduling tasks and meetings, inviting others to meetings, and printing and coordinating calendars.

Chapter 14

E-mailing with Microsoft Outlook

If you read the introduction to this part of the book, you already know Microsoft Outlook is far more than an e-mail application. Developed as a kind of personal data assistant to help you keep track of the myriad details of your daily life, Outlook includes a task scheduler, a calendar, a contact manager, a journal, and a notepad. But because e-mail has become so central to our personal and professional lives, it's nice to know that Outlook has at its core one of the best e-mail programs around. This chapter focuses on introducing you to the Outlook window and exploring the basics of e-mail.

What Can You Do with Outlook?

But first let's brainstorm about what you can use Outlook to do in your life and work. Here are just a few ideas:

- The obvious: Use Outlook to organize your business contacts and appointments.

- Keep track of your children's baseball, skating, and trumpet lessons.

- Keep a journal of new ideas you want to research for upcoming campaigns.

- Set up and use a daily to-do list that helps you see easily what you've accomplished in a week.

- Schedule meetings and reserve meeting rooms after coordinating times with coworkers also using Outlook.

- Keep your contacts and schedule up-to-date by downloading them to your favorite personal digital assistant (PDA).

A Walk Around the Outlook Window

When you double-click the Microsoft Outlook icon on your desktop or choose Microsoft Outlook from the All Programs menu, the Outlook Today window appears (as shown in Figure 14-1). This window, after you begin working with your calendar, scheduling tasks, and using it for sending and receiving e-mail, will offer you reminders of all the important things you need to do today.

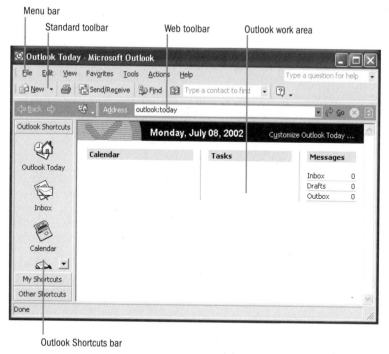

Figure 14-1   The Outlook Today window is where you begin your work with Outlook and all its features.

Outlook Menus

The Outlook menu bar probably looks familiar. At the top of the Outlook window, you find seven menus—File, Edit, View, Favorites, Tools, Actions, and Help. The File menu contains commands for displaying all the elements you create in Outlook—messages, folders, appointments, contacts, tasks, journal entries, and more. You can also manage your Outlook data, archive old stuff, and print. The Edit menu is all about copying, pasting, cutting, moving, and marking items as read or unread; View enables you to display one of the several different views, panes, and windows you open in Outlook.

Favorites lets you move quickly to various Web sites already programmed into Outlook. Choosing one of these Web pages opens the page in the Outlook work area if you're already online, which means you can use Outlook to view Web pages quickly, if you choose. The Tools menu allows you to send and receive messages, log on to your instant messaging program, work with the Address Book, work with forms, and more. You also can activate the speech-recognition feature so that you can dictate e-mail to your computer. Finally, Actions gives you e-mail-specific options for dealing with junk mail, finding messages, and creating messages. And Help, of course, offers help.

Outlook Toolbar

The Outlook toolbar contains the tools you'll use to create, send, and print messages quickly, locate a contact, and find specific information. Here's a glance at the Outlook toolbar:

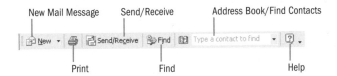

Web Toolbar

Because we want instant access to the Web in just about everything we do, Outlook 2002 packs a Web toolbar right into the Outlook window. The Web toolbar includes all the tools you need in any standard browser, as shown here:

> **Tip**   You can click the Outlook Today button to jump quickly to another Outlook application while you're surfing the Web. Just click the down arrow to the right of the tool and choose the item you want from the displayed list.

Outlook Shortcuts

The panel along the left side of the Outlook window is called the Outlook Shortcuts bar. This panel contains the different icons you'll select to use the different features of Outlook. The following list introduces them in a nutshell:

- Outlook Today displays the Outlook opening window that appears when you first start the program. This page gives you information about the appointments, tasks, and messages you've got today.

- Inbox takes you to the e-mail component of Outlook from which you can create, send, organize, respond to, and print your e-mail messages.

- Calendar displays the Outlook Calendar, as well as a TaskPad that displays your current tasks, a daily log, and monthly calendars.

- Contacts opens your Contacts list. Don't be alarmed if the first time you display this view, you get a message saying there's nothing to show. You'll learn how to import an Address Book in the sidebar "Importing an Address Book," later in this chapter.

- Tasks shows you the list of tasks that are waiting to have your undivided attention. Tasks are listed by Subject and Due Date.

- Notes displays a page of notes you've added in previous sessions. If you haven't yet created any notes, this page is blank.

- Deleted Items is a folder that stores the messages, tasks, appointments, notes, and journal entries you delete—until you choose Empty "Deleted Items" Folder from the Tools menu.

Click the My Shortcuts and Other Shortcuts buttons beneath the Outlook Shortcut area to display additional items you can display. In My Shortcuts, you'll find links to your e-mail Drafts folder, as well as Outbox, Sent Items, Journal, and Outlook Update. Other Shortcuts contains links to your My Computer, My Documents, and Favorites folders. Clicking any one of the items displays its contents in the Outlook work area.

Tip   You can add your own shortcut groups by right-clicking on the Outlook Shortcut bar. A context menu appears, giving you a number of options for customizing the Outlook panel. Click Add New Group and a new group is added beneath the Other Shortcuts button. Type the name you want to assign to the group. You can then drag other items—for example, Journal from My Shortcuts—to the new group. Just another way to get organized.

Folders List

The Folders List isn't visible when you first begin working with Outlook. To display it, choose Folder List from the View menu. The list is displayed between the Shortcut bar and the Outlook Today window (as shown in Figure 14-2).

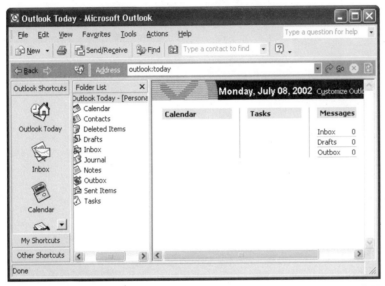

Figure 14-2   If you'd rather see a folder-style version of items you can select, use Folder List.

Tip   Outlook Shortcuts and the Folder List both enable you to choose the utility you want to use and navigate to the folder you need. To save workspace, hide the Outlook Shortcut bar if you'd rather use Folder List. To do that, right-click Outlook Shortcuts and choose Hide Outlook Bar from the displayed menu.

Using Outlook as Your E-mail Program

When you first begin working with Outlook, the program searches your computer for existing e-mail programs and accounts you've set up. Luckily, if you have existing e-mail accounts on your computer, Outlook imports the information so that it knows automatically how to send and receive mail using those accounts. To start the e-mail component of Outlook, follow these steps:

1   Connect to the Internet.

2   Choose Inbox in the Outlook Shortcut bar. Figure 14-3 shows the Inbox window and points out the important elements you need to know.

Received messages   Double-click a message to open it.

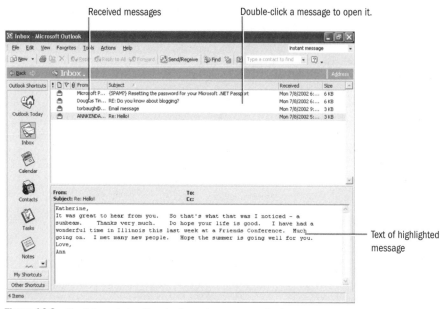

Text of highlighted message

Figure 14-3   The Inbox window lists the incoming messages in the upper pane and displays a preview of the selected message in the lower pane.

Adding New E-mail Accounts   When you want to add an account to Outlook, choose Options from the Tools menu. Click Mail Setup in the Options dialog box and then click E-mail Accounts. This displays a page on which you can change e-mail accounts or add new ones. Click Add A New E-mail Account and then click Next. On the Server Type page, choose the type of server your new e-mail account will use. (Most standard service providers use POP3 servers; Web-based servers use HTTP. If you're unsure which type your e-mail account requires, contact your Internet service provider for the necessary information.) Click Next to continue.

The Internet E-mail Settings page asks you for several kinds of information. You'll need your account user name, the e-mail address, the information about the server for incoming and outgoing messages. After you fill in the necessary data (again, contact your ISP if you're unsure), click Test Account Settings to see whether the settings you've entered will work as planned. Finally, click Finish and your account is set up and ready to use.

Composing an E-mail Message

When you're ready to create an e-mail message, click the New button on the Standard toolbar. This opens the message window.

To create the message, follow these steps:

1 Choose your recipient by typing his or her e-mail address in the To line. If you are sending the message to more than one person, separate the e-mail addresses with a semicolon.

Tip You can change the font, size, color, style, and alignment of the text in your e-mail message by clicking the formatting tools you want on the message toolbar. You can further customize messages by adding a background picture or color or choosing special stationery.

---

2 If you want to send a copy of the message to someone else, enter the e-mail address in the Cc line.

3 Type a subject for the message that helps describe it briefly for the recipient.

4 Click in the message area and type your message.

Tip If you don't know the e-mail address of the person to whom you're sending the message, but you know it's in your Outlook Address Book, you can click the To button to display the Select Names dialog box. Click the name of the person to whom you want to forward the message; then click the To button to add the person's name to the Message Recipients list. Finally, click OK to add the name to the To line in the message window.

---

5 Click Send and Outlook sends the message immediately.

If you want to verify that your message was sent, click My Shortcuts in the Office Shortcut bar pane and click Sent Items. A list of sent items appears in the right pane.

Tip Be sure to use the spelling checker on those important messages. Choose Spelling from the Tools menu or press F7 to start the checker. A Spelling dialog box appears when an unrecognized word is discovered so that you can change it, ignore it, or add it to your dictionary.

Retrieving and Reading Your E-mail

When you first open the Inbox, you click the Send/Receive tool on the Standard toolbar (or press F5) to tell Outlook to go out to the server and retrieve any e-mail stored there in your account. An Outlook Send/Receive Progress status window appears while the message is retrieved and delivered. If you've previously created any e-mail to be sent, you can also see that transmission in this status window. When the new e-mail arrives, your computer plays a chime and the messages appear boldfaced in the upper pane. In addition, a note symbol appears at the far right end of the notification area on the Windows toolbar.

To read a new message, double-click it. The message opens in its own window, showing the Subject line as the window title (as shown in Figure 14-4).

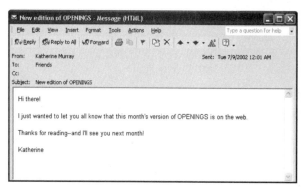

Figure 14-4   The received message opens in its own window.

Replying to and Forwarding E-mail

Sending a response is simple. While the e-mail message is open on your screen, simply click Reply. The message is displayed in a new message window, as shown in Figure 14-5. The header information from the original message, which gives you information about the sender, the subject, and the date and time the message was sent, is copied into the body of the message. An InfoBar also appears above the To line, giving you additional information about the message you're about to send.

When you receive an e-mail message that you think someone else needs to see, you can forward it. To do that, click the e-mail message and click Forward on the Message toolbar. Again, the header information is copied into the message. Type the person's e-mail address into the To line or choose it from the Select Names dialog box, add whatever text you need to introduce the forwarded message, and click Send. Outlook forwards the message immediately.

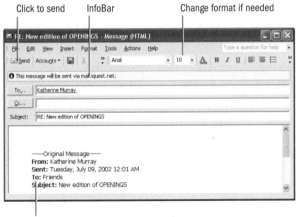

Click to send   InfoBar   Change format if needed

Header information of original message

Figure 14-5   Replying to a message is almost as easy as receiving it.

Attaching a File to an E-mail Message

But there's more to life than e-mail. There are files, too. You'll no doubt want to send files with your e-mail messages—files about the new product, report files, photo files, baby pictures, and more. To attach a file to a message, follow these steps:

1 Create the message as usual.

2 Choose File from the Insert menu.

3 In the Insert File dialog box, navigate to the folder storing the file you want to attach.

4 Click the file and then click Insert. The file name and an icon are added in a new Attach line beneath the Subject line.

Finish typing and formatting your message and then click Send. The message—and the attached file—are transmitted to your server to be delivered to the recipient you specified.

Printing Messages

When you receive a message you want to print for posterity, you can do so quickly by selecting it in the Inbox window and clicking the Print tool on the Standard toolbar. A Printing status box appears for a moment while the message is sent to the printer.

If you want to change the print options before you print, take the longer route by choosing Print from the File menu. This action displays the Print dialog box, where you can select additional options. You'll notice that your choices are fairly limited if you stick with the Memo Style (the default print format); you can choose only to print attached files. If you select Table Style, however, you can click Page Setup to control the format, font, margins, and more; specify the number of copies you want; and choose the range of rows you want to print. Click Preview after you've made your selections to see how the message will look when printed.

Try This!   You can print a number of e-mail messages at once by following these steps:

1   In the Inbox, select the messages you want to print. (Click the first message and then press and hold Ctrl while clicking the additional messages.)

2   Right-click in the selected messages.

3   Choose Print from the context menu.

4   Click OK in the Print dialog box to send all selected messages to the printer.

Tip   Remember that you also can copy information from messages into Microsoft Word, Microsoft PowerPoint, Microscoft Access, or even Microsoft Excel. Simply select the text you want to copy, press Ctrl+C to place a copy of the information on the Office Clipboard, open the desired application and then the file you want to copy the information into, and press Ctrl+V to paste.

Deleting Messages

If you're like most of us, you're going to get many more messages you want to delete than messages you want to keep. *Spam*—junk mail—is big business and until you learn how to filter out unwanted messages (which is covered in Chapter 15, "Organizing with Microsoft Outlook"), just expect to get lots of messages you don't want to read.

To delete the unwanted messages (or messages you've read and no longer need), select the messages and click the Delete tool on the Standard toolbar or press the Delete key. You also can press Ctrl+D if you like, or choose Delete from the Edit menu. Any way you do it, the messages are sent to the Deleted Items folder and they will remain there (just in case you want to retrieve something) until you empty the folder by choosing Empty "Deleted Items" Folder from the Tools menu. When you choose this command, Outlook displays a message box asking you to confirm that you do, in fact, want to delete the messages. Click Yes to continue and those messages are outta here.

Instant Messaging

Depending on how you look at it, instant messaging is either a great time-saver and loads of fun or a real pain in the neck. Instant messaging is a relatively new phenomenon, a combination of e-mail and chat, which allows you to know which of your friends or coworkers are online with you and gives you the ability to trade quick little messages with them in real time.

To start instant messaging in Outlook, choose Instant Messaging from the Tools menu; then choose Log On from the submenu that appears. The .NET Messenger Service dialog box appears so that you can enter your e-mail address and password (as shown in Figure 14-6). If you don't have a .NET account, click the Get A .NET Passport link at the bottom of the window and you are taken online to a Web page where you can sign up.

Figure 14-6 When you start Instant Messaging, you are asked for your .NET Passport user name and password.

Note The .NET Passport is a free account you are given automatically if you use Hotmail or MSN as your e-mail service; if you don't use either of these services, you'll have to click the link to get your Passport.

Once you have your .NET Passport user name and password, you can use the Log On command to start sending and receiving instant messages.

Setting Instant Messaging Options You can customize all kinds of details about the way Instant Messaging works. By choosing Instant Messaging from the Tools menu and selecting Options, you can change your on-screen name, create or edit a profile that tells other people about you and your interests, and choose a different font. You also can alter the way the Instant Messaging program starts and choose to disable some of the alerts that sound automatically. You can even screen out some users with whom you'd rather not trade messages. If you plan to spend any time with Instant Messaging, check out the available options to see whether there's something there that will make your life easier.

Receiving an Instant Message

When someone sends you an instant message, the message pops up over whatever you're working on, like this:

When you click the message to respond to it, the message opens in a larger window (as shown in Figure 14-7). In the Instant Messaging window, you can do all kinds of things in addition to sending quick messages back and forth—including sending photos and files, making a phone call, share applications, and more.

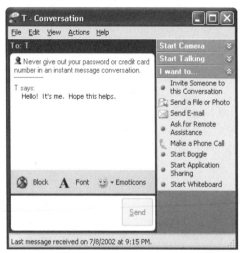

Figure 14-7   Trading text is only one part of what you can do with Instant Messaging.

Sending an Instant Message

Outlook uses the InfoBar to let you know whether the user you are corresponding with is online. When you open an e-mail message from a person who is logged on to Instant Messaging, for example, the InfoBar tells you that the person is online. You can send an instant message by clicking the InfoBar. A message window opens and you can simply type your message and click Send.

Changing Online Status

The pain-in-the-neck part of Instant Messaging lies in the fact that, once you're online, everyone who has your e-mail address listed as a contact can see you. And if you're popular, you might get lots of messages you didn't expect. There are two ways to handle this—the first is to log on only at the hours nobody else is online. A more practical answer is to learn how to change your online status so people know when you're busy or otherwise engaged.

To change your status while you're online, follow these steps:

1   Choose Instant Messaging from the Tools menu.

2   Click Status. The different status settings are Online (the default value), Busy, Be Right Back, Away, On The Phone, Out To Lunch, and Appear Offline. Select the desired option and then click OK.

The status change remains in effect for the rest of your online session unless you repeat the steps and choose a different status setting.

Key Points

■   Outlook is a multifeatured program that enables you to organize your appointments, tasks, e-mail, journal entries, and more.

■   The Outlook window includes everything you need to start and work with the various Outlook components. You use the Outlook Shortcut bar to move among applications.

■   When you want to create a new message, click Inbox on the Outlook Shortcut bar; then click New. When the new message window appears, enter the recipient in the To line and type a Subject and the body text of the message; then click Send.

■   Attach a file to an e-mail message by choosing File from the Insert menu. Find the file you want to send, click it, and click Insert to attach the file.

■   Instant Messaging in Outlook enables you to swap short-and-sweet messages with others you know who are currently online.

Chapter 15

Organizing with Microsoft Outlook

The best data organizer in the world can't help you if you just throw all your data in a corner. If you want to get organized and *stay* organized, you first have to create places in which to store different pieces of information—and then discipline yourself to use the system you've created. Doesn't sound like fun, does it? Many of us prefer to deal with things as they come and "remember" where things are on our desks or in the filing cabinet. Gradually, we learn that getting organized—without driving ourselves nuts in the process—helps us work smarter and more efficiently, no matter what we're doing.

This chapter focuses on how you can use Microsoft Outlook to get organized. Specifically, you'll learn how to manage the volumes of e-mail you receive and filter out the junk. You'll also learn to organize your contact information and work with the Address Book to record important items you'll need to know later.

Managing Your E-mail

Anyone who's had an e-mail address for any length of time has learned that getting control of messages right away is crucial. Otherwise, you'll wind up as I did—with 1,400 messages in your Inbox and only a few folders to put them in. Most of us simply skip the messages we don't want to read and move on to the next. The problem with such an out-of-sight, out-of-mind strategy is that it becomes a problem when you have to find that one message about the meeting you had back in November when Tom was hoping to introduce the new timing belt...

Better to bring your e-mail under control right off the bat, before you have piles of it to dig through (metaphorically speaking). Outlook gives you a number of ways to organize your e-mail and your e-mail data. We'll start by creating folders in which to store the messages you want to keep.

Creating Folders to Store Your E-mail

When you begin to amass messages that you need to keep (such as e-mail related to a current project), you can create a folder to store the messages. Creating such a folder helps you find those e-mails later and prevents them from being deleted or archived accidentally.

You can start the folder-creation process in several ways:

■ Click the New down arrow on the Standard toolbar, and then click Folder.

■ Press Ctrl+Shift+E.

■ Choose New from the File menu, and then select Folder.

■ Right-click a message in your Inbox, choose Move to Folder, and then click New.

Whichever route you choose, you reach the Create New Folder dialog box (as shown in Figure 15-1). Type the name you want to assign to the folder. In the center of the dialog box, the Folder Contains field displays the kind of Outlook information that will be stored in the folder. The default selection is the one you want. You also can see that the Inbox in the Folder List pane is highlighted, indicating that the new folder will be a subfolder of the Inbox (which also is the setting you want). Click OK to create the folder.

Outlook asks whether you'd like to create a shortcut on the Outlook Bar to the folder you just created. Click Yes if you do; otherwise, click No.

If you choose not to add a shortcut to the Outlook Bar, Outlook displays the Folder List pane and places your new folder beneath the Inbox folder.

Figure 15-1   Enter a name for the new folder and click OK to create it.

Moving Messages to Folders

When you're ready to do some housecleaning and want to move your messages to their respective folders, begin by selecting the messages you want to move. To move messages, first select them using one of the following three methods:

- Select a single message by clicking it.

- To select a group of contiguous messages, click the first message and press and hold the Shift key as you click the last message in the group. The entire group is highlighted.

- To select messages that are not contiguous, click the first message and press and hold Ctrl as you click additional messages. Only the messages you clicked are selected.

Now right-click one of the selected messages and choose Move To Folder from the Context menu. (If you've selected more than one message, right-clicking one of the selected items will move the entire block.) In the Move Items dialog box (shown in Figure 15-2), click the name of the folder to which the message or messages will be moved, and then click OK.

> **Tip**   A faster way to move messages to folders is to display the Folder List pane by choosing Folder List from the View menu. Then select the messages you want to move to a folder and drag the selected message group to the folder in the Folder List. When you release the mouse button, the messages are moved with no further action required. Pretty simple, eh? It's a process that's easy to reverse, as well—if you accidentally move the message to the wrong folder, press Ctrl+Z to undo the operation immediately afterwards.

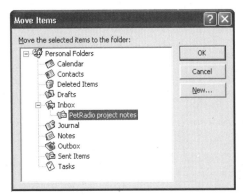

Figure 15-2   You can move selected messages to the folder by right-clicking and choosing Move To Folder; then select the folder you want and click OK.

Try This!   In Chapter 14, "E-mailing with Microsoft Outlook," you learned how to delete unwanted e-mail messages. You can instruct Outlook to empty the Deleted Items folder for you at the end of every work session if you like. This saves you the trouble of remembering to do it periodically. (Remember, one of the first rules of organizing is: Delegate everything possible—and automate the rest.) To clean out your Deleted Items folder automatically, follow these steps:

1   Choose Tools from the Outlook menu and click Options.

2   Click the Other tab and click the Empty The Deleted Items Folder Upon Exiting check box.

3   Click Apply to invoke your changes, and then click OK to close the Options dialog box. (If you don't want to look at your changes before you finalize them, simply click OK.) Now, every time you exit Outlook, the items in your Deleted Items folder will vanish.

Automatically Filing E-mail

You also can use the Organize button in the Outlook toolbar to display a panel that allows you to make choices about folders, colors, views, and junk e-mail. You can use this feature to have Outlook automatically file e-mail from a certain person or organization in a folder that you specify. Here's how to do that:

1   Click Organize on the toolbar and click Using Folders, as shown below:

2   In the Create A Rule area, leave From selected and type the name of the sender (individual or company), then click the down arrow and choose the name of the destination folder for that sender's e-mail.

3   Click Create to create the rule.

A message box appears, telling you that the rule will be applied to all incoming messages and asking whether you want to apply the rule to current messages. If you want the rule applied, click Yes (you might as well, if just to save a few keystrokes).

Controlling Junk E-mail

Is there anyone who actually *likes* junk e-mail? Finding a mountain of colorful-but-unnecessary brochures and advertisements stuffed into your mailbox when you get home from vacation is disheartening enough, but logging on after a week away and finding 447 e-mail advertisements for working at home, finding the perfect mate, getting online college degrees, and improving your memory is downright disgusting. What can we do to eliminate this waste of our time? Happily, Outlook can help scuttle those unwanted e-mails. You can instruct Outlook to do the following things:

■   Send junk e-mail directly to the Deleted Items folder

■   Create a Junk E-mail folder and deposit suspected junk e-mail in that folder

■   Download junk e-mail to the Inbox but color-code it so you can see it clearly

■   Create a junk e-mail list that blocks future messages from the sender

---

Tip   Junk e-mail, also called *spam*, is unsolicited, undesired, and unwelcome e-mail. These people want to sell you something and they probably purchased your e-mail address from a list somewhere. Most spam isn't dangerous, just annoying.

Color-Coding or Moving Junk E-mail

You can use the Organize panel to color-code the junk e-mail in your Inbox. Click the Organize tool, and then click the Junk E-mail link, as shown below:

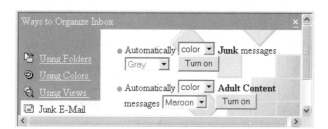

In the top selection, click the down arrow in the Color box. Your two choices are Color and Move.

■   To move the offending e-mail to another folder (such as the Deleted Items folder or the Junk E-mail folder Outlook creates), click Move. Select the destination folder, and click Turn On. The feature is now set.

■   To change the color of junk e-mail, leave Color selected, and then choose the color you want from the list that appears when you click the down arrow. Click the Turn On button to activate the feature.

Note   Outlook distinguishes between junk e-mail and messages with adult content and allows you to set the features individually for those two kinds of e-mail.

Creating a Junk Senders List

Another way to weed out those dastardly messages is to add the names to a junk e-mail senders (or adult-content e-mail senders) list. To do this, right-click a junk or adult content message and select Junk E-mail from the Context menu. Choose Add To Junk Senders List or Add To Adult Content Senders List, depending on the content of the message. Outlook records the entry and checks against the list each time you receive new e-mail. If Outlook detects e-mail from that sender, the e-mail is treated according to the options you've chosen, either moving the e-mail to the Deleted Items (or another) folder or color-coding the e-mail message so that you can spot it easily.

Tip   You can edit the Senders lists by clicking the Organize tool in the Outlook toolbar, clicking Junk E-mail, and scrolling to the bottom of the pane. Click the Edit Junk Senders or Edit Adult Content Senders links to edit or revise the lists.

Archiving E-mail

If you're like me and you're too busy to clean out your old e-mail messages regularly, you can use Outlook's AutoArchive feature to archive your old messages and move them to the location you specify. To use AutoArchive, follow these steps:

1   In Outlook, choose Options from the Tools menu.

2   Click the Other tab in the Options dialog box.

3   Click the AutoArchive button. The AutoArchive dialog box appears, offering a number of options for customizing how AutoArchive works (as shown in Figure 15-3).

4 Change any items necessary. In particular, look at how often you want to run AutoArchive, what period of time you want to set for archiving (six months is the default setting), and whether you want to move the old items to a new location (click Browse if you want to change this setting to a different folder) or permanently delete old items.

5 Click the Apply These Settings To All Folders Now if you want the settings to go into effect immediately.

6 Click OK to return to the Outlook window.

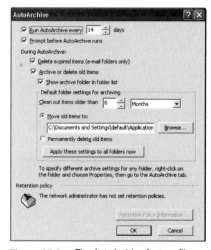

Figure 15-3   The AutoArchive feature files away or deletes old e-mail messages according to your instructions.

Tip   Outlook includes another feature, Mailbox Cleanup, to help you keep your Inbox orderly. This feature works hand-in-hand with AutoArchive and relies on the Deleted Items folder as well. Choose Mailbox Cleanup from the Tools menu to display the dialog box. Choose the features you want to use (including AutoArchive and Deleted Items) and click OK to save your settings.

Working with Contacts

Did you ever have trouble fitting all the information you needed on those little Rolodex cards? I did—and the cards became dog-eared and tattered; I wrote on them with different-colored pens, updating information over the years. Sometimes I pulled one out of the little stand and tucked it in my pocket on the way out the door, intending to call the person while I was on the road. But that card was never seen again. What might have been an important contact was lost.

Outlook's Contacts feature doesn't get tattered, doesn't show signs of scribbled-in updates, and it doesn't fall out of your pocket and get lost. In fact, with

Outlook Contacts, you have an almost unlimited amount of room to store information about the people important to your business and your life. As your relationships with others grow, the data you store about them can, too.

Getting Started with Contacts

To display Contacts in Outlook, click the Contacts icon in the Outlook Shortcuts bar. Depending on the number of contacts you've entered (and if you imported your address book from another program, as the exercise in Chapter 14 described, you may have quite a number of contacts), the names and e-mail addresses appear in the Contact window.

To display your data on a specific person, double-click the entry in the Contacts window. The Contacts window for that person opens on your screen, filled with any information you've entered. Along the top of the Contact window, you'll notice a new toolbar to help as you work with contact data, as shown below:

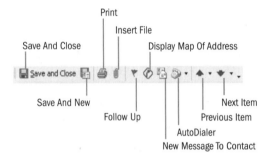

Here's a quick list to give you an overview of what you'll do with the tools in the Contact window:

- Save And Close updates information you've changed and closes the window.

- Save And New saves and closes the current contact and opens a new Contact window.

- Print prints the selected entry (for more about printing, see the section entitled "Printing Contact Information," later in this chapter).

- Insert File lets you save a file along with the contact information (this might be helpful for adding an organization's annual report to the Development Director's data, for example).

- Follow Up enables you to flag an entry and remind yourself that you need to make contact by a specific time on a specific day.

■   Display Map Of Address does just that—it shows a map of how to get to the contact's office—and New Message opens the e-mail window.

■   AutoDialer opens a New Call dialog box so that you can enter a phone number and dial the person.

■   Previous Item and Next Item allow you to scroll through the contacts preceding and following the current one in your Contacts list.

Where Does the Address Book Fit In? If you've been working with Microsoft Office XP or its predecessors for any length of time, you're familiar with the Address Book. This feature allows you to store names, e-mail addresses, telephone numbers and other contact information for the people with whom you work regularly. The Address Book is available within Contacts—it's a tool on the Outlook toolbar (to the left of the Contact Search box). If you click the Address Book, you'll see that it's pretty spare in the features department compared to the huge Contacts utility.

If you're more comfortable working with Address Book to select, enter, and find data, feel free—when you go to edit contact information or add a new contact, Address Book moves seamlessly into Contacts, so you're working with the same Contacts window anyway. All data goes to the same place, which is the most important thing when you're trying to get organized and stay organized.

Creating a Contact

But let's assume for a moment that you don't have any contacts in your Contacts list. How do you add one? The process is simple:

1   Click the Contacts shortcut to display the Contacts window.

2   Click New. A blank Contact window appears (as shown in Figure 15-4).

3   Click the individual fields and enter the information you have to record.

4   When you're finished, click Save And Close to save the information you've added.

More Data! More Data! Are you wondering what all these other tabs are for? As your experience with Outlook grows, you'll find that you can track *all kinds* of information—including free-form notes you've added about meetings, projects, interests, and more. The General tab, as you've seen, records all the important business contact information; the Details tab gives you room to add details about the person and records NetMeeting settings. The Activities tab tracks the interaction you've had with the person by listing e-mail contacts, journal entries, notes, scheduled tasks or appointments. The Certificates tab lists any digital signatures you use to correspond with the person; and the All Fields tab lets you create fields for recording additional information.

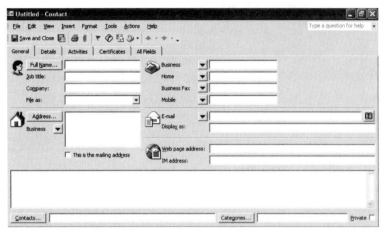

Figure 15-4   Use the Contact window to record pertinent information.

Finding a Contact

When you're trying to track down your information on a specific person, you can do it quickly by typing a name. Click the Contact Search box in the Outlook toolbar, type the person's name, and then press Enter. Outlook immediately finds the person's data and displays it in the Contact window, ready for your editing or review.

Tip   To speed your search, you can enter only the person's first name (for example, **Larry**) in the Contact Search box. If your contact list includes more than one Larry, the Choose Contact dialog box will appear, asking you to select the Larry you want. Click the name you need, and then click OK.

Revising Contact Information

When you need to change contact information, simply display the contact's data by clicking Contacts in the Outlook Shortcuts bar and then double-clicking the contact's entry. The Contact window for that person then appears and you can click in the fields you want to change and type the new information.

Printing Contact Information

Printing your contact information is a good idea, especially if there's a chance that your computer system could go south someday and leave you dataless. (A frightening thought, isn't it?) One of the downsides of keeping our former Rolodex information in electronic format is that it may be beyond our reach if something disastrous were to happen to our computer access, such as going into work and finding the office has been moved to a secret location and you weren't invited along.

When you want to print your contact information, you can choose to print individual contact information or print the whole list. Here are the steps for doing both:

■ To create a printout of contact information for an individual, right-click the entry in the Contacts list and choose Print from the Context menu. (You also can display the Contact window by double-clicking the entry and choose Print from the toolbar.)

■ To print the entire list, display the Contacts list and choose Print from the File menu. In the Print dialog box, choose the Print style you want: Card Style, Small Booklet Style, Medium Booklet Style, Memo Style, or Phone Directory Style. Then select the number of copies you want and click Preview to see how the document will look when printed.

Tip   If you want to print only a few entries, select them in the Contacts list (click the first entry you want to print, and then press and hold Ctrl while clicking the other entries). Right-click a highlighted entry and click Print. In the Print dialog box, choose the Print style you want to use; then, in the Print range area, click Only selected items. Choose the number of copies you want, and then click OK to print the selected entries.

Try This!   This is simply a cool, time-saving feature that helps keep you from getting lost on the way to an appointment. To display a map to your contact's address, follow these steps:

1   Select a contact for which you've entered a full address (or if you haven't entered one, create a contact for yourself and enter your address information).

2   Display the contact by double-clicking it if necessary.

3   Verify that you're connected to the Internet.

4   Now click the Display Map Of Address button and, after a moment or two, MSN Map-Point appears, displaying a map to your destination.

You can print, e-mail, or download the map to your personal digital assistant (PDA). You can also save the file to your hard disk and then attach it to your contact information using the Insert File tool. Cool stuff!

As you can see, there's a lot more you can do with Contacts in Outlook. In fact, the way in which you can use the data in different Office XP applications is enough to fill a book. Experiment as you have time and you'll soon discover favorite time-saving features in Outlook.

Journaling in Outlook

As an avid journal writer myself, I was thrilled to find the Journal feature in Outlook. "Oh, good!" I thought, "A place to record my deep thoughts while I'm working on other things!" Unfortunately (or fortunately, depending on your perspective), that's not what Outlook's Journal is about. Outlook's Journal feature enables you to record your involvement with a particular contact or task. By storing the information on a daily, weekly, or monthly timeline, the Journal can show you how you spent your time and which of your clients gets the most of your time. This can be especially helpful when you work in a service-related area and need to keep track of how much to bill different clients when you work on multiple projects during a day.

To start the Journal in Outlook, begin by clicking My Shortcuts on the Outlook Shortcuts bar. The first time you choose Journal, Outlook will tell you that the Activities tab in the Contacts window does a good job of tracking information related to specific clients. If you want to use Journal only for those items you enter, click No when Outlook asks you whether you want to use it for automatic recording. If you want Journal to record items such as e-mail correspondence, scheduling, task entries and updates, and working with files, click Yes. And the Journal Options dialog box appears so that you can choose the items you want to track. If you choose this route, click the items you want Journal to record, and then click OK to begin working with the Journal.

To record a new Journal entry, click New on the Outlook toolbar. The Journal Entry window appears (as shown in Figure 15-5). Enter the subject for the entry, then click the Entry Type down arrow and choose the type of activity from the displayed list. Enter the name of the company the item relates to, and then select the Start time by choosing the date and time you want to begin tracking the activity. You can then minimize the Journal entry and go on about your work for that client company.

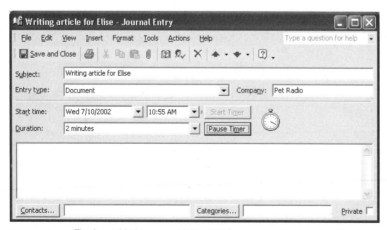

Figure 15-5   The Journal helps you track how much time you spend on individual pieces in a project.

When you're finished with the task at hand, redisplay the Journal entry by clicking the entry in the taskbar, and then click Save And Close. The item is then added to the timeline, as shown below, and you can redisplay it, add to it, or edit the entry by double-clicking it.

> **Note**   There's much more you can do with the Journal in Outlook—and multiple views you can use to review the way your time information is tracked. Experiment with the different displays by choosing the different timeline views on the Outlook toolbar or by choosing Current View from the View menu.

Working with Tasks and Notes

Does your to-do list grow during the day? Do things fall off the list accidentally, leaving unfinished details that are sure to catch up with you later? Do you have trouble reminding yourself about what you wanted to remember? Outlook includes two more features—Tasks and Notes—that can help you capture details that are in danger of falling through the cracks. Tasks enables you to reduce your larger projects into a series of manageable steps, while Notes helps you remember those great ideas that occur to you as you're doing a project.

First Tasks First

My mother had lists for everything. Her morning list began with "Make coffee" and ended with "Defrost chicken for dinner." I must admit that I'm not half the organizer my mother is—but, luckily, I know how to use Outlook's Task feature. I can track projects and people and personal events. And if you're on the road to better organization, Tasks can help you get that sense of accomplishment at the end of the day.

To start Tasks, click the Tasks shortcut in the Outlook Shortcuts bar. The window shown in Figure 15-6 appears.

To add a new task, click New on the Outlook toolbar. In the New Task dialog box, click in the Subject line and type a name for the task. Click the Due Date down arrow to display a calendar and click the due date you need. Fill in additional items, such as the Status, Priority, and Start Date if needed. You will automatically be reminded of the approaching deadline until you click the Reminder check box to clear the checkmark (as shown in Figure 15-7).

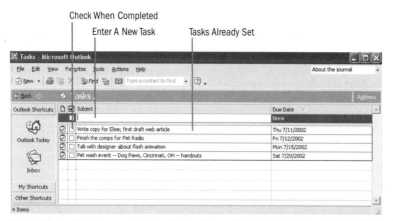

Figure 15-6   Create a new task by clicking New on the Outlook toolbar when the Tasks window is displayed.

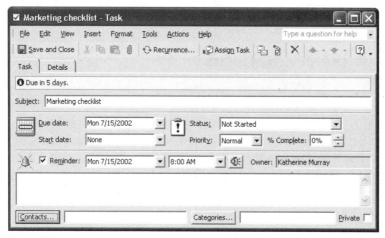

Figure 15-7   Outlook lets you know how many days you have before the task is due. Pressure, pressure.

Tip   If you prefer to enter a task the fast way, click in the Click Here To Add A New Task box and type the task; then press Tab to move to the Due Date column. Click the down arrow to display a calendar and click the date the task is due. Press Enter to save the task.

After you've entered the task information, click Save And Close to save the task. Outlook displays the task in the Task list. You can change the task data at any time by double-clicking the task in the list. When you complete an item, click the Complete check box (just to the left of the task). Outlook then marks out the task, like this:

Closure. Nice. (Omigosh—did someone remember to defrost the chicken?)

Now the Notes

Notes is a rather small but powerful feature in Outlook. Start Notes by clicking the Notes shortcut in the Outlook Shortcuts bar. If you've previously entered notes, they appear in the Notes area of your screen.

To create a note, click New. A notepad appears, showing the date and time along the bottom of the notepad. Type your note and then either leave the note open on the screen or click the close box to save the note in the Notes area. You can open a note later by displaying Notes view and then double-clicking the note. The note appears over your work area, looking something like this:

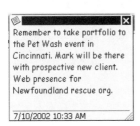

As you can see, there are many features in Outlook that can help you get organized, whether you need to control e-mail messages, contact data, time, tasks, or thoughts. The only problem is: which one will you tackle first?

Key Points

■ As you begin receiving more and more e-mail, you'll need to create folders to store messages you want to keep. You can create a new folder by clicking the New down arrow in the Outlook toolbar and choosing Folder (or by pressing Ctrl+Shift+E).

■ Move messages to folders easily by right-clicking the message group and choosing Move To Folder.

■ You can have Outlook automatically save messages to specific folders by using the Organize tool in the Outlook toolbar.

■ Rid your Inbox of junk e-mail (or color-code your e-mail so it will stand out) by choosing Junk E-mail in the Organize pane.

■ The Contacts feature in Outlook is an extensive data management tool that enables you to gather, update, sort, print, and use information about clients, companies, coworkers, and companions.

- Journaling in Outlook enables you to keep track of the time you spend on specific tasks during the day.

- Use Tasks to help you break down large projects into smaller, manageable chunks. You enter the task and due date and check off the tasks when they're finished.

- Outlook Notes are pop-up boxes you can leave open on your screen as you work to remind you of important things you might forget.

Chapter 16

Scheduling with Microsoft Outlook

If you've ever felt like the frantic White Rabbit ("I'm late! I'm late!") from *Alice in Wonderland*, you know what a great thing it can be to discover a few extra minutes in the day. How often have you sighed with relief when a meeting was cancelled at the last minute or when a project you were dreading was moved down the priority list?

Microsoft Outlook includes a number of features that can help you discover more time in your day. Using the Outlook's Calendar, for example, you can bring your tasks and appointments together and create schedules that make sense for everyone in your group. Sound ambitious? It's not too tough—but, like everything in Outlook, if you use the feature religiously, you'll stay organized and discover you have more free time than you thought you did. So let's get started. There's no time to waste.

Understanding Outlook's Calendar

Now we're getting to the point where we can bring together all the organizing features in Outlook to make your life easier, your desktop cleaner, and free you up to do other things. Here are just some of the things you can do with the Outlook Calendar:

■ Schedule daily, weekly, monthly, or annual appointments.

■ Set up reminders to play a sound or message when it's time for an appointment.

■ Set up and organize meetings.

■ Work with items on your Tasks list.

■ Coordinate group schedules.

To start the Calendar, click the Calendar icon in the Outlook Shortcuts bar. Figure 16-1 shows what the Calendar window looks like and the important features you'll use.

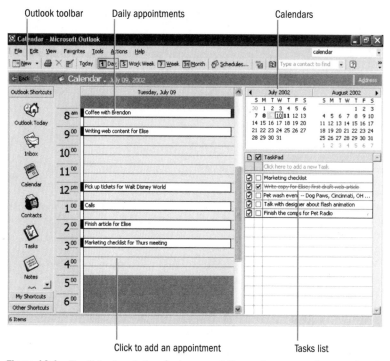

Figure 16-1   The Calendar window displays your daily appointments and your assigned tasks.

At the top of the window, beneath the menu bar, you see the Outlook toolbar. This toolbar contains the tools you'll use to create appointments, print your schedule, color-code your calendar, change the calendar view, work with group schedules, and find contacts.

The Calendars window displays several panels you can use to set appointments and complete tasks. The main area of the screen shows the schedule for the current day, organized in 30-minute increments. In the top-right corner of the window, you see the Calendars area, displaying the current month and next month. (You can display different months by clicking the arrows at either end of the Calendars title bar.) The Tasks list appears in the lower-right portion of the window, showing the tasks you've finished as well as the tasks you need to do.

Try This!   When you're working with the Calendar in Outlook, it's helpful to view entries in different ways. You might use the Day view to enter appointments or review your appointments for the morning; but looking at the entire Work Week is helpful when you've got to make a guesstimate about how long it will take you to complete a report. Viewing your calendar in Month view helps you decide the best time for a vacation day, especially when vacation seems a long way off.

To change the Calendar view, click the Outlook tool you want to see. Click Work Week to view a five-weekday schedule; click Week to show all seven days; or click Month to see the current month, complete with any appointments you've entered. You can enter, update, or delete appointments using any of the Calendar views.

Creating Appointments

There is a fast way and a detailed way to create an appointment. Which do you want first? Okay, let's take the short road. The fastest way to add an appointment is to display the Calendar in Day view, click the line corresponding to the time you want to add the appointment, type the text, and then click outside the entry.

When you want to create a more detailed appointment, however, with start and end times, reminders and more, you need to click the New Appointment tool in the Outlook toolbar (or double-click a line in the Calendar in Day view). This action brings up the Appointment window, in which you enter the information you need to set up the appointment (as shown in Figure 16-2).

To create the appointment, follow these steps:

1   In the Subject line, type a phrase describing the appointment.

2   Enter a location or click the down arrow to choose a location you've entered previously.

> **See Also**   *If you will be using Microsoft NetMeeting to meet online, see the section, "Setting Up an Online Meeting," later in this chapter.*

---

3   If the appointment is to be set for a day other than the current day, click the Start Date down arrow and choose the date from the calendar that appears.

4 Set the Start Time by clicking the down arrow and choosing the time
from the list.

Note   If the meeting is an all-day event, select the All-Day Event check box and the
Calendar removes the time selections.

---

5 Repeat steps 3 and 4, choosing the date and time your appointment
will end.

6 Click Save And Close to save the appointment and add it to your daily
calendar.

Tip   You also can create specific types of appointments by choosing Options from
the Actions menu. Choose from New Appointment, New All-Day Event, New Meeting
Request, New Recurring Appointment, or New Recurring Meeting to start with the
appointment type you want.

Changing an Appointment

When you want to revise details for an appointment you've already entered, you
can do so easily by double-clicking the appointment in any Calendar view. This
opens the Appointment window, showing all the appointment information
you've entered. Click in the field you need to change, make your modifications,
and then click Save And Close to update the appointment.

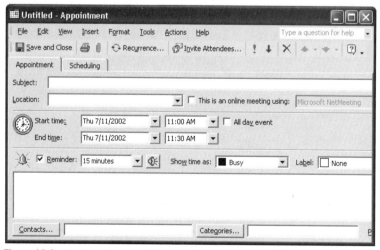

Figure 16-2   The Appointment window enables you to choose the start and end times for your appointment
and add other details as well.

Creating a Recurring Appointment

If you have regularly scheduled appointments (such as the Monday-morning staff meetings or the Thursday-at-noon book club), you can create what Outlook likes to call a "recurrence." To do so, follow these steps:

1 Display the Appointment window. If you're starting a new appointment, click New on the Outlook toolbar; if you're transforming an existing appointment into a recurring appointment, display the appointment by double-clicking it in any Calendar view.

2 Click Recurrence on the Appointment toolbar.

3 In the Appointment Recurrence dialog box, enter a Start Time and an End Time. (You don't need to enter the Duration value; Outlook will figure that out.)

4 In the Recurrence Pattern area, choose whether you want the appointment to repeat Daily, Weekly, Monthly, or Yearly. Depending on what you select (Weekly is selected in Figure 16-3, for example), the options in the right side of the dialog box change to allow you to specify when you want the recurrence to happen.

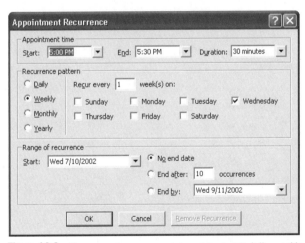

Figure 16-3   You can set up an appointment to repeat daily, weekly, monthly, or yearly.

5 Choose the date you want the recurring appointment to begin. (The current date is selected by default.)

6 Specify when you want the appointment to end. If you're setting an appointment to watch each of Bill Moyers's new PBS shows in a 13-week series, for example, you would click the End After: box and type **13**. If you know a specific date on which these appointments should end, you can enter it in the End By: box. And, of course, if you want the appointment to continue indefinitely, leave No End Date selected.

7   Click OK to create your recurring appointment. When Outlook displays your message in a Calendar view, a small Recurring symbol appears to the left of the appointment subject, as shown here:

↻ Book club dinner (Charlene's house)

Canceling a Repeating Appointment   If you later decide to cancel the "recurring" aspect of an appointment, you can do so by double-clicking the recurring appointment. Outlook displays a small message box, as shown below, asking whether you want to open only this appointment or the entire series of recurring appointments. Click Open The Series, and then click OK.

In the Appointment window, click Recurrence, and then click the Remove Recurrence button at the bottom of the Appointment Recurrence dialog box. That's all there is to it.

Using Reminders

You've probably already noticed the Reminder check box in the lower portion of the Appointment window. By default, Outlook activates the Reminder feature when you create an appointment (until you turn the feature off in one appointment; and then subsequent appointments appear without Reminder selected). A reminder, in Outlook, simply lets you know a few minutes (or however long you specify) in advance of the appointment that you've got something to do. A reminder works like this:

When Outlook sees that it's time to remind you about something, a chime plays (you can customize this feature, by the way—you'll learn how in the next section) and the Reminder dialog box appears (as shown in Figure 16-4). You then have the following choices:

■   Click Dismiss All to cancel all reminders on the current day.

■   Click Open Item to display the appointment for editing or review.

■   Click Dismiss to cancel the reminder on this item only.

■   Click Snooze to reset the reminder to ring again in the period of time you specify.

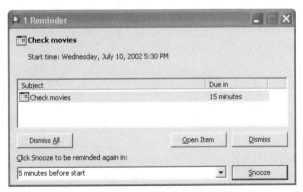

Figure 16-4   The Reminder window pops up when it's almost time for a task or appointment you've scheduled.

Modifying Reminders

You can customize when and how the Reminder lets you know what's coming. To change the amount of time, click the down arrow and choose a new time interval (from 0 minutes to two weeks) to let Outlook know how much forewarning you want.

If you want Outlook to play a different reminder sound, click the Reminder Sound button (which is labeled with a megaphone symbol) to the right of the time text box. The Reminder Sound dialog box appears, as shown below.

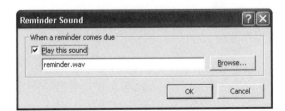

Click the Browse button to navigate to other sound files. If you want to disable the sound altogether, click the Play This Sound check box to clear it. After you select the new sound, click OK.

Tip   Any sound you've saved with a .wav extension (including ones you've recorded yourself) can be used as a Reminder Sound.

Scheduling with Outlook

In addition to setting up appointments and events that affect your work and personal time, you can use Outlook to set up and schedule a meeting, invite participants, and reserve meeting rooms. While you're doing this, you can block out your time so that you can easily see when you're busy, when you're out of the office, and when you have free time. Once you set up your schedule in this way, you can allow others to see the information as well, so they can make informed decisions about when to schedule their own meetings, if they want you to attend.

Planning a Meeting and Inviting Attendees

What if you held a meeting and nobody came? Hey, it happens to the best of us. (In my case, I scheduled an informal meeting at Starbucks and then went to the wrong one. Oh well.) When you want to schedule a meeting that you'll be sure people will attend, you can use Outlook's scheduling features to help you. Here's how it works:

1   Click the Calendar shortcut on the Outlook Shortcuts bar.

2   Choose Plan A Meeting on the Actions menu.

3   Click Add Others in the Plan A Meeting dialog box.

4   Choose Add from the Address Book, and then go through the names, clicking the ones you want. Then click one of the following buttons:

- Required adds the name to the top group. These are the people who must attend in order to you to have the meeting.

- Optional puts the names in the middle group. You care about whether these people come, but if they can't make it, it's no big deal. You'll have the meeting anyway.

- Resources isn't a category for humans—it's for conference rooms and overheads. Okay, I admit that doesn't seem to make much sense. But before you can reserve resources using this category in Outlook, the item must have its own mailbox for reservations. If this is a bit too techie for you, check with your network administrator for the hows and whys about scheduling resources electronically.

5   Click OK. The names are added to the All Attendees list in the Plan A Meeting dialog box (as shown in Figure 16-5).

Note   The first time you use this feature, the Microsoft Office Internet Free/Busy dialog box appears, asking whether you'd like to join the Microsoft Office Internet Free/Busy Service. This is a service that publishes your free times and busy times to the Internet so that people who can't view your calendar can see when you are available. This is a protected service so that only those people who are members of the service, and who have your explicit permission, can view your calendar information. If you want to try the service, click Join; otherwise, click Cancel.

---

6   Enter the start and end times for the meeting.

7 Click the Make Meeting button. In the Meeting dialog box, type the Subject for the meeting and enter the location. In the message box, type a note to participants explaining the meeting, if you like.

8 Click Send. Outlook sends the message as an invitation to the people you selected, enabling them to check their calendars and respond to the invitation.

Attendees to be invited will appear here.

Planned meeting time

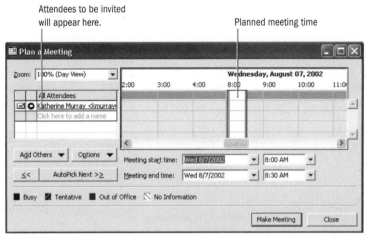

Figure 16-5 After you select attendees using the Add Others button, they appear in the All Attendees list.

Tip Don't forget to invite yourself if you want to see what the invitations look like (and gauge when they arrive in your attendees' e-mailboxes).

Setting Your Schedule Are you wondering how to tell Outlook to display time as free time, busy time, or out-of-office time? The Show Time As option in the Appointment or Message windows is the key. In either dialog box, enter the other items as normal, and then click the Show Time As down arrow, as shown below:

Click Free if you want the time you selected in the start and end times to be shown as available time. Choose Tentative if you've sent out invitations for another meeting during that time or have an appointment pending. Select Busy if you're already scheduled for that time; or click Out Of Office if you plan to go swimming with the kids that afternoon.

Holding an Online Meeting

In today's world, you may be as likely to have teleconferences or cyberspace meetings as you are to have real, face-to-face meetings. Outlook provides a feature that helps you schedule online meetings, using NetMeeting or another conferencing utility and an online meeting space. To schedule an online meeting, follow these steps:

1   Click the time in your daily calendar when you'd like to schedule the meeting.

2   Click the New down arrow on the Outlook toolbar and choose Meeting Request. (You also can press Ctrl+Shift+Q if you prefer.)

3   In the Meeting dialog box, enter the people you'd like to invite in the To line. (If necessary, click the To button to select the names, and then click OK to return to the Message window.)

4   Enter a Subject for the meeting.

5   Click the check box to the left of This Is An Online Meeting. The dialog box changes to display additional options, as shown in Figure 16-6.

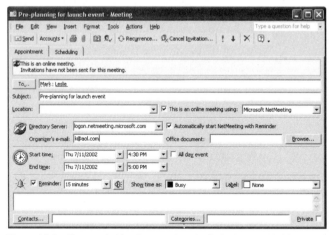

Figure 16-6   You can hold online meetings in Outlook using NetMeeting or another online conferencing service.

6   If you plan to use a conferencing service other than NetMeeting, click the drop-down arrow to see what other services you have available, then click the one you plan to use.

7   A default Directory Server name appears. This is the place online where you can "gather" with the other meeting participants. If you have a dedicated server used for this purpose in your organization, enter the address here.

8 As the meeting's planner, your e-mail address will be entered automatically. If you want to change this to another contact person, click in the box and type the new e-mail address.

9 If you want NetMeeting to start automatically whenever Outlook reminds you of the meeting, click the Automatically Start NetMeeting With Reminder check box.

10 Set the other options as usual, entering the start and end times and customizing the Reminder if you choose.

11 Click Send to send the meeting invitation to the people you want to attend.

Note If you are scheduling a meeting and inviting attendees who work in another time zone, their calendars are automatically adjusted for the time change, which means you won't have to recalculate their free times. Saves you trouble. Nice.

Tip When you set up an event (which is an appointment that lasts 24 hours or longer, such as a convention, a workshop, or a business trip), the appointment appears as a banner rather than as a block of time on your schedule.

Printing Your Calendar

Having all your appointments, events, tasks, and meetings on your desktop is a great convenience, but there will be times when you're away from your desk and out of reach of a laptop and you'll need a reminder to advise you of what's coming next. You can print your Outlook Calendar in several different styles:

- Daily Style prints a listing of all scheduled appointments in a day's time.

- Weekly Style prints the entire week in a two-column format.

- Monthly Style prints the calendar in traditional monthly format.

- Tri-fold Style displays a three-column format with the daily calendar on the left, the Tasks list in the center, and the weekly calendar on the right.

- Calendar Detail prints only the items you have scheduled for the current day.

To print your calendar, click Print on the Outlook toolbar. In the Print dialog box, select the printer you want to use, then click the Print Style that fits the look you want. Specify a Start date and an End date for the calendar entries you want to print and enter the Number Of Copies you need. Finally, click Preview to see how the calendar will look before you print it. If everything looks good, click Print in the Preview window to display the Print dialog box a second time and click OK to begin printing.

As you can see, Outlook contains many features that help you keep your wits about you when it seems that the whole world is knocking at your office door, wanting a moment of your time. If you use Outlook's e-mail, organizing, and scheduling features regularly, you'll find that you spend less time in panic mode, trying to remember to whom you promised you'd do what, and more time working faster and smarter with Office XP.

Key Points

■   You use Outlook's Calendar to schedule your appointments, events, and meetings.

■   Calendar gives you four views for your appointments: Day, Work Week, Week, and Month.

■   Any tasks that you've added are displayed in the Day view.

■   You set new appointments by clicking New on the Outlook toolbar, entering a Subject and Location, and scheduling a start and end time.

■   Outlook allows you to create recurring meetings of any frequency you choose—weekly, biweekly, monthly, or annually.

■   You can use Reminders to let you know when a meeting or appointment is approaching. The Reminder plays a chime and displays a dialog box to alert you.

■   Outlook uses a schedule to keep track of your time. You can create individual and group schedules to coordinate collaborative work.

■   You can hold online meetings in Outlook, using NetMeeting or another online conferencing utility.

Part VI

Managing Data with Microsoft Access

How many times have you heard that we live in the "Information Age"? We don't have to look far to be convinced. Everything seems to be about lists and data and donors and inventory. We have mountains of data to store—data about ourselves, our clients, our pets, our projects, our *stuff*. How will we store it? How will we make sense of it? And how will we retrieve it when we need it? Microsoft Access is all about answering those questions, whether you need a complex programmable database that drives the ordering and fulfillment system for your online enterprise or whether you need a simple database that records the inoculation records of your new litter of Newfoundland pups.

In this part of the book, you'll learn how to create a simple database, retrieve information from it, and print a report based on the results you find. Chapter 17, "Getting Started with Databases," provides the foundation for the rest of your work with Access by showing you how to create and save a new database, and enter data. Chapter 18, "Working with Your Data," focuses on what you're likely to do with the data once you've entered it into Access—sort, organize, and display the data you want to see. By the time you get to Chapter 19, "Preparing and Printing Reports in Microsoft Access," you'll be ready to find ways to produce reports that can be printed, saved to a file, or published on the Web.

Chapter 17

Getting Started with Databases

The word *database* is one of those intimidating, techno-speak words that seem to suggest that you'd need a lab coat, a pocket protector, and a computer science degree to understand its meaning. Not so. A base of data is simply a collection of information, organized around a specific topic. That list of your top 10 favorite tennis shoes is a form of database. The donor list of the American Red Cross is also a database. The parts inventory at your local car repair shop, the names and addresses in your Rolodex, even the pile of bills sitting on your kitchen counter—are all forms of databases, collections of information related to a specific topic.

This chapter will help you get comfortable with the necessary practicalities of databases and show you how to create your first simple database in Microsoft Access.

Note   Note that if you are using Microsoft Office XP Standard Edition, Access is not included as part of your suite. Access is included with the Professional and Developer editions of Office XP.

What Can You Do with Access?

Let's start with the issue of function. What are *you* most likely to do with Access? There is an incredibly wide range of possibilities here. For example, you could use Access at home to do any of the following:

■ Create an inventory of your CD collection, complete with album title, artist name, song or track selections, and song or track durations or timings.

■ Organize all your monthly bills, citing the creditor, due date, amount, and balance.

■ Create a household inventory (nice for the insurance company to have) that lists individual items, tells what room they are in, estimates their value, and gives their quantity.

■ Finally put the names, birthdays, ages, and anniversaries for all your relatives in one place.

■ Create a list of all the books and videotaped movies you lend to friends (and never get back). You would track the item name, the type (book or movie), and the name, address, e-mail address, and phone number of the "borrower."

The larger use of Access, of course, is found in the workplace. Here are just a few ways someone might use Access at work:

■ Develop a sales inventory database that interacts with point-of-sale software, updating inventory levels automatically at the close of each business day.

■ Create a database for patient accounts in your optometrist's office that stores individual patient records, includes examination results, tracks office visits and prescription changes, and prints out a reminder card automatically one month before each patient's yearly checkup.

■ Design a "back end" for a Web application in which users take an online survey and answer questions about your company's product. The results are saved in an Access database and can be used in further analyses and reports.

■ Add a personnel database to your system that keeps track of each employee's start date, semiannual reviews, performance, payroll, bonuses, commendations, and vacation time.

> **Note**   As you begin to work with Access, you'll no doubt discover ways in which you can put the
> program to work for simple and not-so-simple data management uses. Once you discover how
> easy it is to create and work with data tables in Access, you won't have an excuse *not* to organize
> your data better.

A Walk Around the Access Window

Ready to get started? Let's begin with a tour. Start Access by clicking the Start
menu, choosing All Programs, and then selecting Microsoft Access. After a
moment, the Access window appears on your screen (as shown in Figure 17-1).

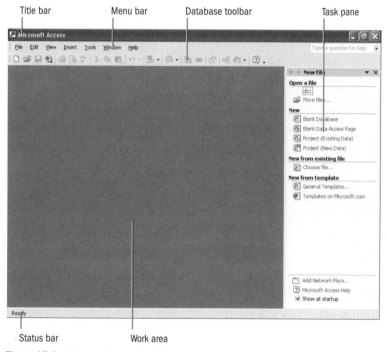

Figure 17-1   The Access window includes the tools and menus for creating, working with, and building
relationships among data tables.

Access Menus

You're probably not surprised to see that Access has the familiar menus you've
found in other Office XP applications. The File menu provides the means to open,
save, print, and preview databases. You also can export database information and
preview the database as a Web page. On the Edit menu, you'll find commands for
copying, cutting, and pasting data cells, columns, and rows, as well as for undoing
changes, creating groups, and working with the Office Clipboard.

The View menu enables you to look at your database in different ways, a feature that's particularly helpful when you work with large amounts of data. For example, you might want to display only the forms attached to a particular database, or switch from Datasheet view to Design view. (More detail about each of these items will be given later in this chapter.)

The Tools menu contains the tools you need to work with the data within your database. Whether you want to check spelling, establish a relationship between two databases, beef up your security measures, replicate your database, or work with a team online, you'll find the appropriate commands in the Tools menu.

The last two menus in Access, Window and Help, are similar to those menus in other Office applications. Window includes commands for arranging your data windows on the screen; in addition, you can choose to hide or "unhide" data windows. The Help menu offers you the familiar means of assistance and provides one extra important selection: Sample Databases. If you don't have a database to work with as we go through these next chapters, you may want to choose Sample Databases from the Tools menu and choose Northwind Sample Data so you can follow along.

Access Toolbars

The *Database toolbar* stretches left to right just below the menu bar. The toolbar contains a wide variety of tools, each of which has a comparable command in one of the Access menus. Figure 17-2 shows all the important tools on the Database toolbar.

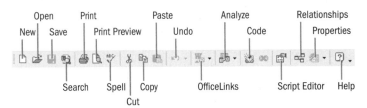

Figure 17-2   You can select tools for the most common Access operations from the Database toolbar.

> **Note**   If you have previously opened a database table in Access, you might also see the Formatting toolbar, which appears beneath the Database toolbar. Access also features a Web toolbar that looks just like the Web toolbars in the other Office applications.

Database Window

You will do all your work with data in Access in the Access database window. When you start Access, there is no database window displayed on the screen.

After you open a database, however, a window such as the one shown in Figure 17-3 appears.

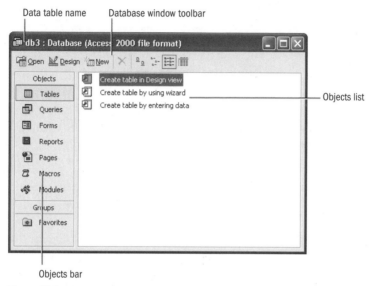

Figure 17-3   The database window is where you'll choose the Access elements you want to work with.

Database Basics

So let's bring Access into the picture and apply it to the databases I mentioned at the outset of this chapter. Suppose that you want to create a database that tracks information about the new litter of Newfoundland puppies you have.

There is an array of information items to capture about each pup, including birth weight, sex, dam, and sire. As time goes on, you will add weight data to track how quickly the pups are growing. You might add fields categorizing the individual characteristics—this pup has a white star on her chest; that pup is the leader of the group; another pup is the wallflower, and so on. You'll also record the amount of food the pups are eating, veterinary check-ups and shots, and any comments or additional bits of data you want to keep with each puppy's data. You'll enter the individual items you want to record—weight, sex, food, and so on—within *fields* in the data table. A collection of information about one pup is known as that pup's *record*. And the entire collection of data—all the pup records together—comprises the *database*.

Tip   You can add pictures, video, and sound to your database tables as well as text and numbers. This means you can put a photograph of each Newfoundland puppy on the record to help identify the pup later—and even add a sound clip of his bark if you choose. (Okay, okay, maybe I'm taking this example a bit far. Forget the bark.)

Once you have entered all the data, you might create a relationship between this database of puppies and your database of potential pup buyers. In the "potential buyer" database, you'd have the names, addresses, location, and desires of each prospective owner. This owner wants an all-black Newfie, so the pup with the white star is out. But this one wants a female with a laid-back temperament. By creating relationships and then querying the database (asking the database to display records with the characteristics you specify), you can match buyers with puppies and print a report.

> **Note**   Of course, a database doesn't have to be anything more complicated than a simple list of items, perhaps the names of your relatives and their birth dates. This example just shows you how the different features of Access can be used together to get the most use from the data you've already got (which helps you work faster *and* smarter).

Starting a New Database

When you're ready to start a new database, you have two options. You can use the Access Database Wizard to walk you through the process, or you can do it yourself from scratch by creating a new data table.

Help Me, Mr. Wizard!

The first time you create a database, it's a good idea to use the wizard and see how Access does it. You begin by choosing a template of the style you want, and then the automated wizard leads you through everything you need to know—all you do is answer the questions and select the options you want to use. Here's the process:

1   Start Access and choose New from the File menu.

2   Click General Templates in the task pane.

3   In the Templates dialog box, click the Databases tab.

4   Select the type of database you want to create and click OK. (For this example, something simple like Contact Management works well.)

5   In the File New Database dialog box, navigate to the folder where you want to store the file and enter a file name. Click OK. The Database Wizard starts and tells you what the type of database you selected will be used to do. Click Next.

6   The wizard shows you what tables will be created in your database and, in the right panel, lists the fields included for the selected table. (To see the fields for other tables, click the name of the table you want

to see.) Scroll down through the field list and clear the check boxes of any fields that you *don't* want to include and click the blank check boxes of fields that you *do* want to include. When you're finished specifying fields for your tables, click Next.

7   Choose how you want the data form to look on the screen. Click the different styles and watch the preview window to find one you like. When you've selected the style you want, click Next.

8   The next choice involves how you want your printed reports to look. Again, scroll through the list and when you find one you like, and then click Next.

9   Enter a name for the database.

10 If you want to include a picture on the records (for example, if you have a business logo, a special symbol, or yes, a puppy picture you like to include), click the Yes, I'd Like To Include A Picture check box. Navigate to the folder containing the picture you want to use, select it, and click OK to return to the Database Wizard.

11 Click Finish to complete the wizard and create the new database.

Access displays a status window as it goes through and creates all the elements and tables for the new database. After a moment, the Main Switchboard appears in your Access work area (as shown in Figure 17-4). This is the menu you'll use to add, view, update, and print the data in the new database.

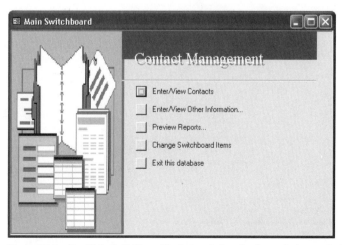

Figure 17-4   The Main Switchboard includes choices for the main Access tasks you're likely to perform.

> **Tip**   The Main Switchboard is available only if you have used the Database Wizard to create a database. It's a great way to put a friendly face on what can be complicated databases, especially if other people will be adding information to the database you've created. You can customize the Switchboard if you choose by selecting Change Switchboard Items.

Create a New Database from Scratch

If you're one of those people who'd rather do things yourself ("Wizards are for sissies," you say?), you can create a database with a few simple clicks of the mouse. The process isn't difficult, but what you miss is the create-it-all-at-once technique that the wizard offers. You also won't have the same look and feel for your data-entry form and your reports, but that's no big deal. You can learn those things as you go. (And besides, you'll learn how to create, format, and print reports in Chapter 19, "Preparing and Printing Reports in Microsoft Access.")

Here are the steps for creating a database from scratch:

1   Start Access and choose New from the File menu.

2   Click Blank Database in the New area of the task pane.

3   In the File New Database window, navigate to a folder in which you want to store the database file and enter a name for the file, and then click Create. The new database is created (in this case, the database for Newfie pups), and displayed in a database window with the file name you specified, as shown in Figure 17-5.

Figure 17-5   The new database file is created and displayed as a data table in your Access work area.

Creating Tables and Fields

If you created your database from scratch, you need to set up the tables and the fields you want to use in your database. (For the moment, all you have is a created database file.) The tables collect the records related to a specific item (for example, you might have a "puppies" table and a "potential buyers" table). Fields store the individual data items that comprise each record—for example, name, address, city, state, product name, and so on. You'll use a different wizard to help automate the process of creating the tables and fields for your new database file. Here are the steps:

1 Open your database (if necessary) by choosing Open from the File menu and clicking the new database name in the task pane. The database window opens in the Access work area.

2 Double-click Create Table By Using Wizard. The Table Wizard appears, as shown in Figure 17-6.

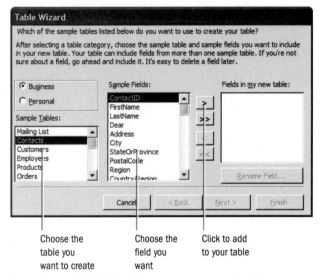

Choose the table you want to create

Choose the field you want

Click to add to your table

Figure 17-6 The Table Wizard prompts you to choose the fields you want to include in the new table.

3 In the Sample Tables list, click the table type you want to create. The Sample Fields list in the center of the dialog box changes to show the fields typically used in that table.

4 Click a field you want and click the Add button to add it to your table. If you want to add all the fields in the Sample Fields list, click Add All.

Tip   If you plan to use the majority of the fields, a quick way of adding the fields you want is to click Add All, and then, in the list showing your database fields, click the individual fields you *don't* want, and then click Remove to put them back in the Sample Fields list.

---

5   If you want to change the names of any field you add to your form, click the field you want to change, and then click Rename Field. In the Rename Field dialog box, type the new name and then click OK.

6   Enter a name for the table and leave the primary key option set the way it is. (The primary key is the field by which Access first sorts your data. For example, Customer ID would be a good candidate for a primary key because it uniquely identifies each customer record. For most purposes, you can let Access set this for you.) Then click Next.

7   Choose whether you want to modify the table, enter data, or have the wizard create a form in which you can enter data. We'll create a form later in this chapter, so leave the middle option selected and then click Finish to create the table. The table appears, showing the fields you added, in Datasheet view, ready for you to add data (as shown in Figure 17-7).

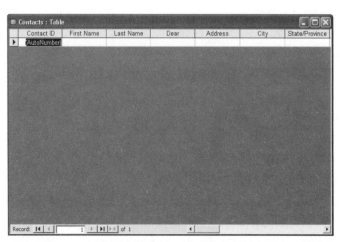

Figure 17-7   The Table Wizard creates the table and displays it in Datasheet view, with your field names as column headings and the first row selected, ready to receive the data you enter.

Tip   Oh, no! Forgot a field you need? You can add it easily by clicking the column label to the right of the column you want to add. Choose Column from the Insert menu and Access adds a new column with the label Field1. Double-click the field name to select it; then type a name for that field, and press Enter.

More Than One Way to Create a Table The database window offers you two additional ways to create a table in your database. You can use Design view to create the table and add fields, or you can simply create the table by entering data. When you choose Create Table In Design View, Design view is displayed so that you add the field name, type, and a description for each field you create. Your field names can include as many as 64 characters, and you can choose a field type, which refers to the type of data that is to be stored in the field, by clicking in the Data Type column and clicking the down arrow that appears. Simply click the data type you want to assign to the field. (You can choose from Text, Memo, Number, Date/Time, Currency, AutoNumber, Yes/No, OLE Object, HyperLink, or Lookup Wizard.)

If you choose Create Table By Entering Data, Access creates the table, names it Table1, and displays a spreadsheet-like grid in which you want to enter data. Change the field names by double-clicking the Field1, Field2 and similar labels, and type the name you want: **Name**, **Address**, and so on. You can then enter the information directly into the table, pressing Tab to move from field to field.

Adding Data

Now that you've created the database, you're ready to add information to it. In database parlance, this is known as "populating" the fields. Depending on how you created your database, you can use one of two methods to fill it with data:

- If you used the Access Database Wizard to create the database, you can use the Main Switchboard to enter data. This displays the data in a pre-designed form that makes it easy for you to add data.

- If you created the table from scratch, you can enter data in Datasheet view. You also can create your own form in place of the Datasheet (but I'll save that discussion for the section entitled "Creating a New Form," later in this chapter).

Entering Data with the Switchboard

If the Main Switchboard is available (meaning that you used the wizard to create the database), click Enter/View Contacts and a data form appears on your screen (as shown in Figure 17-8).

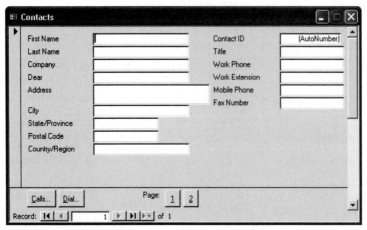

Figure 17-8   You add data in a simple form the Table Wizard creates for you.

Enter the information for each record by following these steps:

1   Click in the fields where you want to add information.

2   Type the data.

3   Press Tab to move to the next field (or click another field).

4   Click Page 2 to display additional fields.

5   When you're ready to move to the next record, click Next Record to display the next blank form.

Navigating Forms   There's a collection of buttons at the bottom of the Switchboard data entry form that you'll use to move among the records in your database and add records. This is what the different buttons do:

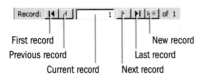

You can use the buttons to move to different records within the data table after you've entered your data; but you can also click in the Current Record box and type the number of the record if you know it.

Entering Data in the Datasheet

If you use the Tables Wizard to create the table in your database or you choose the Create A Table By Entering Data option, the resulting table is automatically displayed in Datasheet view (as previously shown in Figure 17-7). There are two details about working in Datasheet view you need to remember:

■ Each column is a unique field in the table. Column names might include Name, Address, Product ID, Customer Number, Social Security Number, or ZIP Code.

■ Each row in the Datasheet is a unique record in the table. A record is a collection of fields related to one specific person, item, or product. In a Customer table, for example, each customer has his or her own record, and individual data fields (or columns) store the data for Name, Address, and so on.

Tip   Even if you are using the Main Switchboard, you can enter data in Datasheet view. To do that, close the Switchboard by clicking the Close box; then open the database window (which is mini-mized in the lower-left corner of the Access window) by clicking the Restore button. In the database window, click Tables and then double-click the name of the table to which you want to add data. The table will open in Datasheet view and you can type the data items and press Tab after each one.

To enter data in the datasheet, simply type the information and press Tab or Enter. The cursor moves to the next cell, until you get to the last field in the record (row); then the cursor moves to the first field in the next record.

Importing Data   You don't have to type all your data into the database; you also can import files you've already created. When you want to add data from another program into Access, use the Get External Data option on the File menu to do the job. Before you import a file, however, be sure that both files have the same fields and data types; otherwise, some of your data can be lost. To import data into an Access database, follow these steps:

1   Open the database window for the database to which you want to add data.

2   Choose Get External Data from the File menu and then choose Import.

3   In the Files Of Type box in the Import dialog box, select the program used to create the data.

4   Navigate to the folder containing the file you want to import and select it.

5   Click Import. The Import Wizard steps in to help you import your data into Access. Answer the questions on the screen, and then click Next when prompted. When you click Finish, Access lets you know that the table was imported or linked successfully. Click OK to return to the database.

Working with Forms

Many people find it easier (and friendlier) to work with forms over the datasheet. You can easily create forms that you or others can use with your Access data tables. And once you create the form, adding data is simply a matter of clicking and typing.

Creating a Form

To create a form, follow these steps:

1   Open the database you want to use.

2   In the database window, click Forms.

3   Choose Create Form By Using Wizard. The Form Wizard steps in to help you create a data entry form for your database (as shown in Figure 17-9).

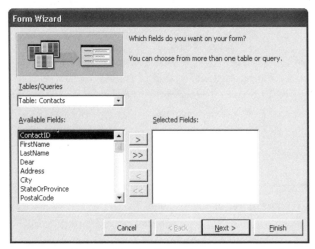

Figure 17-9   The Form Wizard walks you through the process of creating a data entry form for your data table.

Tip   You also can choose Create Form In Design View if you want to create a customized form on which you control where the fields and labels appears. This technique is a bit too advanced for our purposes here (*fast* and *smart*, remember?), but feel free to experiment on your own.

---

4   Click the fields in the Available Fields list that you want to add to your form, and then click Add after each one. The fields are added to your Selected Fields list.

5 When you're finished choosing fields, click Next. The Form Wizard asks you to choose a layout for the form you're creating. Select different options until you find the one you want, and then click Next.

6 Choose the form style you like by scrolling through the list and selecting the one you want. Click Next.

7 Add a title for the form. You can choose to open the form after you create it or modify it. If you want to display a help window with information on working with forms, click the check box at the bottom of the Form Wizard window.

8 Click Finish to create the form.

Tip   If you choose to modify the form after you click Finish, the form is displayed in Design view. You can then change the look, color, alignment, and format of the labels and fields using tools on the Formatting toolbar and the options available when you right-click the elements in the form.

Using a Form

When you are ready to add data by using the form you just created, display the database window and click Forms. Your new form appears in the right side of the database window. Add data to your data table using the form by following these steps:

1 Double-click the form name to open the form.

2 Click Last Record to move to the last record in the data table (if you've already entered data).

3 Click New Record to display a blank form.

4 Type the data in the fields, pressing Tab after each entry. At the end of the form, Access displays another blank form so that you can continue entering data.

5 When you're finished adding data, click the form's Close box. Access saves your data automatically and closes the form.

Saving a Database

Once you enter a database name and save the database file in the File New Database window, Access takes care of saving your information for you automatically. Each time you add data to a form, Access saves the information and updates the data table. Whenever you close a datasheet view, Access asks whether you want to save what you've done. This is a nice feature, which saves you from entering an hour's worth of data and then forgetting to save the file before you exit. All programs should be this thoughtful.

You can save Access data tables in other formats, however, so that you can use them with other things. Here are two options:

■ You can choose Save As on the File menu to save a database as a data access page (a Web page that also has a connection to a database).

■ You can select Export from the File menu to save the database in other popular formats, including XML documents, Microsoft Active Server Pages, HTML, Rich Text Format, and Microsoft Excel.

For now, however, let's keep Access in Access and move on to the fun part—juggling all this interesting data you've collected.

Key Points

■ Microsoft Access is a database program that enables you to collect, store, organize, use, and report on the data you collect.

■ Access gives you two methods for creating a database: You can use the Access Database Wizard or do it from scratch.

■ The database window contains the tables, forms, queries, reports, and other elements you'll work with in Access.

■ The Access Database Wizard suggests tables, fields, formats, and styles you can use for your data tables, forms, and reports.

■ When you create a database from scratch, you create only the database file; you'll need to add your own table, fields, forms, and reports.

■ When you create a database using the Access Database Wizard, the Main Switchboard enables you to enter, update, and report on data from a central menu.

■ Entering data in Datasheet view or in a data-entry form is a simple matter of typing the data and pressing Tab.

■ You can create a new table using the Table Wizard and a new form using the Form Wizard.

■ You customize a table or a form, arranging the layout and look of fields, by using Design view.

Chapter 18

Working with Your Data

So now that you're comfortable with the idea and practice of creating databases (you *are* comfortable, aren't you?), let's move on to what you'll actually do with the information you store. Although databases make great data receptacles, their primary benefit is that they enable you to work with the data you've saved to see data trends, sales results, and future projects in new and enlightening ways. By sorting your data in a certain way, you'll be able to tell whether you sell more on the West coast or the East coast, for example, thereby helping you decide where to spend your advertising dollars. By searching for your top salespeople in the Northeast region, you can easily see who you need to take to dinner on your next trip north. And when you need to do damage control and orchestrate a recall—who purchased Model 2332 in Maine between July 15 and September 15 of last year?—you can use a query in Microsoft Access to find that information almost as quickly as you can type.

See Also   Once you display the data you want to see, you might want to print the information in a report. See Chapter 19, "Preparing and Printing Reports in Microsoft Access," to find out how.

Try This!   In Chapter 17, "Getting Started with Databases," you learned to enter the information in your database. Before we move on to searching, sorting, and querying the database, let's consider how to correct outdated or incorrect entries. If you find that some data needs to be changed, you can make the changes by following these steps:

1   Open the database you want to edit.

2   In the database window, double-click the name of the table with the data you want to change.

3   In the datasheet, click the cell containing the data you need to change and type the new data.

   That's all there is to it.

Sorting Data Records

One of the simplest operations you'll perform with your Access data involves sorting it. You can sort data by using either the datasheet or the data-entry form for a particular table. To sort records, follow these steps:

1   Open the database you want to use.

2   In the database window, double-click the data table or form you want to sort.

3   Click in the field that will be the organizing point for arranging your records. (For example, if you want to sort the records alphabetically by company name, click in the Company field. If you want the records sorted by customers' last names, click in the Lastname field.

4   Click Sort Ascending or Sort Descending in the Standard toolbar. If you clicked Sort Ascending, the records are arranged from A to Z. If you click Sort Descending, the records appear arranged from Z to A.

Note   If you prefer to use the menus, you can choose Sort from the Records menu and then choose Sort Ascending or Sort Descending from the submenu.

Searching for Data

Depending on what you want to do with the information you find, you can use a couple of techniques for searching for data. The first technique helps you find a record you want. You might choose to search for a customer's address, for example, or update a product code in your Products table. The second method involves searching for groups of records by applying a filter that eliminates those records that are irrelevant. This section introduces you to both procedures.

Finding Specific Data

When you want to move to a specific record in your database, you first need to know what you're looking for. Are you looking for the record of a customer with the last name of Davis? That's enough to do a search. Here are the steps:

1 Display the data table or form you want to search.

2 Click in the field you want to search.

3 Choose Find from the Edit menu or press Ctrl+F. The Find And Replace dialog box appears (as shown in Figure 18-1). Notice that the selected field appears in the Look In box.

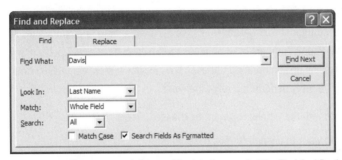

Figure 18-1 You can search for specific data items using the Find And Replace dialog box.

Tip If you are uncertain where the data you need to change is stored, you can have Access search the entire database by clicking the Look In down arrow and choosing the name of the table.

---

4 In the Find What box, type the word, phrase, or characters you want to find.

5 Click the Match down arrow and choose whether you want Access to look for the information you typed in any part of the field, as the whole field (meaning that Access will display only records that show exactly what you typed in the field you selected), or as the beginning of the field entry.

6 In the Search list, choose whether you want Access to search Down through the database from the current selection, Up to the beginning of the database, or All the way through the entire database.

7 If you want Access to search for the capitalization you entered in the Find What box, click the Match Case check box.

Tip   The Search Fields As Formatted check box enables you to search for data as it is displayed, instead of how it is stored. This means, for example, that although a value might be stored as 2345, you can search for $2,345 if that's the way the information appears. This search feature can add extra time while you're waiting for results, however, so if you want your data fast, leave this box unchecked.

---

8   Click Find Next. If you are using a form, Access displays the next form with the information you're looking for. If you are using datasheet view, Access highlights the field entry that matches your criteria.

...And Don't Forget Replace   The Replace feature comes in handy for times when you need to make a change throughout your database. For some reason, here in Indiana, they keep changing our area codes. Phone numbers in some areas that used to have a 317 prefix now have a 765 prefix. Talk about messing up someone's database! Now all your entries for Madison County are wrong. How will you fix it? Simply perform the following steps:

1   Open the data table with the entries you want to change.

2   Click in the field you want to change (in this case, Phone).

3   Press Ctrl+H (or choose Replace from the Edit menu).

4   In the Find What box, type the data you want to find (in this case, 317).

5   In the Replace With box, type the information you want to insert (in this case, 765).

6   Set the Match and Search options and then click Replace to replace the next occurrence of the data or click Replace All to search the entire database and change all occurrences within the data table.

Applying Filters

A filter is a bit like a water purifier—it strains out all the elements you don't want. When you apply a filter to your data table, you tell Access to display only the data records that match what you're looking for. Here's the process:

1   Display the table or form to which you want to apply the filter.

2   Choose Filter from the Records menu and then choose one of the following:

   ● Filter By Form displays a form in which you can enter your filter conditions.

   ● Filter By Selection allows you to choose the filter by clicking existing data in the record.

- Filter Excluding Selection eliminates the selected data and displays everything else.

- Advanced Filter/Sort displays a window in which you can construct a more detailed filter for your database.

3 For this example, select Filter By Form. A blank form appears (if you're viewing the datasheet, a blank table with one row appears).

4 Click in the field you want to use as a filter; then click the drop-down arrow that appears and select your choice from the list. Figure 18-2 shows a Sales Manager filter applied to the Contact Title field.

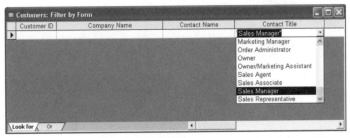

Figure 18-2   When you choose Filter By Form, you use a blank form or datasheet row to choose the data by which you want to filter your records.

5 Select any additional fields you'd like to use as part of the filter.

6 Click Apply Filter in the toolbar. Only the records that pass muster with your filter are displayed.

Tip   Use Remove Filter/Sort from the Records menu (or click the Remove Filter tool on the toolbar) when you want to return the table or form to its full record display. If you want to use the filter again, you can choose Apply Filter/Sort from the Records menu (or click Apply Filter in the toolbar) to reapply the most recently used filter.

Creating and Using Queries

The word "query" is one of those fancy-sounding words for something really simple. A query is a question. When you query an Access database, you ask it a question, such as:

- How many salespeople in Oregon sold more than 1,200 books last March?

- Which of our regional offices works the longest hours?

- How many students took advantage of our online courses last semester? And which classes were most popular?

You might think answering these types of questions would take hours of fact-digging. In fact, they can be answered in less than a minute in Access, if you've set up your fields correctly and know how to use queries. This section introduces you to this amazing feature.

Composing a Query

Your first task in creating a query that delivers the results you want is to tell Access what you want to find. Start that process by pressing F11 to display the database window of the database you want to query (as shown in Figure 18-3).

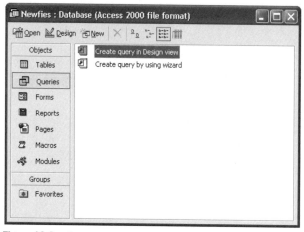

Figure 18-3   Start a query in the Database window.

Here are the steps for creating your first query:

1   Click Queries.

2   Double-click Create Query By Using Wizard. The Simple Query Wizard appears.

3   In the Tables/Queries box, choose the name of the table you want to use.

4   Click the field (or fields) from the Available Fields list that you want to add to the Selected Fields list (these are the fields you will use in the query). Click the Add button to add each field. Click Next.

5   Add a title for your query. Leave the other settings as they are. Click Finish. Click the Close box of the query window that appears.

Applying a Query

Now that you've created the query, you need to apply it to your database. Because you assigned the query a name, you can use that query on this table or other tables at any time by selecting it from the Queries list in the database window. To apply a query to a table, follow these steps:

1 Display the database window for the database you want to query.

2 Click Queries in the left panel.

3 Double-click the query name from the list on the right. The information appears in the Query results window, showing you the latest query results based on the data in the data table as it currently stands.

> **Tip** Queries are very helpful when you need to know similar things periodically, such as who took the greatest number of vacation days last month or which employees are due for rate increases. Once you create a query and name it, that query is available in the database window and you can select it to apply it on your database monthly, weekly, and so on, to get the most up-to-date picture your data can present.

Modifying a Query

If you want to change a query you've created, you can simply edit the selections you've made. You do this using Design view. Here's how:

1 Display the database window for the database you want to use.

2 Click Queries in the left panel.

3 Double-click the query you want to use. The query opens in the query results window as usual.

4 Click Design View on the far left side of the Standard toolbar. The query appears in Design View (as shown in Figure 18-4).

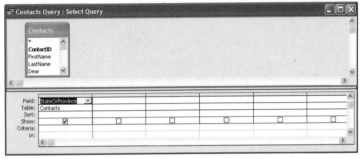

Figure 18-4   To modify a query, display it in Design View and change your selections.

5 To choose a different field, click in the Field entry and a down arrow appears. Click the arrow and select the field you want from the displayed list.

6   If you want to choose a different table, click in the Table entry and, again, choose the table you want from the list that appears when you click the down arrow.

7   Make any other modifications as needed, and then click Run on the toolbar. The modifications are applied to your data and the query is saved in the new form.

Tip   If you want to do away with a query, simply click Queries in the database window, select the query you want to delete, and press Delete. Access will ask you to confirm that you want to delete the query. Click Yes to complete the operation.

More Fun with Queries Queries are really wonderful and can be quite complex, depending on what you want to do with them. Access includes five types of queries:

- A *select query* allows you to select the data you're looking for.

- A *crosstab* (short for cross-tabulation) *query* enables you to perform calculations based on the data values in query results.

- A *make-table query* creates a table with the results of the query.

- An *update query* goes through your database and updates records with new information.

- An *append query* allows you to add information to the selected database.

For more information about working with these more specialized forms of queries, see *Microsoft Access Version 2002 Inside Out* by Helen Feddema, also from Microsoft Press.

Linking Tables

As you create tables and work with your data, you will begin to see ways that you can do even more with your data. By linking tables, you can extend the functionality of your data by joining tables and looking at the data in different ways. This section gives you a glimpse at relationships among tables so that you can explore more thoroughly on your own.

Understanding Relationships

Access allows three kinds of relationships between tables:

- **One-to-one relationship**   This relationship is rarely used because it typically can be handled within a single data table. However, an example of a one-to-one relationship might be when you want to link an employee's attendance record with a bonus schedule. The Employee ID field is the field unique to both tables on which the tables would be linked.

- **One-to-many relationship**   This relationship is the most common data relationship, in which one item in one table can be linked to many items in the second table. An example of a one-to-many relationship would be a link between a Sales Staff table and the Orders database. One salesperson can submit many different orders, but each order can have only one salesperson.

- **Many-to-many relationship**   This type of relationship is for complex data relationships in which each item can be linked to multiple items. Access uses a third table, called a *junction table*, to store the primary and foreign keys (the fields on which the relationships are linked). An example of a many-to-many relationships is a book database in which each book can be sold to multiple customers and be purchased from multiple vendors.

Creating Relationships

To create a link between tables, perform these steps:

1   Close any tables you have open, and display the database window by pressing F11.

2   Click Relationships on the Standard toolbar. If there are no relationships established in your database, the Show Table dialog box appears (as shown in Figure 18-5).

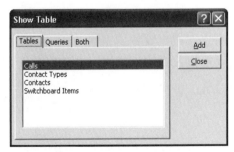

Figure 18-5   Use Show Table to choose the tables you want use to set up relationships.

Note   If you used the Access Database Wizard to create your database, links may already be established between your tables. In this case, the ShowTable dialog box does not appear; instead, the Relationship window opens, showing the tables and the links established between them.

3   In the Show Table dialog box, click the Table, Queries, or Both tabs,
depending on the items you want to include in your relationships.
Select the tables you want to use by clicking each one and clicking
Add. When you're finished adding tables and queries, click Close and
the Relationships window is displayed (as shown in Figure 18-6).

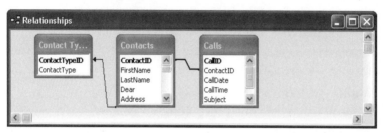

Figure 18-6   The Relationships window shows the tables among which you'll establish
relationships.

4   To create a relationship between tables, drag the field from one table
to the corresponding field in the second table. In the Edit Relationships
dialog box, click Create. The link is made between the tables.

5   Close the Relationships window by clicking the close box. Access asks
whether you want to save the layout of the tables. Click Yes.

As you can see, there is much more to working with data than simply entering it into tables. With Access you can easily sort information, search for specific
data, apply filters, establish relationships, and query the database to find information. Chapter 19, "Preparing and Printing Reports in Microsoft Access," rounds out
your introduction to Access by showing you how to generate reports.

Key Points

■   Access enables you to sort your data easily—A to Z or Z to A—by
clicking the tool you want on the Standard toolbar.

■   When you search for data in Access, you can use Ctrl+F to find a specific item; Ctrl+H to search and replace existing data; or a filter to display a group of records with the items you specify.

■   You can use queries to ask the database to show you something related
to the data stored in the data tables. Access includes a wizard to help
you create a query that will provide the best results to your question.

■   You can link tables to establish relationships among them. This enables
you to perform operations—including sorts, searches, and queries—on
a large table with many linked tables.

Chapter 19

Preparing and Printing Reports in Microsoft Access

Once you have spent your time entering and arranging your data, you'd probably like to see something concrete for your efforts. Microsoft Access enables you to create reports—from simple to complex—that help others understand the important aspects of the data you're gathering. A report can show how well your business is growing—or where you need to cut back. A report can list your best-selling items or shine a light on customer-service problems most likely to cause complaints. With Access, not only can you put your data in a logical, easy-to-understand form, but you can also make the results truly report-like, adding headers and footers and even charts and pictures that make your report visually appealing.

Note Once you create a report, Access makes it available in the database window so that you can select it at any time. When you open the report, Access reads the data in the data table to which it is attached, which means that the report shows you the most current data you've entered each time you view the report. So an Access report is not like a static report you create in Microsoft Word or Microsoft Excel; a report in Access retrieves any new data so that you're always getting the most current picture of your database.

Creating a Report

Access once again comes to the rescue for the novice report writer by providing a wizard to do the difficult part for you. The main steps for creating a report involve starting the wizard, answering the questions, and plugging in your own data. Here's the process:

1 Open the database for which you want to create the report.

2 Display the database window by pressing F11.

3 Click Reports in the left side of the database window.

4 Click Create Report By Using Wizard. The Report Wizard starts (as shown in Figure 19-1).

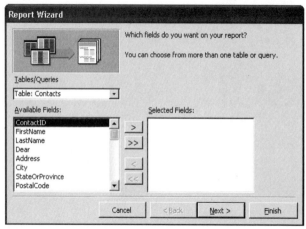

Figure 19-1 The Report Wizard leads you through the steps of generating a report based on the selected database.

5 In the Tables/Queries list, choose the name of the table or query that you want to use for the report.

6 In the Available Fields list, click the fields you want to add to the report; then click Add to display the field in the Selected Fields list. Click Next.

Tip   If you want to add all fields to the Selected Fields list at one time, click Add All in the center of the Report Wizard dialog box.

---

7 The next page of the wizard asks you to choose a grouping level for the report. If you want to add a *grouping level*, click the field you want to use and click Add. Then click Next to move to the next page of the wizard.

Lingo   A *grouping level* is a field by which the data is grouped. For example, when you group records by state, you display records with matching state values together.

---

8 Next, you must choose the sort order for your records. You can choose from one to four fields, each arranged in either ascending or descending order. If you first want to sort your records by state and then alphabetically by last name, you would choose State, Ascending for the first entry in this window and Last Name, Ascending for the second entry.

Note   Because Access tailors your choices depending on the type of table and fields you select, your options may be different from the ones I mention here. The process is the same, but the actual fields you select for reporting will be related to the data you are reporting on.

---

9 Choose a format for the report by selecting one of the following choices:
- Columnar format displays all data fields together in a list, with each entry representing one record.
- Tabular format shows data in datasheet array, with columns representing fields and rows representing records.
- Justified format displays the report in a form-like array, showing one record per page.

    On this page of the wizard, you also choose whether you want the report to appear in Portrait or Landscape orientation. (As you learned earlier in the book, Portrait orientation prints the page in standard 8.5-by-11-inch vertical format, while Landscape orientation prints the report in horizontal, 11-by-8.5-inch format. Make your selections and click Next.

10 Choose a style for your report. Click through the list to find the style you want. When you've found it, click Next.

11 Type a name for the report and click Finish. The report appears in Print Preview so that you can view the report, customize it, and then print it.

Sprucing Up Your Report

Once you generate a report in Access, you can make some changes to give it a different look. Start by displaying the database window and clicking Reports. The report you generated appears in the list to the right. Double-click it to open it. The report appears automatically in Print Preview, which presents you with a new toolbar. Here are the tools you'll use to work with your Access reports:

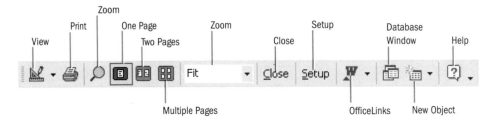

On the Print Preview toolbar, you find the selections you need to display the report in Design view (which enables you to add cool details such as headers, footers, and graphics), change the way the report is shown in Print Preview, use the report in Word or Excel, display the database window, add an object to the report, or print the report. The sections that follow show you how to use these tools to make a few changes to the report you have created.

Caution   Once you step outside the familiar wizard territory in Access, you'll find that things can quickly get very complicated. Before you begin experimenting with modifying the report in Design view, be sure that you've gotten the whole story on how those changes will affect the display of your data. To learn how to navigate like an expert in Design view, see *Microsoft Access Version 2002 Inside Out*, by Helen Feddema, published by Microsoft Press.

Changing Margin, Page, and Column Settings

You use the Setup tool on the Print Preview toolbar to display the Page Setup dialog box (as shown in Figure 19-2). In this dialog box, you can use the Margins tab to change the margins for your report (you might need to do this, for example, if you're putting the report in a binder). To change the margins for your report, click the Margin setting you want to change and type a new value. The Sample window changes to show you how the new setting will look.

Figure 19-2 You can change the print margins for your report using the Page Setup dialog box.

Click the Page tab if you want to change the orientation of the report. You might want to print the document in Landscape orientation, for example, if you are trying to fit as many columns on the page as possible. You also use the choices on the Page tab to choose the paper size and source and to select the printer on which you'll print this report.

The Columns tab enables you to control the columns in which your report is printed. One tricky point here: the word *columns*, in this context, does not refer to the fields in your report—instead, it refers to the column printout of the entire report. By default, this is set to one column, and unless you have a special use for columns in Access, leave the default as it is to avoid unwanted changes in your report.

Note   Are you wishing for an easier way to make your reports look good? The next section shows you how to publish your reports in Word so that you can fine-tune their layout and make them professional and polished.

Publishing Reports in Word

One of the great advantages about working with a suite of programs such as Microsoft Office is that you can share the talents of the different programs no matter what kind of data you are working with. After you create a report in Access, you can use the OfficeLinks command to send it to Word, where you can fix it up with your favorite formats and frills. To publish a report in Word, follow these steps:

1   Display the database window by pressing F11 if necessary.

2   Click Reports and select the report you want in the right panel.

3   Click Preview. The report appears in Print Preview.

4   Click the OfficeLinks down arrow on the toolbar; then select Publish It With Microsoft Word. A message box appears, telling you that the report is being printed to Word. The document is saved in a file with the same name as your Access report, but it is given the .rtf (rich text format) extension. The report appears in the Word window (as shown in Figure 19-3). You can now change the report in any way you choose, formatting or enhancing the report as a Word document.

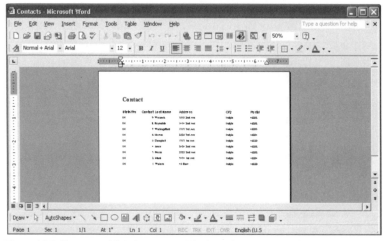

Figure 19-3 You can publish the report to Word to take advantage of Word's formatting features.

Note   When you publish Access data in Word, the data does not remain linked to its original source in your Access database. This means that if you change the data in Access, the report published in Word will not reflect those changes. To make sure you have the most accurate, up-to-date information in your Access reports published in Word, be sure to use Publish It With Microsoft Word in OfficeLinks regularly.

Deleting Reports

When a report no longer serves your purpose, you can easily delete it from the database window to free up room for other new, improved reports. Here are the steps:

1   Press F11 to display the database window if necessary.

2   Click Reports.

3   Click the report you want to delete.

4   Click the Delete button or press Delete. Access asks you whether you want to continue with the deletion of the report and warns you that you cannot recover the file once it's deleted.

5   Click Yes to delete the report.

Tip   When you delete a report, you aren't doing anything to the data used to *create* the report. The data remains intact within the data table in which it is stored.

Printing Reports

When you're ready to print the report you've created in Access, you can do so in several ways:

■ Right-click the report in the database window and select Print from the context menu.

■ Select the report in the database window and press Ctrl+P.

■ Choose Print from the File menu.

■ Click Print when the report is displayed in Print Preview.

The first three methods display the Print dialog box so that you can choose your printer, specify the print range, and enter the number of copies you want. If you click Print while you're viewing the report in Print Preview, however, the report is sent directly to the printer with the default options.

Try This! If you send a report to the home office regularly, you can e-mail it directly from Access. Here's how to do it:

1 Display the database window by pressing F11.

2 Click Reports.

3 Right-click the report you want to send in the right panel of the database window.

4 Select Send To in the context menu; then choose Mail Recipient (as Attachment). The Send dialog box appears, as shown below:

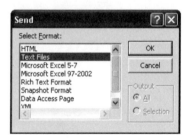

5 Select Text Files (which saves data in a tabular format), and then click OK.

6 If the Choose Profile dialog box appears, click the Profile Name down arrow and choose the name of the e-mail program you want to use to send the report. Click OK. A new e-mail message then appears, with your Access report included as an attachment.

Key Points

■ The Report Wizard in Access helps you generate a quick report and prompts you to choose the fields, sort order, style, and title you want.

- Once you create a report, you use Print Preview to display it and review the data.

- You can add page and report headers and footers by working in Design view.

- If you want to add formatting enhancements to your report, you can use the OfficeLinks feature to publish the report in Word.

- You can print a report by pressing Ctrl+P, right-clicking the report name and clicking Print, or selecting Print while in Print Preview mode.

- To delete a report, simply select it in the database window and press Delete.

- You can e-mail a report by choosing Send To from the File menu and choosing Mail Recipient (as Attachment).

Part VII

Fast Web Pages with Microsoft FrontPage

Mark my words: Sooner or later, everything goes to the Web. Basic communication and data management has taken a turn toward the invisible. We no longer need printouts of everything and pages and pages (and volumes and volumes) of bound documents to record our decisions and practices. Today we can post our documents to the Web and burn them on CD to archive them.

Microsoft FrontPage is one part of this Web-centric revolution, as an easy-to-use but powerful Web creation and management program that takes coding off your shoulders and helps you create sites the fast, easy, and smart way. This part of the book shows you how to create your Web site the way you want it and publish it to the Web.

Specifically, Chapter 20, "First, the Basics," takes you on a tour of the FrontPage window and introduces you to all the tools you'll use as you create your first Web site. Chapter 21, "Special Tasks in Microsoft FrontPage," shows you how to add text boxes, frames, and rollovers to your pages. By the time you get to Chapter 22, "Publishing Your Pages," you'll be ready to learn how to prepare your files and publish your site using Server Extensions. This chapter also includes a troubleshooting section, just in case things don't work out quite as you expect.

Chapter 20

First, the Basics

At its essence, a Web page is nothing more than a document coded in a certain way that allows headings, text, and graphics to be displayed in a browser window. The codes themselves are quite simple and the rules are pretty easy to remember. You create a *link* in your document that enables visitors to move to another page by clicking it. The page links to another page, which links to another page, and so on. Before long, you have the World Wide Web.

So if creating Web pages is so easy, why do we need Microsoft FrontPage? FrontPage is a powerful and yet surprisingly easy Web creation program that gives you a friendly way to create sites without having to work with Hypertext Markup Language (HTML) code. You can use the menus, tools, options, and palettes to add the items you want in the way you want them to appear. FrontPage also helps you work with what could be very complicated elements—forms, rollovers, animations, and more—in an easy-to-use, no-coding interface. For those of us who slept through most of computer science, that's good news. So let's knock out that first Web site.

Tip FrontPage is a standard part of Microsoft Office XP Professional and may be available in some special-promotion packages as well. If you don't have FrontPage 2002 but you'd like to learn it, check out Microsoft's Web site at *http://www.microsoft.com* to purchase your copy.

What Can You Do with FrontPage?

The most obvious answer to this question is, of course, *create a Web site*. But perhaps the bigger question—and the one you'll need to spend some time considering before you start work—is, What do you want to do with your Web site?

In its relatively short life span, the World Wide Web has grown from being a fairly ugly, primarily text-based medium to a high-energy, moving, colorful communications channel that offers text, graphics, video, and sound. The Web has gone from clunky to cool in a few short years. Now everybody—and I mean *everybody*, from governments to companies, from grandparents to schoolteachers—wants a Web site to share the information most important to them.

So, what will you do with a Web site you create in FrontPage? Here are just a few possibilities:

- Create a professional Web site for your company complete with an About Us page, a corporate directory, a customer-service page, and a page describing your products and services.

- Publish your college coursework to the Web so that your distant students can follow along with the presentations you give in class.

See Also   *Chapter 22, "Publishing Your Pages," walks you through the steps involved in actually getting your pages on the Web where everyone—students and others—can enjoy them.*

- Make the annual reports of your nonprofit organization available online so that potential donors can find out more about you and what you do.

- Create an e-commerce site for your small business that enables you to sell items from an online catalog (see the section on Microsoft bCentral later in this chapter).

- Create a family Web site that includes one page for each family member and, yes, even the dog.

- Design a team site your employees can create and use collaboratively (this kind of site requires Microsoft SharePoint Team Services, an additional service).

A Walk Around the FrontPage Window

Start Microsoft FrontPage by clicking Start, choosing All Programs, and selecting Microsoft FrontPage. The FrontPage window opens in a familiar-but-somewhat-different Office XP interface (as shown in Figure 20-1). The sections that follow give you a quick introduction to the elements you'll use most often in the FrontPage window.

Tip   The first time you fire up FrontPage, the program asks whether you'd like to designate FrontPage as your default Web page editor. If you'd like to use FrontPage by default, click Yes. This means that whenever you view or edit an HTML file, FrontPage will start. Microsoft Word is the application selected for the Web page editor by default.

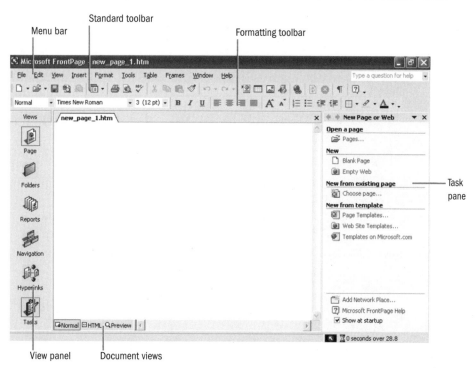

Figure 20-1 The FrontPage window looks similar to the other Office applications, but with special features related to Web work.

FrontPage Menus

Do you feel that you're experiencing *déjà vu*? The FrontPage menus seem very similar to the menus you've seen in other Office applications. When you look inside the menus, however, you'll see that the options are quite different. Here's what you'll find in the various menus:

■   The File menu contains the commands you need for starting, opening, closing, saving, previewing, printing, and setting up Web pages.

■   The Edit menu houses the commands you'll use for cutting, copying, finding, pasting, and selecting page content. The almighty Undo command is also here.

- The View menu controls the different ways in which you can display the FrontPage window. The Views bar offers a number of different view perspectives and lets you display the Folders List, the Navigation pane, Reveal Tags, and different report styles.

- The Insert menu lets you add just about anything imaginable to your Web page—including a page break, a line, a picture or video, frames, forms, and more.

- The Format menu includes everything you need for formatting the text and objects on your Web page. Choose to add bullets and numbering, borders, styles, page transitions, and more.

- The Tools menu houses the special tools you'll use to check spelling and word usage, use add-ins, work with AutoCorrect, and specify the options you want.

- The Table menu gives you all the options you need for working with tables, including distributing data, inserting tables, adding and deleting rows and columns, filling with data, converting table data, and more.

- The Frames menu enables you to add, work with, split, save, and delete frame content.

- The Window and Help menus include any open windows and the standard Help commands available in all other Office applications.

FrontPage Toolbars

You'll also recognize the FrontPage toolbars. The Standard toolbar contains all the expected tools for opening, saving, printing, searching, and previewing pages, but there's one important addition: the Web Component tool. Web Component displays the Insert Web Component dialog box so that you can add ready-made Web features.

Lingo   What's a *Web component*? An object or feature you can use on your Web site to add functionality or fun to your page. A Web component might be a search feature, a top-10 list, a banner ad, or a hit counter.

FrontPage Views

The FrontPage Views bar displays six icons, each showing you a different view of an open Web site. The Page view displays the selected Web page. The Folders view shows the folders and files of the open Web page. The Reports view shows the status of the links on the current page. Navigation view displays the navigation bar for the current page; Hyperlinks checks the status of the links; and Tasks displays anything that remains to be done on the current site.

Along the bottom of the page area, you see three tabs: Normal, HTML, and Preview, as shown below. Normal displays the page in editable page view, complete with text and graphics frames; HTML displays the page as the source HTML code; and Preview is a read-only mode that shows you how the page will look on the Web.

`⌐Normal ⊟HTML ⌕Preview |`

Where Will Your Web Site Go? Before you create a Web page, you need to think about where it will appear. You'll need to have a hosting location for the site—an account with an Internet service provider, or ISP. There are many national and local ISPs who can set you up with a Web account and give you a Universal Resource Locator, or URL (also known as a *Web address*). The URL is the piece of information you need to tell FrontPage where your finished Web site will appear.

Creating a Web Site

The process for creating a Web site is easier than you might think. If you don't need to add anything fancy—perhaps just a couple of headings, some body text, and a picture or two—you can create a Web page in just minutes. Ready? Let's go through the process from start to finish:

1 Start Microsoft FrontPage. If the task pane doesn't appear, choose New from the File menu and select Page Or Web.

2 In the New From Templates area, click Web Site Templates.

3 In the Web Site Templates dialog box, shown in Figure 20-2, click the different template icons to find the one you want. The Description area changes to show you what each of the Web sites are meant to do. Select the template you want to use, and then click OK.

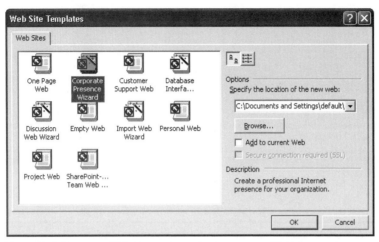

Figure 20-2 To create a Web site the fast and easy way, use a Web site template.

4 A wizard starts, ready to lead you through the creation of the Web site you selected. Depending on the template you select, the wizard will ask you to choose your preferences for a number of items related to the site. For example, the Corporate Presence Web Wizard asks about the following:

- The main pages you want on your site (for example, What's New, Products/Services, and so on).

- The topics you want to be displayed on your home page.

- The topics you want to address on your What's New page (assuming that you selected it as a main page you want to include).

- The number of products and services pages you want to create.

- Specific details about what you want to include for information about your products and services.

- The information you want to request from visitors filling in the feedback form on your site.

- Whether the information in the feedback form should be saved in tab-delimited format so that you can easily use it in a database.

- Items about your table of contents page, such as whether you want to update it automatically and use bullets to identify main pages.

- What you want to appear at the top (header) and bottom (footer) of each Web page in your site.

- Whether you want to display an "under construction" icon on those pages that you're working on.

- The title of your company, the short name (if you have one), and the company address.

- Your company's contact info, including telephone, fax, and e-mail addresses.

Whew! As you can see, the FrontPage Web Wizard doesn't leave much to chance. Once you answer all these different questions, you're almost finished. Next, you need to choose the look you want for your Web page.

Note If you select the One Page Web template, a wizard does not start; instead, FrontPage creates a single-page Web site and displays the Folder List so that you can customize the page as needed.

---

5   Click Choose Web Theme if you want FrontPage to design the Web site with coordinated buttons, fonts, rules, and other elements. The Choose Theme dialog box appears so that you can browse the different themes and choose the one you like (as shown in Figure 20-3). When you find your favorite, click it and click OK.

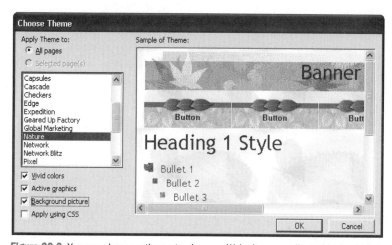

Figure 20-3 You can choose a theme to give your Web site a coordinated look and feel.

Tip   Be sure to select the Vivid Colors, Active Graphics, and Background Picture check boxes to see how the site design will look in full color and with all its effects. There's a significant difference for some themes in the way you see them on the screen in the Sample window and how they appear on the Web, with all systems go. Another variable you should know about: Not all browsers display Web pages the same way. What looks great in Internet Explorer might be less attractive in Netscape. So even though you enable these options to make your site look the best it can, be sure to test the display in more than one browser.

---

6   The last page of the wizard asks whether you want to see Tasks view
after the Web site is created. Leave the option selected, and then click
Finish. The wizard creates the site and displays a list of tasks in the
main section of the FrontPage window.

Working in Tasks View

Tasks view (shown in Figure 20-4) isn't the prettiest display in the world, especially if you are eager to see what your newly created Web site will look like.
But Tasks view serves a useful purpose, and that's why we're exploring it here.
Especially when you are new to creating Web sites, remembering what you
need to do—in what order—can be difficult. Tasks view takes that guesswork
out of Web creation by giving you a list of tasks to complete. Once you finish
them, you're done. It's that simple.

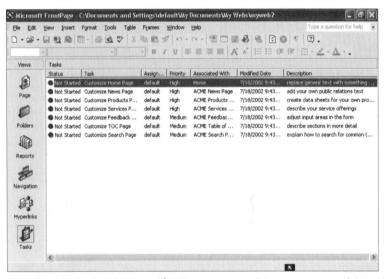

Figure 20-4 Tasks view gives you a list of items to accomplish on your way to a finished Web site.

Double-click the first task in the list. The Task Details dialog box appears,
showing you the status of the task and information about it. Click Start Task to
begin working on your new Web site. FrontPage changes to Page view and displays the new site in the work area (as shown in Figure 20-5).

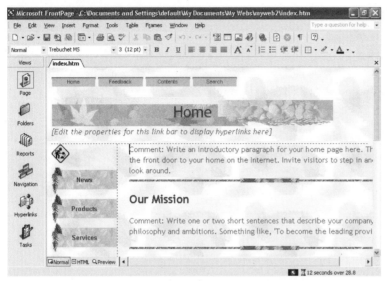

Figure 20-5 The new Web site appears in Normal view, ready for you to add your text and graphics.

Web Lingo   The new frontier of the Web has brought with it a new language. The following list gives you a quick overview of what each of these terms means:

- **Hand-coding**   Using HTML codes to prepare a document for the Web. You can use any text editor (such as WordPad in Microsoft Windows XP) to hand-code Web pages. FrontPage allows you to use menus and tools to bypass coding (although you can still work with code if you like by clicking the HTML tab at the bottom of the work area).

- **Home page**   The page of a Web site that appears when a visitor first logs on to the site.

- **HTML**   An acronym for Hypertext Markup Language, HTML is the simple coding system used to prepare documents for display on the Web.

- **Hyperlink**   Also called a *link*, this is a connection established between pages that enables a visitor to move from one page to another.

- **URL**   An acronym for Universal Resource Locator, the URL is the Web address of the site, often appearing in the form *http://www.webaddress.com*.

- **Web site**   A collection of Web pages organized around a particular topic, company, school, or group.

- **Web page**   An individual page within a Web site.

Adding Text to a Web Page

Your next step in making your Web site your own is adding your text to the home page. When you open that first task, the page you'll see is the home page created by the Web Wizard. Prompts are entered in the various areas on the page to give you ideas about what you might enter there.

To replace a comment with your text, follow these steps:

1   Click in the Comment to select it, highlighting the entire paragraph.

2   Type the text you want to add. Depending on the template you used to create the site, the text you enter might appear in a different color than the prompt text (this is a helpful feature that keeps you from accidentally leaving prompt text on the page); the font and style of the text you enter is the same as the prompt text.

3   Continue replacing the prompt text with your text until you've added everything you need to add.

Tip   You also can copy text from another Office XP program into FrontPage. If you select and copy a bulleted list in Word, for example, the list appears in FrontPage with the same formatting applied in the original document. This gives you a quick way to use text you've already entered once (and can help you make sure your Web site is consistent with other documents you've created for your company).

Modifying Text

You can change the font, style, and color used on your Web site in much the same way you change text in a Word document: Highlight the text you want to change, and then click the tool you want to use on the Formatting toolbar. Here are a few ideas of the types of text changes you might want to make while you're working on your Web site:

■   Click Font Color to change the color of selected text.

■   Click the Font down arrow to choose a different font.

■   Click Align Center or Align Right to change the text alignment.

■   Click Increase Font Size or Decrease Font Size to make the selected text a size larger or smaller.

■   Click the Border tool to add a border around selected text.

Inserting Graphics for the Web

One of the great advantages of the Web wizards in FrontPage is that they take care of a lot of the design for you. But when you have your own images to import, how do you do it? Simple. Start in Normal view, and then choose Picture from the Insert menu. A drop-down list of choices appear.

The following list explains your choices for the different kinds of graphics you can add to your Web page:

- Clip Art displays the Clip Organizer so that you can choose a piece of clip art to include on the page or download clips from the Web.

- From File displays the Picture dialog box so that you can navigate to the folder you want and select the file you want to insert.

- From Scanner Or Camera displays the Insert Picture From Scanner Or Camera dialog box so that you can begin scanning or downloading images from your scanner or camera.

- New Photo Gallery opens the Photo Gallery Properties dialog box so that you can create and insert a collection of photos on your page.

- New Drawing displays the drawing tools so that you can add your own art to the Web page.

- AutoShapes displays the AutoShapes palette, enabling you to add pre-drawn shapes on your site. AutoShapes are great for adding buttons quickly or creating special design elements for your site.

- WordArt is a feature that allows you to do special things with text. To use WordArt, choose the option from the menu, and then select the style you want from the WordArt Gallery. In the Edit WordArt Text dialog box, type the text you want to add to the Web page, and then click OK. The text item is placed as an object on your page so you can move it, resize it, or rotate it as needed.

- Video displays the Video dialog box so that you can choose a video file you've prepared for the Web.

Try This!   If you have a collection of photos you'd like to display on a favorite Web site, you can use FrontPage's Photo Gallery feature to gather and display them in the format you want. The process is simple and the effect is cool. Here are the steps:

1   In Normal view, click the point on the Web page where you want to add the collection of photos.

2   Choose Picture from the Insert menu, and then select New Photo Gallery.

3   In the Photo Gallery Properties dialog box, click Add; then choose Pictures From Files or Pictures From Scanner Or Camera, depending on whether you are using files you've saved or scanning or importing digital images.

4   Navigate to the folder in which the files are stored, click the image you want, and then click Open. Repeat to add more photos.

5   Click the Layout tab and choose the layout you want for your images. Some layouts allow you to add descriptive text; others don't. Click the different layouts and read the text below the Preview window to find out more about them, as shown below.

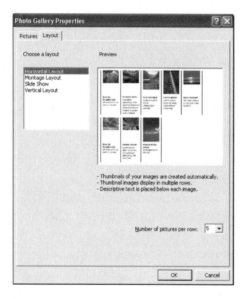

6   Click OK to save the gallery and insert it at the cursor position on your Web page.

If you want to modify the photo gallery later, simply double-click it in Normal view to display the Photo Gallery Properties dialog box and make your desired changes.

Viewing Navigation Paths and Links

Once you create the Web site, add the text, and insert the pictures, you're ready to see how your site fits together. When you use a wizard to create the site, the navigation system (the way in which you move from page to page) and the linking is already done. The navigation buttons appear along the left, top, and bottom of the page (depending on the choices you selected in the wizard); and the links are already made so that when you click the Preview tab and click one of the buttons, you are taken to that page.

When you want to view the navigation system the wizard established for you, display the site in Navigation view by clicking the Navigation icon on the Views bar. The Navigation window shows icons of each page, with lines connecting the pages to which they are linked. You can collapse and expand the navigation diagram by clicking the minus (-) and plus (+) buttons in the bottom center of linked pages (as shown in Figure 20-6).

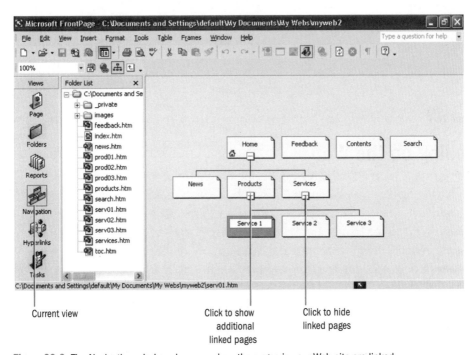

Figure 20-6 The Navigation window shows you how the pages in your Web site are linked.

While you're working in Navigation view, you can add new pages, move linked pages to a different page, include selected pages on navigation bars, rename pages, and delete pages. To work with an individual page, right-click the page and choose the option you want from the context menu that appears.

You also can use Hyperlinks view to see which pages are linked. This is a pretty amazing view—worth at least a quick look. When you have displayed some of the links by clicking the + buttons beside each page icon, the display looks something like Figure 20-7. Staggering, eh? By viewing the links on this simple wizard-generated site, you get the idea why this medium is known as the "Web."

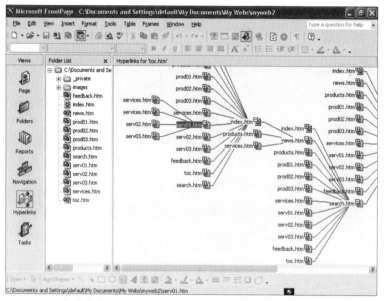

Figure 20-7   The links between pages (and between sites) are the sticky fibers that make this online world a Web.

Selling on the Web

Selling on the Web is becoming big business, although most retail outlets are still having trouble maintaining their equilibrium in a rapidly changing online marketplace. Not to be daunted by folding dot-coms, however, new Internet businesses spring to life hourly around the globe. And everybody is thinking about e-commerce. How will your business make money on the Web? And how much do you have to shell out to create a professional—and profitable—e-commerce-capable Web site?

Tip   Microsoft has at least one answer for small businesses who want to dip a toe into the Internet marketplace without mortgaging the farm to do it. Microsoft bCentral is a FrontPage add-in and service that helps you build e-commerce capability into your Web site. When you download the bCentral add-in, you are given templates that help you design your own catalog and e-commerce pages, add a shopping cart, create an online store, manage your sales, and process the orders you receive. Then, once your site is in place, you can subscribe to the bCentral.com service and pay a monthly fee to have bCentral manage all these different e-commerce components for you. For more information about these and other bCentral.com services, visit *http://www.bcentral.com*.

Previewing the Page

Previewing the Web site is simple—just click Preview in the page view tabs along the bottom-left side of the work area. The text and graphic frames are hidden so that you see what the visitors to your Web page will see.

Preview is a read-only mode, which means that you can only view—and not edit—the page in Preview mode. If you see changes you want to make, click Normal and make your changes in that view.

If you want to get the full effect of the way your pages will look and operate on the Web, you can preview the site in your Web browser. Choose Preview In Browser from the File menu and then, when the Preview In Browser dialog box appears, select your browser and then click Preview. The site will appear in the browser window and you'll be able to click links and move from page to page as you would if the site were live on the Web.

Tip   To get a quick printout of the current page as it will appear on the Web, click the Print button on your browser's toolbar. This prints the page without frame lines so that you can review how the page shows up on the Web.

Saving the Page

When you're ready to save your Web site, choose Save from the File menu. If you had opened the page from Tasks view, a pop-up box appears asking whether you want to mark the task as completed. If you do, click Yes. If you plan to work more on the task later, click No.

Note   Because the wizard generates the pages and names them so that each link refers to the correct page file, you do not specify a new name during the Save procedure as you would when saving other application files. It's important that the home page is named index.htm and the additional main pages keep their original names.

Okay, now you've been through the process of creating a Web site with FrontPage. It's easier than you thought, isn't it? This chapter has only touched on the basic instructions for creating a site. In Chapter 21, "Special Tasks in Microsoft FrontPage," you'll learn how to add some bells and whistles, and then we'll publish the site to the Web in Chapter 22, "Publishing Your Pages." Although this chapter has given you only the basic process for generating that first site, I hope you'll take these ideas and then explore on your own. FrontPage is an amazing program with too many features to soak in at one sitting. When you find yourself with a rainy afternoon on your hands, sit down and experiment with FrontPage. Be creative! Have fun!

Key Points

- FrontPage 2002 is a Web site creation and management program that is part of the Office XP Professional suite of applications.

- You can use FrontPage to create sites quickly from scratch using the program's Web templates.

- FrontPage uses six different views—Page, Folders, Reports, Navigation, Hyperlinks, and Tasks—to enable you to see different aspects of the site you're creating.

- The FrontPage toolbars are similar to those in other Office XP applications: the Standard toolbar includes the tools you'll use to work with files in various ways; and the Formatting toolbar enables you to control and change the formats of elements on your pages.

- The Tasks view lists the items you need to accomplish during the creation of your site.

- Add your own text to a Web page by clicking the prompt text to highlight it and then typing. You can change the font, style, color, and alignment of text as you would in a word-processing document. You also can copy text from other programs into FrontPage.

- FrontPage includes a number of options for the types of graphics you can add to your pages. You can use clip art, scanned images, WordArt, AutoShapes, and more. You also can create your own Photo Gallery, complete with captions, for display on a specific page.

- Preview your page in Preview mode (by clicking the Preview tab at the bottom of the work area) or by choosing Preview In Browser from the File menu. This shows you the way your site will appear on the Web, complete with working links.

Chapter 21

Special Tasks in Microsoft FrontPage

In the last chapter, you learned to use a Web Wizard to create a Web site and then add your text and graphics to your pages. Neat stuff, isn't it? Makes you wonder why Web development companies charge an arm and a leg to do this kind of thing. But rest assured that although you are now a Web designer in your own right, there are still *many* things to learn. We've only scratched the surface of Microsoft FrontPage's capabilities, and this chapter takes you a little further into some of the specialized tasks you might want to try as you develop your Web pages.

The tasks and techniques in this chapter all pertain to making it easier for visitors to read and understand your site. People who browse the Web really have just two needs: They need to be able to see clearly how to get around on your site, and they need to know what you want them to click. Adding tables, frames, lines, boxes, and rollover effects all help communicate the organization and structure of your site so that they will enjoy their visit enough to come back again—a concept known in Web parlance as *stickiness*.

Adding Tables to Your Pages

If you're familiar with tables in Microsoft Word (and if you've read that part of this book, you will be), you won't be caught unaware by the Table feature in FrontPage. Adding a table to FrontPage is a simple matter of positioning the cursor where you want the table to go and then choosing one of the following from the Table menu:

See Also   *If you want to get a refresher on Word tables, see Chapter 6, "Formatting in Microsoft Word."*

■   Draw Table enables you to draw a table freehand in the space you have available on the Web page. Using the pencil tool, draw the table in the size you want; then click and drag to draw the separator lines for rows and columns. Use the Tables toolbar, shown below, to customize your table to appear the way you want it.

■   Insert Table displays the Insert Table dialog box, shown below. Enter the number of rows and columns you want, and then choose the layout settings that fit the space you have available on the page. Click OK to add the table. You can then use the Table toolbar to customize the table further by adding rows and columns, changing the alignment of text, changing the table color, or applying an AutoFormat.

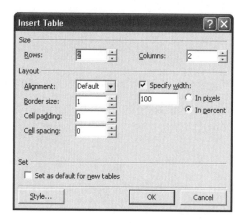

To add text to your table, simply click in one of the cells and type the information you want to place there. You also can add graphics, clip art, WordArt, and other objects to the cells in a table.

Try This!　Depending on the type of content you're adding to your site, you might want to create an invisible table that helps add behind-the-scenes structure to your site. For example, if you are creating a listing of product summaries and you want to position the pictures of the products in the left column and the short description on the right, you can make sure that the pictures and descriptions line up by putting the content in a table. To add an invisible table to your page, follow these steps:

1　Create the table on your Web page as usual.

2　Click in the table to select it.

3　Select Table Properties from the Table menu.

4　Click Table.

5　In the Borders area of the Table Properties dialog box, change the Size setting to 0.

6　Click Apply, and then click OK.

When you return to the Web page, the outline of your table has changed to a dotted line. When you click the Preview tab to see how the table will look on your Web page, the border is gone but the data remains, formatted nicely in an invisible table structure.

Working with Frames

If you've been tuned in to Web talk for any length of time, you know that there are some people who love *frames* and some people who can't stand them. Some people think that frames are helpful navigation devices; others think that frames are clunky, interruptive, and annoying. For some reason, there seem to be few people who don't have an opinion—either for or against—about frames.

Lingo　A *frame* is a panel on your Web page that visitors can control independently of the other panels on the screen.

If you're one of those people who want to give frames a try, you'll be pleased to know you can add frames to your pages easily in FrontPage. Some people choose to create vertical frames, positioning the navigation frame on the left and the content area on the right. (If you save your Microsoft PowerPoint presentations as a Web page, that is the way it's done.)

Here's the process for adding frames to a Web page in your site:

1　Open the Web site you want to work with.

2　Choose New from the File menu and select Page Or Web. The task pane opens on the right side of the FrontPage work area.

3   Click Page Templates, and then click the Frames Pages tab in the Page
Templates dialog box.

4   Select the different frame templates and watch the Preview window to
see which one is right for your site. When you have selected the one
you want, click OK.

   The new page appears, showing the frame style you have
selected. As Figure 21-1 shows, the design isn't very exciting. But
design isn't the next thing you need to worry about; you'll first need to
tell FrontPage what to display in the different frame areas.

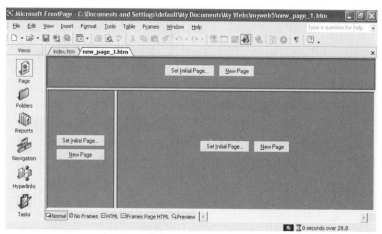

Figure 21-1 When you add a frame page to your site, you must specify to FrontPage which
content to display where.

5   If you want to add existing page content to a frame, click Initial Page
to display the Insert Hyperlink dialog box (as shown in Figure 21-2).
Select the page you want to display in the selected frame, and then
click OK.

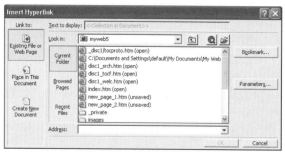

Figure 21-2 When you click Initial Page, FrontPage displays the Insert Hyperlink dialog box so
that you can choose the page you want to use in that frame.

   If you want to add new content to a frame, click New Page. A
blank page appears, ready for you to add text, pictures, and links.

6 Add the information and links as normal. Then resize the frames, if necessary, by dragging the frame border in the direction you want to resize the frame.

7 Preview the page by clicking the Preview tab at the bottom of the work area, and save and close your file as usual.

Tip Because frames can behave differently in different browsers, for best results, test the display of your frames in at least two or three popular browsers before you publish your site to the Web. This helps you reduce the "Oops!" factor when you find out that people using Netscape Navigator can't see a heading underline or that your boxes are cut off in Internet Explorer.

Adding Lines and Borders

In the last chapter, you learned how easy it is to add pictures, WordArt, AutoShapes, and more to your Web pages. Other special items you might want to add are the ever-present graphical lines and boxes. Lines can help you show readers where one section begins and another ends on your Web page; borders can draw visitors' attention to an important point that you don't want them to miss.

To add a dividing line to your Web page, follow these steps:

1 Display the page on which you want to add the line.

2 Display the Drawing toolbar, if necessary, by choosing Toolbars from the View menu, and then clicking Drawing.

3 Click the Line tool (to the left of the AutoShapes down arrow) on the Drawing toolbar at the bottom of the FrontPage work area.

4 Click the starting point for the line; drag to draw the line, and release the mouse button. Handles appear at either end of the line, showing that it is selected (as shown in Figure 21-3).

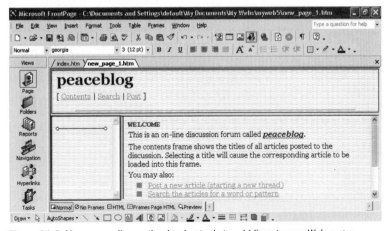

Figure 21-3 You can easily use the drawing tools to add lines to your Web pages.

Tip   Press and hold the Shift key while you draw the line to ensure that it is straight.

Once the line is in place, you can do all sorts of things with it. Here are a few ideas:

■   Press Ctrl+C to copy the line and Ctrl+V to paste it in another place on the site. (You can use this to add identical lines above and below a headline, button, link, or table.)

■   Change the line style by clicking the Line Style tool on the Drawing toolbar and selecting a new line from the pop-up palette, shown below.

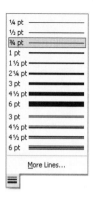

■   Change the line color by clicking the Line Color tool on the Drawing toolbar and choosing a selection from the palette that appears.

■   Add arrows to the line by clicking the Arrow Style tool on the Drawing toolbar and clicking your choice. You can add arrows or shapes on both ends or on one end only.

Tip   Remember that when it comes to adding design elements such as lines and borders, a little goes a long way. Because your ultimate objective is to create a site that is easy to navigate and fun to read (or at least informative), you don't want to make things more difficult for your readers by littering the page with unnecessary lines and boxes. Use the items sparingly and they'll be more effective. When in doubt, do without.

Now that you're aware of that warning, here's how to add a border to items on your current page:

1   Select the text or object around which you want to draw the border.

2   Click the Border down arrow on the Formatting toolbar. A palette of border options appears, as shown in Figure 21-4.

Figure 21-4 FrontPage has a palette for almost everything; here you can choose the border style you want to apply to selected objects.

3   Click the border style you want and it is applied to the selected area.

Tip   If you don't like a border once you've added it, press Ctrl+Z to undo your changes. Instead of doing away with the border altogether, however, you might want to experiment with other borders styles to see whether there's something you like better. In addition, you can add shading to a selected area of your page by choosing Borders And Shading from the Format menu and clicking the Shading tab. Click the Background color down arrow and choose the color you want. Click OK to close the dialog box and return to your Web page.

Creating Rollovers

A *rollover* effect is a simple-but-cool way to help visitors to your Web site know what to do on your site. You can add rollovers to hyperlinks so that the text changes font or color when pointed to; you can add rollovers to pictures so that captions pop up over the image when the user positions the mouse pointer above it; and you can add rollovers that display additional buttons, rotate, or cause some other action to occur.

Lingo   A *rollover* is the name of a special effect that causes a button, link, or image to change when the visitor positions the mouse on the object.

To start the rollover feature in FrontPage, follow these steps:

1   Begin with the page open in the FrontPage window. Make sure that Page view is selected.

2   Right-click the page area; and then choose Page Properties from the context menu.

3   In the Page Properties dialog box, click the Background tab.

> **Note**   You cannot apply rollover effects to a site that uses themes, so if you selected a theme when you created your site (as we did in Chapter 20, "First, the Basics"), rollovers won't be available to you. You can either create a new page with no theme or remove the theme from your existing site by choosing Theme from the Format menu, selecting (No Theme) in the Theme list, and then clicking OK.

4   Click the Enable Hyperlinks Rollover Effects check box; and then click Rollover to display a Font dialog box where you can make the changes the rollover will display (as shown in Figure 21-5).

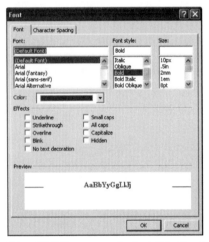

Figure 21-5 You can use the Font dialog box to add a rollover effect to a hyperlink to make the link stand out when the visitor points to it.

5   Scroll through the Font, Font Style, and Size lists and select the settings you want for the text when it is in its rollover state.

> **Note**   You don't have to change these settings to create an eye-catching rollover; using a simple color change and perhaps adding an effect also works.

6   Click the Color down arrow and choose the color you want for the text in its rollover state. Red is selected by default but you can choose any color on the palette.

7   Choose an Effect if you want to change the look of the hyperlink further. To see how each effect looks, click it and watch the Preview window.

> **Tip** Displaying a rollover link in a different color and underlining it is a common way to handle rollovers on Web pages. As you explore the Web, take a look at the different ways designers show you what to click on a given page.

8 Click OK to save the rollover effect and click OK again to close the Page Properties dialog box and save your changes.

9 Click the Preview tab to see how the page will look on the Web. Notice that as you point to a hyperlink, it displays the Font characteristics you assigned.

Viewing the Source

All this time we've been talking about ways to use FrontPage's menus and tools to avoid using Hypertext Markup Language (HTML) code. But I don't mean to suggest that coding is a bad thing—in fact, coding your Web page is actually fun, if you like that sort of thing. If you're curious and want to see what all the behind-the-scenes code looks like, click the HTML tab in the lower-left portion of the FrontPage work area. The HTML tags appear within brackets in blue text, while the content you have entered (or that the wizard created for you) is shown in black text, as shown in Figure 21-6.

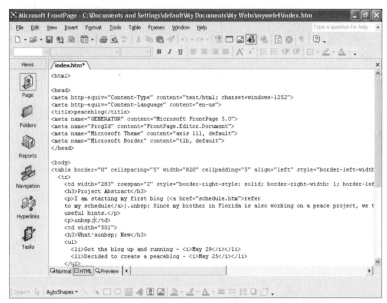

Figure 21-6 You can click the HTML tab to take a look at the HTML source code for your Web page whenever you like.

If you want to try adding or deleting information on your page, you can do it in the HTML tab if you like, but be sure to make a backup copy of the page before you try your hand at coding—just in case something goes wrong. To make changes on the HTML tab, click at the point in the code where you want to make the change and use the Backspace key to delete any unnecessary text. You can select, copy, paste, and cut text in the HTML tab just as you would in any word processing program.

Before taking too much of the coding on yourself, be sure to do some homework to become familiar and comfortable with HTML before you work on something important. Practice makes perfect, but it also involves plenty of mistakes along the way.

Key Points

- FrontPage includes a number of features that enable you to add extra elements easily to your Web page.

- To add a table to your Web page, select the place in the page where you want the table to go and choose Insert Table or Draw Table from the Insert menu.

- Creating frames on a page requires that you use a frames template to add a new page; you then tell FrontPage whether you want to use existing pages or new pages to fill the frames.

- Adding dividing lines on your Web page is as simple as using a pencil—from the Drawing toolbar, that is. Click the Line tool, and then click and drag to draw the line on the page. You can then use Drawing tools to customize the line, making it the color, thickness, and style you want.

- A rollover is a special effect in which a hyperlink changes font, style, or color when the user positions the mouse over it. You can add rollover effects easily to your hyperlinks in FrontPage by displaying Page Properties and choosing the rollover effect you want to apply.

- Although FrontPage makes it possible for you to bypass coding completely, you do have the option of reading and working with the HTML code for your pages if you choose. To see the code behind your page, click the HTML tab. The HTML tags are displayed in blue while the content you've entered appears in black.

Chapter 22

Publishing Your Pages

Okay, now we've come to the part you've been waiting for: putting that slick new site on the Web. Although there aren't many steps left, these last few are very important. In this chapter, you'll learn to prepare your files for the Web, publish the site (using a few different approaches), and then sit back and evaluate (in other words, bask in the glow of) your success.

Preparing Your Web Files

You have one more stop to make in Microsoft FrontPage before you publish your site on the Web. Take a moment to go back through your entire site and make sure it's in the best possible shape. Here are some ideas of things to check for:

- Preview your site in different Web browsers.
- Check all links to make sure they're working correctly.
- Check all contact information—including your address, e-mail, and telephone information—to make sure your visitors will be able to reach you.
- Take a last look at Tasks view to make sure you haven't left anything undone.

■ Click Reports on the Views bar to check the status of all the different elements in your site (as shown in Figure 22-1).

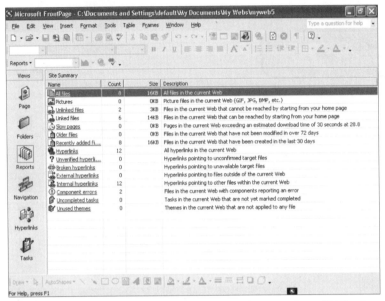

Figure 22-1 You can display Reports to see information about your site and list the elements that still need work.

Try This!   FrontPage has a utility that will check the hyperlinks in your site for you. To start the process, click Reports on the Views bar. The Reporting toolbar appears at the top of the work area. To have FrontPage check your links, follow these steps:

1   Click the Verify Hyperlinks tool on the Reporting toolbar, as shown below.

Click to verify links

2   In the Verify Hyperlinks dialog box, make sure Verify All Hyperlinks is selected, and then click Start. Any broken links are displayed in the Broken Hyperlinks list.

3   Right-click the first link and select Edit Hyperlink.

4   In the Edit Hyperlink dialog box, correct the broken link by editing the page, entering a new hyperlink, or linking to a different page.

5   When you've made modifications to all broken links in the list, select Verify Hyperlinks again to be sure that the problems have been corrected.

About Server Extensions

Microsoft FrontPage Server Extensions are add-in programs that extend the capability of the *Web server* in charge of hosting your site. Extensions enable you to add such items as Web search capability, hit counters, the photo gallery we discussed in Chapter 20, top-10 lists, and document libraries.

Not all Web servers support FrontPage Server Extensions, so you'll need to check with your Internet service provider (ISP) before publishing your site to see whether the ISP has that capability. If not, the features you've included on your site that rely on the extensions won't function—which means that your hit counter or Web search utilities won't work.

Lingo   A Web *server* is the computer that stores your Web site and interacts with users who visit your site.

When you first begin working with FrontPage, Server Extensions are started by default, which means all these features are available to you as you create your site. If you find out that your ISP does not support Server Extensions, you can disable the extension features by choosing Page Options from the Tools menu and clicking the Compatibility tab in the Page Options dialog box. Click the Enabled With Microsoft FrontPage Server Extensions check box to clear it. This turns off Server Extensions, and the features that use them in your Web design will be disabled so that you cannot add them.

If your server does not support extensions, you will publish your site to a File Transfer Protocol (FTP) server. To do this, you must know the server name as well as your user name and password.

Publishing Your Site

Putting your Web site on the Web is called *publishing your site* in FrontPage. The process actually involves packaging your site in a certain way and then copying the files—as well as all the graphics, fonts, bells, and whistles—to the destination folder on the Web server that will host your site. When you're ready to publish your site, follow these steps:

1   Choose Publish Web from the File menu. If you've changed anything on the site since the last time you saved the file, FrontPage will prompt you to save the file before publishing. If you see this prompt, click OK.

2   In the Publish Destination dialog box (shown in Figure 22-2), type the Uniform Resource Locator (URL) address, the FTP address, or the path to the folder that contains your finished Web site.

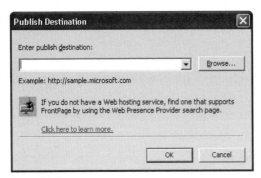

Figure 22-2 The Publish Destination dialog box asks for the location on the Web where your site will appear.

3   Type the address for the Web or ftp site, and then click OK. FrontPage checks the site address you entered and may display the following message:

4   Type the User Name and Password you have been given for access to your Web server space (your ISP or system administrator will give you this information), and then click OK.

5   If you have entered the name of a folder that has not been created, a message appears telling you that the folder does not exist and asks whether you want FrontPage to create it. Click OK and FrontPage creates the folder as needed.

6   FrontPage then displays the Publish Web dialog box, listing all the files that comprise your site (as shown in Figure 22-3). Click Publish to begin posting the files to the Web. FrontPage displays a status bar showing you the progress of the posting.

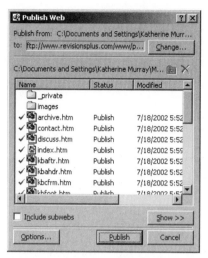

Figure 22-3 The Publish Web dialog box lists all the files that make up your site as FrontPage prepares to publish your site to the Web.

Filling in the Publish Destination Dialog Box Depending on the capabilities of your ISP and where you want the site to reside, you can enter different items in the Enter Publish Destination box:

■   If your ISP supports Microsoft FrontPage Server Extensions, you can type the Web address (the URL) for the site.

■   If your ISP doesn't have Server Extensions, you must publish your site using FTP. In this case, enter the FTP address for the site to which you'll be publishing. (FTP addresses commonly begin with *ftp.*, instead of the *www.* that precedes many Web addresses.)

■   If you are publishing the site on your local company's intranet, type the path to the folder in which you want to store the site.

Tip   If you want to see the destination folder into which the Web files will be copied, click Show in the Publish Web dialog box to extend the display. As the files are uploaded, they appear in the pane on the right side of the dialog box.

As the process begins, FrontPage alerts you if your Web service cannot support any of the features you've used on your site. Click OK to close the message box and the upload will continue. When the files have been published to the Web, FrontPage displays a message box telling you that everything went fine and offering you a link so you can go take a look (as shown in Figure 22-4).

Figure 22-4 After the process is finished, FrontPage lets you know the Web site has been published so that you can check out how it looks "live."

Congratulations! You're a Web site publisher!

Publishing Options for the Future

This first time you publish your site is undoubtedly the first of many times you will update and revise what you've done. The next time you publish the site, you won't need to post all of it; instead, using FrontPage's publishing options, you'll be able to upload only those pages that have changed.

When you click Options in the Publish Web dialog box, a tab of options related to publishing appears. You can have FrontPage upload only the changed pages in your site (which saves time) or have the entire site uploaded each time it is published. In addition, you can choose whether you want FrontPage to compare the new files with the old to make sure that you're uploading the most current files, or you can rely on the timestamps (the date and time the files were created) to show you when the files were created.

Troubleshooting Your Site

Anything worthwhile takes a little effort. Most of the sites I've published have at least one glitch to work out after I publish them. A link doesn't work on this one, or the form looks funny on that one, or an animated image doesn't rotate the way it's supposed to. It's almost inevitable that I'll have some tweaking and moving and resizing and resaving to do. This is all a learning process, and because of the changing nature of the Web, and because of the continual upgrading that goes on at the server level at Web hosting companies, we have to be persistent in figuring our way around the variables that we encounter. When your page isn't loading or working as it should, approach it as a puzzle, not a dead end. There's an answer there somewhere—and if you keep looking for the fly in the ointment, sooner or later you're sure to find it (just remember to wash your hands before you come back to the keyboard, okay?).

Here are some of the more common problems that occur when you are publishing Web sites with FrontPage:

- **The computer is disconnected from the system.**   This may be a server error; the system might be down, or you might have been temporarily disconnected. Check your Internet connection. If the connection is fine, try publishing again shortly to see whether the error has resolved itself.

- **The server isn't recognizing my password.**   Passwords are case-sensitive, so make sure that you're entering the password correctly. If you still get the error, your server might be having difficulties. Wait a few minutes and try again. If all else fails, call your ISP to see whether there is a server problem.

- **My hit counter (or some other site element) isn't working.**   If one of your Web components doesn't work as you thought it would, check with your ISP to make sure FrontPage Server Extensions are installed.

Rating the Effectiveness of Your Site

So how does it look? Does everything work? Do the pages scroll as you intended? Remember that, whether your site looks great or needs a total makeover, designing for the Web is 10 percent splash and sparkle and 90 percent functionality.

Here are some questions to consider (and maybe to ask others, if you're a brave soul) when you want to know whether your Web site hits the mark:

- Is it easy to know where to click to move from page to page?
- Are the colors inviting?
- Is the text easy to read? Is it the right font, size, and style?
- Is the page too crowded?
- Do the special elements work well, or are there too many of them?
- Will users with different kinds of browsers be able to use the frames and see the graphics you've added?

Remember that your site is a work in progress and that the more you experiment, the more you'll learn. Keep your eyes open for the designs you like and try your hand at new, cool Web techniques as they catch your attention. Most of all, have fun with this fascinating new medium, and get comfortable—because it's the fast wave of the future. In fact, it's a fast and *smart* wave of the future, rolling right alongside Microsoft Word, Microsoft Excel, Microsoft Outlook, and Microsoft Access. I hope you've enjoyed your trip through this sweet suite of Microsoft Office XP Professional programs as much as I've enjoyed being your guide. Enjoy your increased productivity and efficiency and, most important, do something fun with all that time you're saving!

Key Points

- Before you publish your Web site with FrontPage, do a quick check to make sure everything is working as you intended.

- Use Reports on the Views bar to show the status of different elements in your site.

- Click Verify Hyperlinks to have FrontPage check all the links in your site and display any problems.

- Fix broken links by right-clicking a broken link and choosing Edit Hyperlink.

- Publish your site to the Web by selecting Publish Web from the File menu.

- If your Web server does not support FrontPage Server Extensions, you must publish your files to an FTP server.

- You can have FrontPage upload only changed files on subsequent publishing operations. Choose Options from the Tools menu and click the Publish tab to set publishing options.

Appendix A
Installing Microsoft Office XP

Once upon a time, installing programs was a hit-or-miss effort that required plenty of coffee and more than a little luck. Today, using Microsoft Windows XP and Microsoft Office XP, installation involves little more than putting the CD in the CD-ROM drive and having the numbers you need handy.

Knowing how to install and uninstall programs is helpful for times when you want to alter the installed components in Office XP, add applications, or remove applications you're not using.

> **Note** If you are using Office XP on a network, be sure to talk with your system administrator for more information before you make any changes to the applications installed with your version of Office XP.

What You Need to Install Office XP

The most important requirements for installing Office XP are, of course, a computer and Office XP. Here are the "essential ingredients" that Office XP needs to run on your computer:

- A personal computer with a Pentium 133-megahertz (MHz) or faster processor (Pentium III is recommended)
- Windows XP, Windows 98, Windows Millennium Edition (Windows Me), Windows NT 4 (with Service Pack 6 or later), or Windows 2000
- Random access memory (RAM) varying between 32 megabytes (MB) and 128 MB, depending on which version of Windows you use
- 245 MB disk storage space
- CD-ROM drive
- SuperVGA or higher resolution monitor
- Mouse, trackball, touchpad, or other pointing device
- Printer (optional)
- Modem (optional, for using Internet-related features)
- Microphone (optional, for using speech features)
- Graphics tablet (optional, for using handwriting recognition)

Before you install, be sure to make a backup of all your important files just in case there's a glitch and something goes wrong. That's not likely to occur, but it's always better to be safe than dataless.

Installing Office XP

To install Office XP on a single-user system, follow these steps:

1 Close any programs you have open.

2 Click Start and choose Control Panel.

3 Select Add Or Remove Programs.

4 In the Add Or Remove Programs window, shown below, click Add New Programs.

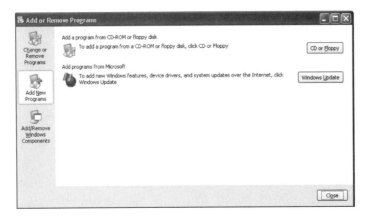

5 In the Add New Programs window, click CD Or Floppy.

6 Insert the Office XP Program CD, and then click Next.

From this point on, the Microsoft Office XP Setup utility takes over and guides you through the process, helping you choose the folder where you want to install the program, allow you to choose the components you want to install, and more. When the installation is complete, Windows displays a message box. Click OK to complete the process.

Changing Office Installation

At some point down the road, you may want to change the way you've got Office XP installed. You might want to install Access even though you skipped it before; or perhaps you aren't using FrontPage and you want to remove it to free up some disk space. When you want to change the installation, choose Add Or Remove Programs from the Control Panel, and then click Change Or Remove Programs.

A list of currently installed programs appears (as shown in Figure A-1). Click Microsoft Office XP and two buttons—Change and Remove—become visible.

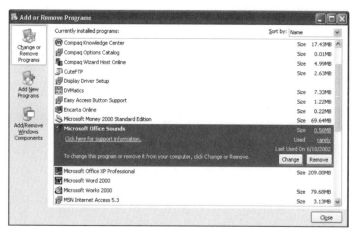

Figure A-1 Use the Add Or Remove Programs feature to change your Office installation.

Click Change. The Windows Installer starts the Microsoft Office XP Setup utility. You can then follow the wizard's prompts to affect the changes you want to make to your Office installation.

All This and Windows XP Updates, Too

Periodically Windows XP will let you know that there are updates available for your system. A prompt will appear over the system tray in your work area, asking whether you'd like to install the updates. If you click the prompt, the Automatic Updates window appears, as shown below. Click Install to begin the process. Windows installs the update and then prompts you to restart your computer so the changes will take effect.

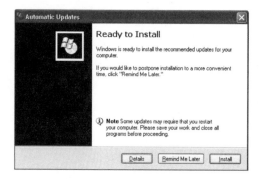

Note that you also can check for Windows Updates by clicking Windows Update in the Add Or Remove Programs window or by clicking Windows Update in the All Programs menu.

Repairing After Installation

If you find that an update file or accessory doesn't work correctly after you've installed it, you can repair the file from the Add Or Remove Programs dialog box by following these steps:

1   Click Start, and then choose Control Panel.

2   Click Add Or Remove Programs and select the program or utility that isn't working properly.

3   Beneath the program name, select Click Here For Support Information.

4   In the Support Info box, shown below, click Repair. Windows Installer starts and reinstalls the program, hopefully correcting the problem.

Tip   I mentioned this earlier in the book, so I'll just add a reminder here: If your version of Office XP begins to act strangely—that is, taking a long time to update the screen, operating slowly, inserting unwanted characters at odd places—it could be that a file the program needs has been damaged. Office XP includes a utility that will fix that for you automatically. To repair the problem, choose Detect And Repair. In the Detect And Repair dialog box, choose whether you want to restore your shortcuts or return the computer to its default settings. Click Start to have Office XP search for problems and repair the files.

Microsoft Office XP Shortcut Keys

As you've learned throughout the book, one of the great advantages of Microsoft Office XP is the way you can learn certain tasks—such as printing, saving, opening, and closing documents—in one Office application and then apply that knowledge (and the same keystrokes) in other applications. This list assembles all the Office shortcut keys you'll use with the various programs. Commands followed by a program name in parentheses, such as Delete (Outlook), indicate that the shortcut key is available only in that program for that purpose.

To Do This	Press This	Found in This Menu
New	Ctrl+N	File
Open	Ctrl+O	File
Save	Ctrl+S	File
Print	Ctrl+P	File
Undo	Ctrl+Z	Edit
Repeat	Ctrl+Y	Edit
Cut	Ctrl+X	Edit
Copy	Ctrl+C	Edit
Delete (Outlook)	Ctrl+D	Edit
Mark as Read (Outlook)	Ctrl+Q	Edit
Move to Folder (Outlook)	Ctrl+Shift+V	Edit
Paste	Ctrl+V	Edit
Select All	Ctrl+A	Edit
Find	Ctrl+F	Edit
Replace	Ctrl+H	Edit
Go To	Ctrl+G	Edit
Rename (Access)	F2	Edit

To Do This	Press This	Found in This Menu
Refresh (Access)	F5	Edit
Reveal Tags (FrontPage)	Ctrl+/	View
Hyperlink	Ctrl+K	Insert
Bookmark (FrontPage)	Ctrl+G	Insert
Cells (Excel)	Ctrl+1	Format
Remove Formatting (FrontPage)	Ctrl+Shift+Z	Format
Properties (FrontPage)	Alt+Enter	Format
View Show (PowerPoint)	F5	Slide Show
Next Pane	F6	Window
Spelling and Grammar	F7	Tools
Thesaurus (FrontPage)	Shift+F7	Tools
Track Changes	Ctrl+Shift+E	Tools
Address Book (Outlook)	Ctrl+Shift+B	Tools
Find (Outlook)	Ctrl+E	Tools
Advanced Find (Outlook)	Ctrl+Shift+F	Tools
New Mail Message (Outlook)	Ctrl+N	Actions
Follow Up (Outlook)	Ctrl+Shift+G	Actions
Reply (Outlook)	Ctrl+R	Actions
Reply to All (Outlook)	Ctrl+Shift+R	Actions
Forward (Outlook)	Ctrl+F	Actions
Help	F1	Help
What's This?	Shift+F1	Help

Index

Katherine Murray

Katherine Murray has been writing about computers and programs since the early 1980s—the stone age of Wordstar 3.3 and the IBM PC. Blessed or cursed with a genetic geekiness (her father *still* programs in RPG) and a fascination with discovering how to work smarter and faster (not harder!) in her own small business, Katherine loves writing about ways people can use technology to improve their productivity so that they have more time for the *real* business of life—playing Super Mario with the kids, walking the dog, reading in the hammock, cooking a gourmet dinner, and listening to James Taylor. Since 1987, Katherine has written more than 40 books on a variety of computer-related subjects, from general PC books to specific program-related books on software of all kinds. In addition to her technical books, Katherine has written a number of books for parents. Her most recent book, *A Different Kind of Kid: Connecting with Unconventional Teens*, was recently published by her own small press, Homeward Bound Publishing (*www.homewardboundpublishing.com*).

Katherine also is the editor of a two online newsletters: *Mom Reporting* shares simple, heartfelt parenting stories, and *Openings* is a monthly newsletter on issues related to spirituality and life discovery. Both newsletters are currently available online at *www.revisionsplus.com/Openings.htm*. Katherine also has written a number of articles for national and local magazines on parenting issues and for a time had a blast writing op-ed pieces for MSNBC Opinions.

In addition to her books, articles, and newsletters, Katherine publishes a blog called BlogOfficeXP that offers tips, quirky bits, and thoughts for Office XP users. (Don't know what a blog is? Visit *www.revisionsplus.com/blogofficexp.html* to find out.) Katherine has had her own business, reVisions Plus, Inc. (*www.revisionsplus.com*), for 15 years, offering writing, publishing support, and communications services to businesses and nonprofit organizations. She enjoys what she does, but most importantly, she loves the people she does it for: Her children, Kelly (21), Christopher (14), and Cameron (9).

The manuscript for this book was prepared and submitted to Microsoft Press in electronic form. Pages were composed by Microsoft Press using Adobe FrameMaker+SGML for Windows, with text in Garamond and display type in ITC Franklin Gothic Condensed. Composed pages were delivered to the printer as electronic pre-press files.

Cover designer:	Tim Girvin Design
Interior Graphic Designer:	James D. Kramer
Principal Compositor:	Joanna Zito
Project Manager:	Susan H. McClung
Copy Editor:	Peter Tietjen
Technical Editor:	Eric Faulkner
Proofreaders:	Jan Cocker, Rebecca Merz, Robert Saley
Indexer:	Edwin Durbin

Get a **Free**
e-mail newsletter, updates,
special offers, links to related books,
and more when you

register on line!

Register your Microsoft Press® title on our Web site and you'll get a FREE subscription to our e-mail newsletter, *Microsoft Press Book Connections*. You'll find out about newly released and upcoming books and learning tools, online events, software downloads, special offers and coupons for Microsoft Press customers, and information about major Microsoft® product releases. You can also read useful additional information about all the titles we publish, such as detailed book descriptions, tables of contents and indexes, sample chapters, links to related books and book series, author biographies, and reviews by other customers.

Registration is easy. Just visit this Web page and fill in your information:

http://www.microsoft.com/mspress/register

Microsoft®
